Speech-Language Pathology Services in the Schools

Second Edition

Joyce S. Taylor
Southern Illinois University of Edwardsville

ALLYN AND BACON
Boston London Toronto Sydney Tokyo Singapore

Series Editor: Ray Short
Series Editorial Assistant: Jo Ellen Caffrey
Production Coordinator: Lisa Feder
Editorial-Production Service: York Production Services
Cover Administrator: Linda Dickinson
Cover Designer: Suzanne Harbison
Manufacturing Buyer: Louise Richardson

Copyright © 1992, 1981 by Allyn and Bacon
A Division of Simon & Schuster, Inc.
160 Gould Street
Needham Heights, Massachusetts 02194

Library of Congress Cataloging-in-Publication Data

Taylor, Joyce S.
  Speech-language pathology : services in the schools / Joyce S.
Taylor. — 2nd ed.
      p.   cm.
  Includes bibliographical references and index.
  ISBN 0-205-13262-6
  1. Handicapped children—Education—United States—Language arts.
2. Language arts—United States—Remedial teaching.
3. Communicative disorders in children—United States. 4. Speech
therapy for children—United States.   I. Title.
LC4028.T39   1992
371.91′4—dc20
                                                          91-27390
                                                          CIP

Printed in the United States of America

10 9 8 7 6 5 4 3 2 1   95 94 93 92 91

In Memory of Little Boy Blue II

BRIEF CONTENTS

CONTENTS

FOREWORD

Dana LeTempt Jerome

"Mewy Kwismas, 'peech teacher!" I smiled and waved goodbye as I inwardly groaned. It was the end of December and I had been referred to as the " 'peech lady," "teach peacher," and various other titles since September when I had first started fulfilling my student teaching requirements in a nearby elementary school. Yet, for all of my techniques, repertoire of therapy materials, and cajolings, to at least one of my students I would remain the 'peech teacher.

I have since graduated with a master's degree in speech pathology and am currently working in a private school. Looking back, I can remember the confusion and anxiety I felt when I thought of being responsible for my own caseload of speech-language-impaired students. I began to realize the scope of my unpreparedness when I thumbed through the first edition of this text. I knew that working in a university speech clinic on a one-to-one basis for two one-half hour sessions per week did not parallel reality within the school setting where one's caseload may be upward of seventy students. I was fortunate enough to have offered at my university a class dealing specifically with procedures in the public school—I promptly enrolled! I went into that class having many unanswered questions: the interpretation of PL 94-142 and how it related to the SLP, the writing and implementation of individualized education programs, assessment procedures, case selections, scheduling models, inservice training, computerized speech and language therapy, and so on. Some of these were issues not specifically addressed in the university speech clinic since they did not always apply. Many of these questions were addressed in this text, and solutions, alternatives, and clarifications were provided. Some questions, however, found solutions through trial and error during my student teaching experience. I have been asked to relate some of these experiences and their relevance to my prestudent teaching preparation. I have attempted to do so in the material that follows.

Initially, PL 94-142 appeared vague and nonspecific with regard to SLPs and how they "fit in." Where were we addressed and what was expected of the profession? Chapter 2 discussed our roles as special education and related personnel and pointed out the role parents played in the educational process. It was in Chapters 2 and 6 that I learned about the Individualized Education Programs (IEPs). While student teaching, I remembered the information regarding the IEP, accountability, and flowchart of procedures and was grateful for the knowledge. Even so, I couldn't help being overwhelmed by the vast amounts of paperwork that seemed to be one of the hallmarks of the profession. Multidisciplinary conference forms, screening forms, parent permission statements, testing protocols, reevaluation forms, tracking sheets, homework, progress reports, and the like littered my desk for the twelve weeks I student-taught; some of these forms were results of PL 94-142.

When it came to identifying and assessing the students, I found a vast variety of testing and screening materials at my disposal. In the text, information regarding the "testing hierarchy" was delineated. For example, parental permission is not needed to screen children, but further evaluation does require parental consent. With regard to hearing screenings, I found that they were not under my jurisdiction in the public school setting. It was the school nurse, not the SLP, who was responsible for the pure tone screenings. Several colleagues related the oft-received frosty looks and curt responses from the school nurses when met with the suggestion that the SLP, not the nurse, be allowed to conduct the hearing screenings as part of the evaluation process.

Once the evaluation process was out of the way, one had to address scheduling of speech-language services. I had "heard" that scheduling therapy was problematic. The text offered several options for both intensive cycle or intermittent scheduling for caseloads from two to five schools and addressed the situations one might encounter when trying to work around the child's class schedule, the SLP's schedule at a particular school, teacher preference, and time constraints. When I looked at the scheduling models suggested in Chapter 5, they appealed to me because they were neat, balanced formulas in which I was sure I could "fit" my students. As useful as the suggestions were, I had not counted on all the exasperating combinations of the aforementioned variables and realized there was more to it than previously surmised. Scheduling became quite the game of strategy, involving the ingenuity of a general, the diplomacy of a diplomat, and the patience of Job. One instance comes to mind when a child at one of the three schools where I student-taught was not able to be taken from his PE or art class, and his teacher felt that absence from his reading class would create problems. Hence, this student was seen twice weekly during my thirty-five-minute lunch period. Thankfully, I was dieting that quarter and didn't mind a shortened lunch break several times a week.

Friday afternoons were scheduled as preparation time and were used to outline lesson plans, schedule parent conferences, monitor students progress, and conduct "make-up" speech sessions. During this time for a five-week span, my cooperating teacher and I developed materials for a first-grade speech enrichment program. Each Friday afternoon for thirty-five minutes we entered the first-grade class and conducted group activities in the areas of auditory sequential memory, discrimination, articulation, fluency, language, and vocal hygiene. Students were asked to participate in activities such as identifying loud/soft, high/low sounds, following two- and three-step directions, identifying common articulatory and grammatical errors, and various vocal abuses. The children enjoyed the exercises and were made aware of the importance of speech and language. It was also an excellent opportunity to provide a bit of public relations and inservice information to the first-grade teachers and aides.

The advent of aides or paraprofessionals and their role in therapy was also addressed in the text. Initially, I was very protective of my profession and felt threatened at the thought of being replaced by an aide. During the Clinical Procedures in Public Schools class, our instructor brought in two guest speakers to allow the class the opportunity to speak with a communication aide and the SLP she assisted in order to obtain the real "scoop" regarding paraprofessionals. After forty minutes of discussion, a reality emerged that we could not ignore: by allowing aides to take over the drill and practice aspect of therapy, the SLP was then free for more evaluations and an increased caseload. The SLP, in effect, takes on the role of consultant or supervisor.

Although the SLP who supervised me did not have an aide per se, I rather served in that capacity. Because I was able to take over the drill and practice, she now had time to create, prepare, and implement a first-grade enrichment program as well as monitor students who were in "carryover" in a wider variety of settings. She was also able to program computer software and develop a more concise speech-language computer therapy program.

Which brings us to the topic of computers and their increasing infiltration into all professional areas. Ours is no exception. The first edition of this text did not delve into this medium; however, it is addressed at some length in the second edition. Consequently, I had no prior knowledge regarding the adaptation and application of computer software for speech-language therapy. True, I had had the benefit of enrolling in a workshop that addressed the various computerized augmentative devices (voice synthesizers, electronic language boards, and so on) available for communicative remediation, but aside from that, I was "computer impaired." However, my cooperating teacher, with infinite patience, introduced me to the world of computers and adaptive software. She showed me how I could program in vocabulary at various levels (graphics for those children who were not yet reading) for instruction in the areas of articulation, language, vocal hygiene, and even fluency. The students looked forward to their "computer sessions." Some communication disorders did not readily lend themselves to computer usage, but who knows, maybe my cooperating teacher obtained the aide she asked for and is even now developing other methods!

I must say that the information gleaned from the first edition of this book was truly helpful in dealing with the public school setting. When the author approached me and asked if I'd offer a few personal experiences and helpful suggestions, I was delighted. She also asked me if I felt there were any other aspects of the public school experience that should be addressed, and I said yes. Until I had spoken with other SLPs, I had not been aware of the tension that often exists between the SLP and the regular classroom teacher. I had never seen this issue addressed in detail in any of my university texts; it appeared to be operating in varying degrees with *all* SLPs I spoke with, and I hadn't seen any formal solutions or suggestions offered toward a resolution of the problem.

The lament of my colleagues revolved around the various comments and descriptions used by many teachers as they perceived the SLP's position. Some examples include:

1. "Wish I could play games all day."
2. "Wish I dealt with only one to two students at a time!"
3. "We *never* see you. We don't know where you are, but you seem to take a leisurely lunch break."
4. "What a gravy job!"

Responses from the SLP to the assailant instructing them to "reenter college for another two years and obtain a master's so they can 'play,' too," although they might sound good at the time, are definitely not the preferred response if one wishes to maintain a positive and workable teacher–SLP relationship. These remarks are infuriating, but are they unfounded? Let's explore this: Human nature sometimes doesn't let us see beyond outward appearances. To some, it *may* appear that we are "playing games," yet research exists that supports the learning of language skills in as naturalistic an environment as possible. And what more natural setting for a child than the context of play? Many SLPs are aware of this, but we mustn't take for granted that *everyone* knows this.

With the advent of whole language classrooms and less occurrence of "pull-out" therapy, we will be seeing less and less of the one-on-one type of service delivery. Admittedly, it must look extremely desirable to have one to three students in a group at any given time, yet many SLPs have caseloads of seventy or more students per week!

Itinerancy carries with it the mystique of "unsupervised activities" and time spent in "idleness" behind the backs of school admininstration. However, accountability measures ensure that the caseload is being addressed and service provided at all prescribed times. Rather difficult to "goof-off" with as many as eighty children being seen weekly!

Any SLP knows that our job is *no* "gravy job." To the untrained eye, sitting in a room with one to three students using colorful and creative materials and the children's apparent willingness to go see the speech teacher may create resentment. There are several options you may wish to keep in mind that may smooth out and clarify pervading misconceptions:

1. *Inservice training*—It is to your advantage to provide information to teachers regarding your position and duties. Though it may seem demeaning to "justify" your existence, a few well-worded materials will go far to elevate the awareness levels.

2. *Post your schedule* — On the door or other highly visible area, post your schedule. I do *not* mean that you should post the names of the students you are serving but rather a general outline of the times you will be present at other schools, your lunch period, and planning time. This is helpful in the event teachers need to speak with you regarding students. It also helps allay any fear that you might have "dead" time in which to imbibe in all those unspeakable activities such as shopping and extended luncheons.

3. *Scheduling* — If you must travel to other schools, it has been my experience as well as that of others, that you do so at midmorning or midafternoon. Leaving fifteen minutes before lunch from School A to travel to School B where you eat lunch and pick up the remainder of your caseload seems innocuous enough. However, cosmetically, it appears to others, as you walk down the hall midway through their lesson, that you are "cutting out" early. Remember, appearances can be deceiving.

4. I suggest that one avoid the lounge as a place for planning time. It is accepted that the lounge is intended for a break or "free" time. Even with the best of intentions and the most fastidious demeanor, being seen frequenting the lounge past the scheduled break time can be a bad public relations move. And may serve to further the poor opinion regarding our services. Teachers and other personnel don't often observe our therapy sessions and they don't see whether we are exemplary therapists or not, *but* they do see the gamelike therapy materials, the small groups of children, and whether or not "too much" time is spent in the lounge area. It must be noted that these negative opinions are *not* shared by all teachers. I had the pleasure of working with many extremely knowledgeable and understanding professionals, who, through their conscientious efforts to augment and maintain my speech goals within the classroom, provided more opportunities for the child to succeed.

Finally, remember you are not superhuman. Not every single child you see will show vast improvements. Oftentimes gains may be gradual, and this can be quite frustrating for both the child and the SLP. But the opportunities provided for the child to broaden and enhance his or her communicative abilities, even if ever so slightly, can make a world of difference. Working within the public school setting brings with it a unique set of circumstances and opportunities not found in other settings. In order to get the maximum amount out of the experience without being overwhelmed by procedures, laws, and paperwork, a generalized knowledge of what to expect and what will be *expected* of you is paramount for making it a smooth and enjoyable transition. I feel this book will assist you greatly in making that transition. Who knows, maybe being the " 'peech teacher" isn't so bad after all.

PREFACE

I first became aware of speech and language specialists when I was in fifth grade. Two boys in my class stuttered. Each week, when the loudspeaker announced that "the speech teacher" was in the building, the two boys left the classroom. As I recall, no one in the class reacted to the announcement or to the fact that the boys stuttered. We also had a mentally retarded girl in class, but she was never seen by the speech teacher, nor was a boy who could not talk above a whisper because he had "screamed too much." If any of the other students had communicative disorders, I was unaware of them.

My next recollection of speech teachers comes from my junior year in high school. During a career-night presentation, I was impressed by a man who was in private practice as a speech correctionist.[1] Two years later, I entered a university program in speech therapy. The lack of significant interest in the field at that time was reflected in class size; some of my classes contained as few as two students. Following completion of the baccalaureate degree, I began work as a public school speech therapist. In that role, I experienced problems that we still encounter today: inadequate physical facilities, restricted budgets, lack of parental involvement, and insufficient training in the various pathologies. I recognized the last-named problem after only one semester in the schools and returned to school on a part-time basis to pursue a master's degree. Five years, seven student teachers, and one master's degree later, I left the public schools for a final encounter with higher education.

The experiences that I had had during my years in the public schools served me well as a Ph.D. candidate; for example, I was able to apply the supervisory skills I had gained in the schools to supervision of student clinicians in a variety of settings. In fact, one observation made while I worked in the public schools served as the hypothesis for my doctoral dissertation. Delinquent tendencies appeared to be the rule rather than the exception in many of the children I had served while in certain schools; my research question was whether the incidence of communicative disorders among delinquent youths

[1] By now the reader will have noted three different titles used to identify the speech-language specialist; there are many others. The problem of this variation is addressed in Chapter 1.

was higher than that found among individuals not so labeled. Using an incarcerated population, my observations were confirmed. I was unable to find a direct relationship between specific kinds of delinquent behavior and various communicative problems, but the incidence of 84 percent was significant.

Following completion of the Ph.D., I accepted a university teaching position. My responsibilities included supervising student teachers and teaching the course in public school methods and materials. As I visited students working under the supervision of state-certified speech clinicians, I was struck by the variation in professional competence. Most clinicians were applying the newest techniques and appeared to have a grasp of current thinking. Some clinicians, however, appeared to persist in using ineffective procedures despite a lack of results and without any clear understanding of why the procedures did not work. Further, techniques of case finding and case selection sometimes seemed inappropriate. The only way to counteract these perceived deficiencies, it appeared, was to provide preservice training to students that would ensure their competence as public school speech and language clinicians.

When I first taught the public school methods course, I searched in vain for a text that would be current and usable. In my view, such a text need not provide extensive information on the various communicative disorders; that material is well covered in a variety of books. Nor should a text claim that there is only one way of managing such logistic details as program scheduling. Instead, it should present sufficient information to make school speech-language pathologists aware of various options and to enable them to make informed and justifiable decisions. Federal regulations concerning the management of handicapped individuals must also be considered in such a text.

Finding no book that met my criteria, I surveyed other instructors of courses in public school methods and materials to see if they also felt a need for a better text. In January 1980, I sent a request for course outlines to the directors of 200 training programs in speech-language pathology; programs accredited by the American Speech-Language-Hearing Association (ASHA) and randomly selected, nonaccredited programs were included. Of the ninety-five responses received, fifty-five indicated that such a course was offered by their departments. Almost without exception, instructors indicated that an appropriate text was not available, and many stated that they did not use a text at all. Surprisingly, the outlines provided were fairly consistent with regard to substantive content although they did show variation in the sequence of presentation of materials.

The first edition of this book represented my attempt to meet the preservice needs of students preparing to work in the school setting. However, the passing of ten years has made some of the information contained in that text obsolete. In addition to updating topics, such as federal and state legislation and the certification of speech-language pathologists, elaboration on such topics as consultation, counseling, and collaboration is included in the current edition. The order in which the materials are presented is one I have found workable, but I have attempted to divide the chapters in such a way as to allow for variation.

ACKNOWLEDGMENTS

My appreciation to a number of individuals must be expressed. First, I thank the SLPs who provided procedural guidelines from their respective states. I am also indebted to Paula Baima who did the research on computer usage among SLPs. Diane Martin reviewed the rough drafts of this text and was brave enough to offer constructive criticism; I am grateful for the feedback. Although Tolly Vassier assumed the responsibility for entering most of the manuscript on the computer, Marie Schreib typed the first two chapters; both must be recognized for their meticulous work. My thanks go to Allyn & Bacon personnel who made preparation of the second edition of this book a pleasure. I am also grateful to Katie, my Golden Retriever Therapy Dog, who slept peacefully under my desk as I prepared this manuscript and never questioned my ability to do so. Finally, my appreciation goes to the students who continue to endure the various phases of my professional growth.

1

Speech-Language Pathology: History and Evolution

POSSIBLY THE OLDEST written reference to speech disorders is a word, included in a papyrus of the Middle Egyptian Dynasty, approximately 2000 B.C. The word has been translated as meaning "to speak haltingly" or "to walk haltingly with the tongue, as one who is sad" (1).

Demosthenes' speech disorder is well known. He has usually been identified as a stutterer, but some feel that his problem could be more clearly described as articulatory. Whether his difficulty was one of fluency or articulation, in the absence of trained personnel, Demosthenes reportedly took it upon himself to treat his own communicative disorder. The success of his "pebbles under the tongue" or "shouting above the roar of the sea" techniques is unclear, but it would appear that Demosthenes presented the first known example of self-treatment for a communicative disorder.

The Origins of the Profession

Stories of individuals with communicative disorders as well as the development of treatment techniques from pre-Renaissance to the mid-1960s are recounted by Margaret Eldridge in *A History of the Treatment of Speech Disorders* (1). Although the absolute accuracy of some of the material may be questioned, Eldridge has offered a chronological picture of the development of the field now recognized as speech-language pathology. She has given the reader some idea of the techniques and procedures employed over the years by those treating communicatively disordered individuals. To provide a perspective from which

1

to view the evolution of the speech, language, and hearing professions, highlights from her book are presented here.

Pre-Renaissance to 1900

In earliest times, concern appeared to be afforded individuals with fluency disorders and impaired hearing; lesser consideration was given to other communicative disorders. With regard to stuttering, Aristotle and others felt that inaccurate movement of the tongue was to blame. Apparently this assertion was accepted by others for years. Aristotle also contemplated the fate of the deaf. Although he was accurate in associating congenital deafness with the inability to acquire language, he expressed pessimism concerning their habilitation. Accordingly, the "deaf and dumb" were excluded from society for thousands of years. Throughout the pre-Renaissance period, the tongue was considered the main organ of speech, and its abnormalities, according to the thinking of the time, could cause stuttering. No significant contributions to the current understanding of communicative disorders were made during this era.

Greater scientific strides were noted from the sixteenth through the eighteenth centuries. Human anatomy was studied, and research and experimentation flourished. Among the contributors of the sixteenth century was Ambroise Paré, a French barber-surgeon; Paré was especially recognized as a designer of prosthetic devices, including an obturator. Paré was apparently a caring man whose interest in his patients did not diminish after the preparation and fitting of the prosthesis; in fact, Eldridge describes Paré as possibly the "first rehabilitation practitioner in history."

Work with the deaf was prominent during the seventeenth century; both manual and oral forms of communication were employed, and divisiveness between those advocating one technique over the other developed. Stuttering continued to be viewed as a disorder resulting from faulty lingual control. Some attention was given to speech following glossectomy and to vocal disorders accompanying hearing impairment.

During the eighteenth century, the first public school for deaf children opened in Germany, and oral communication was emphasized. Little attention was afforded deviant vocal quality, among either deaf speakers or individuals with cleft palates. Although surgical procedures for managing the latter condition were employed, there are no indications that speech intervention was undertaken following surgery. The causes of stuttering remained obscure although Moses Mendelssohn suggested stuttering was due to a "collision between many ideas, flowing simultaneously from the brain" (1). This theory differed from any that had been previously proposed. Continued study of persons who had had glossectomies was apparent during this period.

Investigation of etiological factors and treatment possibilities for stuttering advanced in the nineteenth century. Theories relating stuttering to neural debility and to psychic disturbances were among those advanced. Treatment options ranged from breathing exercises to surgical intervention. Even though surgery was dangerous and painful, a great many people underwent surgery to seek relief from stuttering. A variety of theories was proposed during this period, and it is not altogether surprising that intervention based on those theories did not differ significantly from some techniques employed today.

With regard to other communicative disorders, advances in the areas of cleft palate and deafness were made during the nineteenth century. More sophisticated surgical management of palatal clefts was introduced, and obturators were improved. Although the controversy over oral versus manual communication for the deaf continued, instructional procedures for both became more precise. Surgical removal of the larynx was first accomplished during the nineteenth century; rehabilitation in the form of esophageal speech was apparently not attempted. Research in the area of acquired language disorders also advanced during this period, and physicians and researchers such as Brain, Jackson, Broca, Wernicke, and Head came into prominence. The etiology and nature of acquired language disorders were the concerns of these investigators; they gave little attention to rehabilitation.

During the period from the Renaissance to 1900, investigation into communicative disorders was carried out primarily by physicians. Further, educators and elocutionists assumed responsibility for most habilitative-rehabilitative procedures undertaken. Europeans extensively studied speech, language, and hearing impairments; Americans were less involved. Near the end of the nineteenth century, Dr. John Wyllie published *Disorders of Speech*. This book was apparently the precursor of the many volumes on communicative disorders available today.

1900 to Present: The Initiation of Speech-Language Programs in the Schools

During the early years of the twentieth century, classroom teachers were involved in the treatment of communicatively disordered children. Frequently, the assistance given to children involved placement in a special classroom. In Germany, for example, stutterers were placed together in a special room for both general education and speech therapy. Similar accommodations were provided for children with articulatory disorders, cleft palates, and delayed or disordered language development. It is not clear how teachers assigned to these classrooms were trained. Outside the school setting, elocutionists and voice teachers appeared to have the major responsibility for working with individuals with speech, language, and hearing problems. In the United States, individuals with communicative disorders apparently had to seek assistance from private speech schools; Eldridge described such schools as being "essentially commercial, as well as secretive in character" (1).

Chicago was among the first cities in the United States to offer services for communicatively disordered children in the elementary schools (2). In 1910, the decision to provide speech services to children in that city's schools was apparently based on complaints from parents of "stammering" children. These parents asserted that the schools were doing little to help their children; they felt that aggressive action should be taken. At that time, 1,287 children were reported to be "stammerers." Later assessment determined that not all of the students had fluency problems; some presented other types of communicative disorders. Before assuming positions in the schools, ten promising graduates of the Chicago Teacher's College were given "additional" training. Their pay was $65.00 per month. Meanwhile, in New York City, a survey was conducted to determine whether a need existed for speech training in city schools; although the survey was made in 1911, a program was not established there until 1916. Also, in 1916, a survey of the communicative abilities of school children in Madison, Wisconsin, was conducted; an incidence figure of 5 percent with inferior abilities was derived (3). On the basis of these findings, Smiley Blanton, Director of the Speech Clinic of the University of Wisconsin, suggested that a need existed for special teachers who were conversant with anatomy, physiology, and psychoanalysis. Presumably, these teachers were to work with the speech-defective population. In 1923, the state of Wisconsin acknowledged the need for itinerant teachers; within several years, programs were initiated in large cities on both coasts.

After 1924, programs for the communicatively impaired developed and expanded rapidly. Irwin provides an example of such program development in Ohio. Services were initiated in that state in 1912, but before 1945 there were only seven speech therapists in the state (4). Following passage of a state special education law in 1945, an increasing need for such professionals was recognized; in 1947, thirty-six therapists were employed, and this number increased to forty-six by 1948. It is assumed that program growth in other states paralleled that in Ohio.

According to Saricks, in the 1950s and 1960s, the "speech teacher" or "speech correctionist" had a caseload that consisted primarily of children with articulatory disorders (5). The present author also recalls utilizing the label *delayed speech* to describe a multitude of communicative disorders. Caseloads in the 1950s were sometimes as high as 150–250, and "speech people" were often required to service four or five schools. Space was at a premium, and rooms were frequently shared with others; often, the main function of the room was quite dissimilar (auditorium, furnace room, and so on). Materials were clinician-made and were transported from school to school. In order to service the large numbers of children, speech people conducted speech improvement programs, directing the classroom teacher who then executed the program. In short, the speech person in the days before 1970 was an overworked and probably underprepared professional (5).

The state of the profession has changed since the 1970s, and service delivery has improved. Influencing the growth in professionalism has been state and federal legislation governing the provision of services to the communicatively impaired and stricter certification and licensure requirements. It is the latter topic that is considered next.

Qualifications of Public School Personnel

Certification

As reported earlier, the first public school speech therapists in the United States were teachers who had received "special training"; Blanton suggested such special training should include background in anatomy and physiology and an understanding of psychoanalysis. Many states establishing requirements for public school speech specialists agreed with Blanton that these professionals should be knowledgeable in the area of the anatomy and physiology of the speech and hearing mechanisms, but an understanding of the principles of psychoanalysis was not considered important. Other areas of preparation did not receive such consensus. According to Saricks, because the caseloads of early clinicians consisted of children with articulatory disorders, "many colleges and universities and state boards of education contributed to the restricted view of the clinicians' role by limiting their academic programs and certification requirements" (5).

In order to determine the status of state requirements, Haines analyzed certification requirements in terms of academic and clinical specifications; he reported inconsistencies in many areas (6). With regard to the degree required for certification, for example, forty-one of the forty-five states offering a certificate required a baccalaureate degree; only four required work beyond the bachelor's level. The required number of academic hours in speech, hearing, and related areas ranged from twelve to fifty-one. A 200-clock-hour clinical practicum requirement was specified by eighteen states, and student teaching was required in thirty-five states.

Another attempt to evaluate the consistency of state certification requirements was made in 1979 (7). A request was sent to all state departments of education for certification and procedural information. Responses were received from forty-seven states; because two states required licensure and one appeared to have no certificate, the requirements of only forty-four states were analyzed.

Comparing 1979 standards with 1965 standards, an upgrading of requirements is apparent. In 1965, only four states required work beyond the bachelor's level; the 1979 survey revealed that fourteen states required the master's degree exclusively. An additional twelve states awarded certification at both the bachelor's and master's level, and thirteen states continued to award certification after completion of only the baccalaureate degree. With regard to the number of academic hours in speech, language, and hearing required in 1979, the minimum number of twelve hours had not changed: one state continued to require only twelve semester hours in the major areas. The majority of states specifying semester hour requirements, however, had increased the requirement. The range in 1979 was from 12 to 78 semester hours in speech, language, and hearing; the average number of hours required was 34.63. Clearly, an upgrading of requirements is reflected. In 1965, eighteen states required 200 clock hours of clinical practicum; one state required 220 hours and one state, 100 hours. Other states were not specific in their requirements. The 1979 survey revealed that two states required only 150 clock hours, eight required 200, and fourteen required more than 200 clock hours. Clock hour minima were not reported by the other states. In 1965, Haines reported that thirty-five states required student teaching for certification; only twenty-six states in the 1979 survey indicated that student teaching was required for certification, and of these, just eleven specified the clock hours. This discrepancy in reported student teaching requirements could reflect differing materials furnished to the two investigators. It is doubtful that student teaching experience was required with less frequency in 1979 than it was in 1965.

In 1985, Bullet reported on her survey of the certification requirements for school speech-language pathologists (SLP) (8). Among other things, she reviewed the minimal degree required for certification. At that time (1982–1983), eighteen states required the master's degree for certification, whereas the remainder required only an undergraduate degree. It should be pointed out that several states were in the process of upgrading their requirements; for example, Virginia and Arkansas requirements change in 1992 (9, 10). North Dakota and Wyoming also plan to upgrade requirements (11). The trend seen toward master's level certification should be intensified by the minimum requirement aspect of current federal legislation.

With regard to clock hours required for public school certifications, the variations noted in 1979 continue to exist. Those states reporting clinical practicum requirements in a school setting have requirements that range from 50 to 100 clock hours (8). Do students in Wyoming and Idaho require less practice in the school setting than those in California and Texas? The question is obviously moot but serves to illustrate the inconsistency in state certification requirements.

In analyzing the current information on the certification of public school SLPs, it is apparent that requirements are not consistent. Members of the American Speech-Language-Hearing Association (ASHA) have devoted many hours to the study of minimum requirements for the preparation of competent speech-language pathologists and audiologists. When comparing the requirements of different state certificates to ASHA requirements for the Certificate of Clinical Competence in Speech Pathology (CCC-SP), little conformity is seen. ASHA is specific in its requirements in the basic communication processes area; few state certificates even designate the amount of coursework to be completed in that area. Similarly, a breakdown of coursework in the major area into speech and language disorders is not apparent in most certificate requirements. ASHA requires that all applicants for the CCC-SP have coursework in the area of audiology; only thirteen of the certificates analyzed in the 1979 survey have requirements that equal or exceed ASHA specifications. Finally, in the area of clinical practicum, ASHA requires a minimum amount of experience with children and adults who display all types of communicative disorders. Although some states suggest that applicants should have experience with persons displaying a variety of problems, and some even designate clock hour requirements in specific areas, conformity to ASHA requirements is not seen.

It may be that uniformity in state certification requirements is not possible or even desirable. Although it would be sensible if certain basic academic and clinical requirements were consistent, the educational needs of SLPs in various states are different. SLPs who work in states where there is a high representation of bilingual children should have some knowledge of those children's cultural and linguistic characteristics. Since education is the responsibility of individual states, the latter should exercise the right to establish their own requirements.

The original question posed concerned the special training needed to prepare SLPs for the schools. Early educators did not agree, nor do current experts. Therefore, it behooves the student in training to seek information from individual states about specific requirements for certification; this material is available from teacher certification units of state boards of education. Or, perhaps there is another solution: licensure.

Licensure

The licensing of SLPs and audiologists occurred initially in Florida in 1969 (12). The requirements were identical to ASHA requirements for the Certificates of Clinical Competence. By 1986, 72 percent of the states had licensing laws, most modeled after ASHA requirements (12). Although there is no doubt that licensure helps to ensure uniformity in the academic and clinical preparation of SLPs, in many cases public school personnel were exempted from licensure. As Phillips states, such exemptions "suggest that lesser standards are acceptable in some settings, such as public schools" (12). She suggests that this double standard must be eliminated to ensure consumer protection.

A perusal of the characteristics of licensure laws demonstrates that twenty-nine of the thirty-six states requiring licenses exempted public school employees (13). At that time, twelve additional states were considering licensure, whereas three considered the topic to be "inactive." In one inactive state, there was reported to be reluctance because few persons would be eligible for licensing if public school personnel were exempted (13). As of summer 1990, three additional states had passed licensure bills, but one excluded SLPs. There were varied levels of activity with regard to licensure in the other twelve states (14).

Eugene Cooper has been an active participant in the licensure discussion and, like Phillips, is concerned that two classes of SLPs are emerging: the health care SLP and the public school SLP (15). The latter group, comprising about 70 percent of the work force, are viewed as educators and, therefore, regulated by the departments of education. As noted previously, licensure, for the most part, has not been applicable to public school personnel.

The solution, according to Cooper, is universal exemption-free licensure.

This would eliminate the developing two class system of SLPs, unify standards and salaries, and ensure quality services. Conceding that this will be difficult, Cooper feels that such licensure laws are not impossible and should be pursued.

It would appear that licensure as it exists today may not be the means of assuring uniformity in the preparation of SLPs. One obvious problem occurs when certification requirements are changed by ASHA, which occurs in 1993. Will those states that modeled licensure after the requirements for the Certificates of Clinical Competence modify their licensure requirements as well? It appears to be unlikely. As with certification, it would seem imperative for students to consult individual state agencies to determine if licensure is required for employment in the school setting.

Personal Qualifications

A variety of individuals in education, professional organizations, and state agencies have studied the issues involved in the preparation of competent SLPs. As the previous discussion illustrates, both academic and clinical requirements have been specified although no consensus has been reached. In all these discussions, one critical factor has been ignored: what *kind* of person will be successful as an SLP.

Van Hattum considered the personal characteristics common to successful clinicians (16). He indicated that such people have the ability to understand themselves and others. With regard to personal qualities, Van Hattum acknowledged the need for modesty and humility. In a school setting especially, these traits are essential. Even though most SLPs will embark upon first jobs with a graduate degree, they must be able to relate in a collegial manner to other professionals with less education. These are definitely important virtues.

Honesty is another trait essential to successful functioning in the school setting. According to Van Hattum, honesty requires that you be honest with yourself with regard to personal prejudices and limitations. Perhaps no one is without prejudice, whether it relates to race, gender, disorder, or degree of cleanliness. However, it is important that such prejudices be examined and resolved if intervention is to be successful. Similarly, each individual has educational and clinical gaps and limitations; recognition of these shortcomings and a resolve to correct the situation are mandatory.

Patience is an attribute that may be exaggerated in importance. Granted, it is important to be able to view client improvement in small increments and be satisfied. However, when patience implies repetition of an unsuccessful procedure ad infinitum, then the virtue becomes a fault. Nevertheless, in the positive sense, patience is an important quality.

Van Hattum discussed imagination, creativeness, and originality as important factors in successful intervention. In a sense, the deluge of materials, programs, and cookbooks that have hit the market in recent years has made these attributes less important. However, it is essential that the commercial materials and programs be fitted to the child rather than the child fitted to the program. This requires flexibility and adaptability in addition to Van Hattum's trinity of attributes.

Van Hattum also cited the need for resourcefulness, dependability, and responsibility. Each of these is important and self-explanatory. Finally, he discussed the need for a sense of humor; the ability to laugh at oneself as well as at difficult situations will, in the long run, make one's professional life much more satisfying.

There are other traits that seem to separate effective from ineffective SLPs. Empathy is an overworked term but an important characteristic of an effective SLP. Sensitivity and the ability to be nonjudgmental are equally important. Given the expanding nature of our clients and their needs, it is essential that SLPs be open to cultural differences and have the insight to distinguish differences from deviations, both in the linguistic and behavioral sense. The competent SLP must have the ability to recognize "teachable" moments and take advantage of these opportunities. Finally, the effective SLP must be an active listener; when attending professional conventions, one sometimes wonders if this ability has not been sufficiently stressed. The list of positive personal qualities that characterize an effective SLP is probably endless, and the possessor of *all* these virtues would be a candidate for sainthood. Over a somewhat protracted career in this field, the author has supervised hundreds of students in a variety of settings. In general, it has not been the academic performance of students that has been pivotal in making them successful clinicians. Many straight-A students were unable to relate to clients although they were faultless technicians. Conversely, some average students tended to be sensitive, open, flexible, and responsive. In short, successful SLPs seem to represent a combination of basic knowledge, intellectual curiosity, and positive personal characteristics. The importance of the latter cannot be dismissed.

Professional Titles

In the preceding discussion, it was apparent that questions exist about what constitutes appropriate academic and clinical preparation for school-based SLPs. And, if agreement could be reached on the preparation of speech persons, could agreement also be reached on what these persons should be called?

In the preface, a number of titles were used to refer to the individual who works with persons with communicative disorders. Included among those titles were speech teacher, speech correctionist, speech therapist, speech clinician, and speech-language pathologist; in the literature, other designations are found. From its outset, the profession of speech-language pathology has had some difficulty agreeing on the title its members should assume. *Speech teacher* evolved logically since classroom teachers originally assumed the role of the teacher of speech. Clearly, its application today is inappropriate even though it would not be surprising to hear it still being used in the school setting. Perhaps even some specialists employed in the public schools refer to themselves by that title. *Speech correctionist* was a title that appeared to emerge rather early in the development of the profession (circa 1900). At that time, its use may have been quite descriptive since professionals were dealing with the correction of fluency, vocal, and articulatory problems. Currently, however, members of the profession have responsibilities far greater than the correction of those problems; use of speech correctionist, therefore, appears to be antiquated. Many individuals refer to themselves as *speech therapists;* besides the fact that the language component of the profession is omitted by this designation, the term *therapist* often carries the connotation that the professional is working under the direction of a physician. For example, physical and occupational therapists usually perform services under the supervision of a medical person. However, that is not necessarily true of speech and language professionals. Terms that have enjoyed some popularity throughout the years are *speech clinician* or *speech and language clinician.* As Van Hattum pointed out, this does not indicate that individuals are functioning within a clinical setting but that they are functioning in a clinical manner (17). There were those, however, who felt that the title was too specific. In 1962, the problem of a title for the profession was addressed by the ASHA Executive Council. Although it was acknowledged that some members of the profession were not concerned about the diversity of titles in use at that time, the council studied the issue at some length (18). They suggested that the public does not understand the role of the SLP. The council further stated,

> *Occasionally, we discover that our image is somewhat out of focus. We don't attempt to ask the public to speak our name, for we have yet to give it to them. Until we do get a name, the condition of our absent or distorted image will remain (18).*

Following a discussion of the importance of assuming an identity for the profession, the council suggested the name should meet several criteria. Among these were that the title be a single word that would describe the total activities of its members and that the title could be easily written and spoken. Equally concerned with a name for the profession was Wendell Johnson; one of whose concerns was the inadequacy of the terms *speech pathology* and *audiology.* According to Johnson, the separation of speech pathology and audiology suggested a division that should not occur since these two areas of study are both related to oral communication (19). Johnson deemed it necessary to give the profession a single name, and he, along with others, suggested *communicology.* Such a term would encourage unity rather than diversity among the members of the profession. Those involved in the field of communicology would be called *communicologists.* A review of the literature indicates, however, that Johnson's suggestion of a name for the profession was not taken up by the membership.

Although it was important to be aware of the various titles used by speech, language, and hearing specialists, the concern of this book is with the speech and language specialist in the school setting. Two surveys attempted to determine (1) what title or certificate designations were being used by the certifying agencies at the state level, (2) what certificate designations were thought to be used at the state level by practicing SLPs, and (3) which title the SLPs preferred. The first survey was distributed to state departments of education, and 92 percent of the states responded (7). Table 1-1 lists the certificate designations reported by the various states and the number of states reporting each title. Professional titles and frequency data are also presented in Table 1-1.

Hahn mailed a questionnaire to 150 speech-language pathologists work-

TABLE 1-1 Survey of Certificate Designations and Professional Titles Used by State Education Agencies

	Number of States
Certificate designation	
Speech correctionist	4
Basic speech and language	1
Standard speech and language	1
Speech pathology — Level 1	1
Speech pathology — Level 2	1
Speech and language impaired	1
Speech and communication disorders	1
Basic speech handicapped	1
Standard speech handicapped	1
Speech and hearing	1
Speech and hearing therapy	1
Speech disorders	1
Speech and language pathology	1
Speech and language	1
Professional title	
Speech and language clinician	4
Speech pathologist	4
Speech and language pathologist	4
Speech correctionist	3
Communication disorders specialist	3
Speech and hearing therapist	2
Speech and hearing clinician	2
Speech clinician	2
Speech correctionist/language specialist	1
Teacher of the speech handicapped	1
Teacher of the speech and hearing impaired	1
Language clinician	1
Speech and hearing teacher — therapist	1
School speech and hearing clinician	1
Speech therapist	1
Speech, language, and hearing therapist	1
Speech and hearing specialist	1

ing in the school setting; 45 ASHA-certified persons and 15 non-ASHA-certified individuals responded to the survey (20). Among the questions posed were "What professional title or certificate designation is utilized in your state?" and "By what title do you prefer to be called?" Table 1-2 shows the responses to the first question.

Of those responding to this question, twenty-two indicated that the professional title employed in their states was *speech and language pathologist*. Yet only one state uses that designation on the official certificate, and just four

TABLE 1-2   Survey of Professional Titles Used by Speech-Language Pathologists

	*Number of Responses**
Title or certificate designation used by state	
Speech and language pathologist	22
Speech therapist	12
Speech and language clinician	11
Speech pathologist	9
Speech and hearing therapist	7
Speech clinician	7
Speech correctionist	6
Communication disorders specialist	6
Speech and hearing clinician	3
Teacher of the speech and hearing impaired	3
Speech, language, and hearing clinician	3
Speech-language-hearing specialist	2
Language clinician	2
Speech and hearing specialist	2
Speech and language teacher/clinician	1
Teacher of the speech and hearing handicapped	1
Title preferred by respondents	
Speech and language pathologist	24
Speech and language clinician	13
Speech pathologist	7
Speech therapist	6
Communications disorders specialist	5
Speech-language therapist	4
Communication specialist	4
Speech correctionist	2
Speech and hearing therapist	2
Speech clinician	2
Language clinician	2
Speech, language, and hearing clinician	1
Speech and hearing specialist	1
Speech, language, and hearing pathologist	1
Teacher of the speech and hearing handicapped	1

*Some respondents gave multiple answers (20).

states use this title; it is therefore apparent that the data are skewed or inaccurate.

When asked which title they preferred, respondents replied as indicated in Table 1-2. It is disturbing to realize that persons throughout the United States employ a variety of titles to refer to themselves and that certifying agencies utilize a similar diversity of titles and certificate designations. Even more amazing is that within a single state, various titles may be used. On December 7, 1979, the *Southern Illinois University Placement Service Bulletin* listed the following vacancies for public school positions within the state: speech and language therapist, speech therapist, speech correctionist, speech-language pathologist, speech clinician, speech pathologist, and itinerant speech therapist (21). The official certificate of the state of Illinois is in "speech and language impaired," and the designation given the holder of that certificate is *speech and language clinician* (22). Yet not one of the positions described carried the title of *speech and language clinician.*

In order to determine if disparity continues to exist, the same source was reviewed in the spring of 1990 (23). At that time, six positions were listed for speech therapist; five each for speech pathologist and speech/language therapist; three for speech/language pathologist; and one each for speech clinician, speech/language clinician, speech/hearing therapist, and teacher of speech/language impaired. It does not appear that the eleven-year time lapse has improved the title dilemma.

For a time, it appeared as if the problem of assigning a title to the speech and language specialist was over; in 1976, ASHA officially endorsed the title of *speech-language pathologist* (24). The association hoped that the adoption of this title would end the confusion created by the numerous titles used by members of the profession both in schools and other professional settings. The hope has not materialized. One need only read "Letters" in *Asha* to realize that the controversy continues. For example, one reader suggested that the question of speech-therapist versus speech-language pathologist had "gotten out of hand" when she heard an agency director say that his agency gave physical and occupational therapy and speech-language pathology. The reader's concern was that it sounded as if her colleagues are "giving diseases" (25).

Another reader was asked if, as an SLP, she taught dead people to speak (26). If the title is to be all-inclusive, the reader continued, it should be "speech/language/fluency/articulation/voice pathologists." Other readers explained that the length of our professional title sometimes caused other professionals to use the terms *speech person* or *speech people* instead. This they considered to be disrespectful even though they believed speech therapist to be an acceptable substitution (27). A reader from Tennessee wrote that we are not called SLPs because we do not act like professionals when we deal with such noncommunicative disorders as dysphagia (28). This reader suggests that we focus on "who we are and what we do as communication experts." The inappropriate use of the word *pathologist* received comments from a number of readers.

Additional evidence of the use of diverse titles was collected by ASHA's resource center specialists who surveyed Actionline callers (29). Forty-five percent of the 280 callers who were asked their occupation responded speech pathologist; only 26 percent used the designated SLP title. Other responses included speech therapist (12 percent), speech and language pathologist (5 percent), speech and language therapist (3 percent), speech teacher (3 percent), speech and language specialist (2 percent), speech and language clinician, speech language therapist, and speech and hearing therapist (each 1 percent). And so it goes.

Reviewing the criteria suggested in 1962, the title currently used may not be considered appropriate by all. The Legislative Council indicated that the title (1) should be a single word, (2) should describe all professional activities, and (3) should be easily written and spoken. Speech-language pathologist meets just one of these criteria.

Although professionals within the field may be able to utilize various titles and understand they all relate to the same group of individuals, the public may not be so adept. One of the reasons that speech-language pathologist was adopted as the official title was that it best reflected the training and education of its members and the services delivered to communicatively disordered individuals (24). The consistent use of this title throughout the remainder of the book does not necessarily imply agreement with the designation. Although this title might be a little cumbersome in the public school setting, it is employed because it has been recommended for use in all regulations surrounding the Education for the Handicapped/Individuals with Disabilities Education Act (EHA/IDEA).

The Evolution of ASHA

Thus far, frequent mention has been made of ASHA, and it would seem that this chapter would be incomplete without some discussion of its history. And what better guide through this history than Charles Van Riper? In his guest editorial, "Recollections from a Pioneer," Van Riper reminisces about the year 1930 when there were only twenty-nine association members and dues were $5.00 (30). At that time, the founding fathers believed themselves to be "an elite group of academic scholars" who sought to understand the nature of communicative disorders (30). This research orientation was tempered somewhat by the presence of Van Riper and others who stuttered, as well as four practicing "speech teachers." In 1924, the American Speech Correction Association was born.

There were some members who wished to establish a medical affiliation; however, physicians within the group advised that the creation of an independent profession was better. They further suggested that the work of speech correctionists should be done in the schools. Certainly, the orientation of the profession has expanded since those early days.

In 1936, the first publication of the association appeared in mimeographed form. Edited by a research-oriented gentleman, articles in the *Journal of Speech Disorders* had a pedantic tone. Later, Wendall Johnson took over as editor, and according to Van Riper, "it even became interesting, which is more than one can say for our current publications" (30).

When future editors returned the publication to a research orientation, many complained, and a separate journal (*Journal of Speech and Hearing Research*) evolved. Although Van Riper agrees that subsequent journals (*Asha* and *Language, Speech, and Hearing Services in Schools*) have attempted to meet the needs of practicing clinicians, they have been only partially successful. As Van Riper states, "Some day we may yet have a publication that will serve their needs" (30).

Van Riper reports that governance in the early days was in the hands of the Executive Council. Officers were selected for each position and elected unanimously. That simplistic manner of governance has changed drastically. Other changes involve membership criteria; it is interesting to note that Van Riper would not be eligible to belong to ASHA today since he has never had a course in this field. Van Riper speaks of the conventions, during which every member attended all the sessions and "bedeviled the authors of presented papers with hungry or critical questions" (30).

Van Riper concludes by commenting on the price the profession has paid for the changes made throughout the years. He feels that "we have lost much of the dedication and caring that once was the hallmark of our profession" (30). He notes that we have lost sight of the human beings we serve as we have concentrated on their behaviors. "Once we had a calling; now we have a job" (30).

Summary

It is difficult to fully appreciate the profession without some knowledge of its history and evolution. Of concern to current readers should be the development of services in the schools; as one will see, there are cyclical components in this development. Controversy continues to exist regarding the academic and clinical preparation of SLPs; some of the controversy seems warranted although some is probably academic. Indecision about what to call SLPs also continues despite valiant efforts to achieve uniformity. Finally, attention to the history and impact of ASHA is important since 46 percent of all ASHA members are employed in educational settings (31). Its influence has been felt in the past and most assuredly will be felt in the future.

Endnotes

1. M. Eldridge, *A History of the Treatment of Speech Disorders* (London: E. S. Livingstone, 1968).

2. P. Moore and D. G. Kester, "Historical Notes on Speech Correction in the Pre-Association Era." *Journal of Speech and Hearing Disorders* 18(1953): pp. 48–53.

3. M. E. Black, "The Origins and State of Speech Therapy in the Schools," *Asha* 8(1966): pp. 419–425.

4. R. B. Irwin, "Speech and Hearing Therapy in the Public Schools of Ohio," *Journal of Speech and Hearing Disorders* 14(1949): pp. 63–68.

5. M. Saricks, "School Services and Communication Disorders," *Asha* 31(1989): pp. 79–80.

6. H. H. Haines, "Trends in Public School Speech Therapy," *Asha* 7(1965): pp. 187–190.

7. J. S. Taylor, "Public School Certification Standards: Are They Standard," *Asha* 22(1980): pp. 159–165.

8. M. Bullett, "Certification Requirements of Public School Speech-Language Pathologists in the United States," *Language, Speech, and Hearing Services in the Schools* 16(1985): pp. 124–128.

9. "At Press Time," *Asha* 31(1989): p. 8.

10. "At Press Time," *Asha* 30(1988): p. 5.

11. C. Peters-Johnson, "Action: School Services," *Language, Speech, and Hearing Services in the Schools* 21(1990): pp. 123–125.

12. B. J. Phillips, "President's Page," *Asha* 28(1986): p. 17.

13. C. Lynch, "Characteristics of State Licensure Laws," *Asha* 28(1986): pp. 37–43.

14. C. Lynch, personal conversation, June 19, 1990.

15. E. B. Cooper, "One Lover's Quarrel Revisited," *Asha* 31(1989): pp. 79–82.

16. R. Van Hattum (ed.), *Speech-Language Programming in the Schools,* 2nd ed. (Springfield, IL: Charles C. Thomas, 1982).

17. R. Van Hattum (ed.), *Clinical Speech in the Schools* (Springfield, IL: Charles C. Thomas, 1969).

18. American Speech and Hearing Association Executive Council, "A Name for the Profession of Speech and Hearing," *Asha* 4(1962): pp. 199–203.

19. W. Johnson, "Communicology?" *Asha* 10(1968): pp. 43–56.

20. C. Hahn, "An Investigation into Current Procedures of Case Finding, Case Selection and Scheduling in the Schools," master's thesis, Southern Illinois University at Edwardsville (1980).

21. *Southern Illinois University Placement Service Bulletin,* 10(1979).

22. State Board of Education, Illinois Office of Education, "Rules and Regulations to Govern the Administration and Operation of Special Education" (Springfield, 1979).

23. *Southern Illinois University Placement Service Bulletin,* 20(1990).

24. W. C. Healey and S. Dublinske, "Notes from the School Services Program. Official Title: Speech-Language Pathologist." *Language, Speech, and Hearing Services in Schools* 8(1977): p. 67.

25. K. Newton, "Letters," *Asha* 29(1987): p. 4.

26. I. Weiss, "Letters," *Asha* 29(1987): p. 4.

27. D. Greenman and C. Landman, "Letters," *Asha* 28(1986): p. 5.

28. A. Lane, "Letters," *Asha* 30(1988): p. 7.

29. R. Malone, "Comment," *Asha* 28(1986): p. 2.

30. C. Van Riper, "Guest Editorial: Recollections from a Pioneer," *Asha* 31(1989): pp. 72–73.

31. S. Dublinske, "Action: School Services," *Language, Speech, and Hearing Services in Schools* 20(1989): p. 222.

2

The Communicatively Disordered Individual and Federal Legislation

Introduction

The issue of a person's right to speech, language, and audiological services is a complex one—one with which we must come to grips. Not all communicatively handicapped children are being served by the public school, and I suggest that these children do have a right to such service (1).

The implementation of Public Law 94-142, Education for All Handicapped Children Act of 1975, was heralded by many as signifying the end of a quiet revolution on behalf of handicapped children in the United States. Actually, the educational rights of such individuals were acknowledged in a steady progression of state and federal legislation throughout the years. The concept of free public education, for example, can be traced back as far as 1837; at that time, Massachusetts created a state board to oversee the education of children (2). Provisions for the education of handicapped children were not in evidence, however, until 1911, when New Jersey created a statute that established such provisions. Other states providing education to the handicapped prior to the 1920s included Minnesota, Wisconsin, Illinois, and New York. Another example of state recognition of the needs of the handicapped is the landmark decision in the *Pennsylvania Association for Retarded Children* v. *the Commonwealth of Pennsylvania* case. That case is discussed later in this chapter.

Although education has been considered an obligation of individual states, the federal government has been instrumental in obtaining rights for children and adults with disabilities. In the form of public laws, Congress has encouraged the construction of facilities for the retarded, provided financial assistance to local education agencies, and allocated funds for the education of handicapped children. Each of these laws appears to have had some role in the development of PL 94-142. In the succeeding discussion, the role of the federal government in the expansion of services to individuals with disabilities is explored. The Education of the Handicapped Act/Individuals with Disabilities Education Act and its implementation are analyzed, and continuing concerns for the school speech-language pathologist are considered.[1]

State Participation in Education for the Handicapped

The *Pennsylvania Association for Retarded Children (PARC)* v. *the Commonwealth of Pennsylvania* case is considered critical with regard to education of handicapped children. In this instance, the school code of the state was challenged and found to be unacceptable. On January 7, 1971, thirteen retarded children, along with members of PARC, appeared in the federal district court; their initial goal was to obtain access to free education (3). Although the commonwealth provided education to exceptional children, a loophole in the law allowed for the exclusion of individuals with a mental age (MA) lower than five years. Actually, the education of such a child was "postponed" until an MA of five years was reached; in effect, this meant that a severely retarded child who would never achieve an MA of five would never receive public education. Therefore, the first concern in the PARC case was access to free public education.

A second goal was to ensure that the child received an appropriate education and that both parents and children played a role in determining the nature and quality of that training. What was being sought was justification for placing a child in a specific program, justification for maintaining the child in that program, or justification for changing a child's placement. Further, opportunities for parent and child participation in these decision-making processes were requested.

After hearing the testimony of a variety of witnesses, the commonwealth apparently acknowledged that a more adequate method of meeting the needs of its exceptional children must be found. Through a series of court orders and injunctions, modifications designed to improve the education of handicapped individuals in Pennsylvania were recommended.

Several patterns of reform are exemplified by the PARC decree (4). Access to a free public education for mentally retarded children was mandated, and the identification of children excluded from schools was specified. Comprehensive evaluation of children already identified as retarded and of those previ-

---

[1]The Education of the Handicapped Act (EHA) was changed to Individuals with Disabilities Act (IDEA) late in 1990. Both the familiar and new titles are used throughout the text.

ously excluded from public education was required. These procedures were to ensure that each child was accurately diagnosed and placed. Similarly, biannual reevaluations of all handicapped children were mandated, and due process hearings were made accessible to parents who questioned the accuracy of the diagnosis or the suitability of their child's educational placement. Finally, the decree addressed the issue of appropriate placement; although the "least restrictive" designation was not employed, that concept was described. Significant in the rulings was the stipulation that school officials must be able to justify the placement of children in specific educational programs.

Although total compliance with the *PARC* v. *the Commonwealth of Pennsylvania* recommendation did not occur, significant changes in the educational management of retarded children were brought about. As indicated previously, the right to education irrespective of mental age was established, child-find procedures were implemented, and innovative programming designed to meet the needs of retarded children was initiated. Finally, despite the variations that existed in the due process hearings, parents became active participants in the educational planning for their children.

A similar decision was reached in the *Mills* v. *Board of Education of the District of Columbia* case of 1972 (5). In this instance, a class action suit on behalf of all handicapped children was initiated by the parents and guardians of seven District of Columbia children. The Mills decision concluded with a court order assuring all handicapped children the right to an appropriate free public education.

The right of children with disabilities to education has been reinforced by the passage of a number of state statutes and regulations. By 1972, 70 percent of the states had reportedly adopted legislation requiring the education of children with handicaps, as defined by each state's policy (5). Three years later, all but two states required the education of the majority of its handicapped children, and by 1977, only one state had not enacted such legislation. It is assumed that all states participate now.

It is apparent, then, that legislation at the state level contributed to a recognition of the rights of children with disabilities. Parents were sometimes instrumental in bringing the issue into focus, as were special interest groups. Supplementary pressure has been exerted also in the form of federal legislation; federal government participation is discussed in the next section.

Federal Participation in Education for the Handicapped Prior to PL 94-142

PL 88-164

Throughout the years, the federal government has provided incentives to the states with regard to the management of disabled children. In 1963, Public Law 88-164, titled the Mental Retardation Facilities and Community Health Centers Construction Act of 1963, was enacted. Title I of the law appropriated funds *for project grants to assist in meeting the costs of construction of facilities for research, or research and related purposes, relating to human development, whether biological, medical, social, or behavioral, which may assist in finding the causes, and means of prevention of mental retardation, or in finding means of ameliorating the effects of mental retardation (6).*

Part B of the law authorized appropriations for the construction of university-affiliated facilities for the retarded; such facilities were to provide services to the retarded, as well as training to professional workers. Part C provided grants for the construction of public and nonprofit facilities for the mentally retarded. Finally, Title III dealt with the preparation of teachers of handicapped children. Fellowships, training grants, and traineeships were authorized to educate "speech correctionists" and teachers of the hard of hearing and deaf. This act, inspired by proposals to the Congress by President John F. Kennedy, not only provided incentives for the construction of facilities for the retarded but also attempted to encourage the training of personnel to work with the handicapped (7).

PL 89-10

In 1965, PL 89-10, Elementary and Secondary Education Act of 1965, was enacted. Title I provided financial assistance

to local educational agencies serving areas with concentration of children from low income families and to expand and improve their educational programs by various means (including preschool programs) which contribute particularly to meeting the special education needs of educationally deprived children (8).

According to Hagerty and Howard, many administrators failed to take advantage of Title I even though programming for the handicapped was possible under this section (7).

Title II, School Library Resources, Textbooks, and Other Instructional Materials, required that individual states prepare plans for the acquisition of such materials. Although special resources for the handicapped could be requested in the state plan, little evidence exists to indicate that states sought such funding (7).

Supplementary educational centers and services were encouraged under Title III of PL 89-10; it was reported that some of the most innovative programs developed under this title were designed to assist the handicapped (7). A later revision of the law required that 15 percent of the available funds be allocated to programming for the handicapped. Title IV dealt with the authority of the office of education, and Title V of that act provided grants to strengthen state departments of education. Under that section, states could provide local educational agencies with consultative and technical assistance, as well as services related to a variety of areas, including the education of the handicapped.

PL 89-750

On November 3, 1966, Public Law 89-750, Elementary and Secondary Education Amendments of 1966, was enacted; the most significant amendment was Title VI of the act, Education of Handicapped Children. The purpose of Title VI was to provide grants

> *for the purpose of assisting the states in the initiation, expansion, and improvement of programs and projects (including the acquisition of equipment and where necessary the construction of school facilities) for the education of handicapped children (as defined in section 602) at the preschool, elementary and secondary school levels (9).*

Section 602 defined "handicapped children" and included the hard of hearing, deaf, and speech impaired. In order to receive funding, individual states were required to submit plans to the commissioner of education; eleven criteria were employed to evaluate the state plans. Finally, Title VI established a National Advisory Committee on Handicapped Children and the Bureau for the Education and Training of the Handicapped.

PL 91-230

Additional bills were passed by Congress on behalf of the handicapped. Public Law 91-230, an extension of the Elementary and Secondary Education Act of 1965, was enacted on April 13, 1970. Title VI of that bill codified much of the previously passed legislation (10). In addition to the provisions established in Title VI of PL 89-750, PL 91-230 authorized funding for the development of centers and services to meet the special needs of the handicapped, for the training of personnel for the education of the handicapped (including "speech correctionists"), for research in the education of the handicapped, and for the development of instructional media for the handicapped and special programs for children with specific learning disabilities.

PL 93-380

In 1974, Public Law 93-380, Education Amendments of 1974, was enacted. Among the significant sections of the act was 513, known popularly as the Buckley Amendment or the Family Educational Rights and Privacy Act of 1974. Part a, 1, dealt with the rights of parents "to inspect and review any and all official records, files, and data directly related to their children" (11). Further, Part 2 provided the opportunity for parents to request a hearing

> *to challenge the content of their child's school records, and to ensure that the records are not inaccurate, misleading, or otherwise in violation of the privacy or other rights of students, and to provide an opportunity for the correction or deletion of any such inaccurate, misleading, or otherwise inappropriate data contained therein (11).*

Section 438 also prohibited the release of confidential information without the written permission of the parents.

Sections 611–621 specifically addressed the education of the handicapped and offered financial assistance to the states in developing complete educational programming at the preschool, elementary school, and secondary school levels; the appropriations were applicable to the fiscal year 1975. The rights of parents and children with regard to due process were emphasized in Section 612, as was the concept of least restrictive environment. The law required that the states must ensure that

> *to the maximum extent appropriate, handicapped children including children in public or private institutions or other care facilities are educated with children who are not handicapped, and that special classes, separate schooling, or other removal of handicapped children from the regular education environment occurs only when the nature or severity of the handicap is such that education in regular classes with the use of supplementary aids and services cannot be achieved satisfactorily (11).*

Finally, the act required that the states formulate plans for meeting the needs of all handicapped children and establish a time frame for implementing the plan.

PL 93-112

The purpose of Section 504 of PL 93-112, The Rehabilitation Act of 1973, is to terminate discrimination against handicapped individuals; specifically, it provides that

> *no otherwise qualified handicapped individual in the United States shall, solely by reason of his handicap, be excluded from participation in, be denied the benefits of or be subjected to discrimination under any program or activity receiving federal financial assistance, or under any program conducted by any Executive Agency or by the United States Postal Service (12).*

A civil rights statute, the original Section 504 contained six parts, Subpart A was concerned with general provisions; B with employment practices; C with program accessibility; E with postsecondary education; F with health, welfare, and social services; and G with procedures. Subpart D considered the education of preschool, elementary, and secondary school-age handicapped children. The provisions of this part of the act resemble those of PL 94-142.

> *They require basically, that recipients operating public education programs provide a free appropriate education to each qualified handicapped child in the most normal setting appropriate. The regulation also sets forth evaluation requirements designed to ensure the proper classification and placement of handicapped children, and due process procedures for resolving disputes over placement of students. While the Department does not intend to review individual placement decisions, it does intend to ensure that testing and evaluation procedures required by the regulation are carried out, and that school systems provide an adequate opportunity for parents to challenge and seek review of these critical decisions (12).*

It is apparent, therefore, that concern for the education of children with disabilities evolved over a period of years, and this concern was reflected in the enactment of various public laws. Initially, the federal government provided financial assistance for the construction of facilities for the mentally retarded and encouraged research into the problems experienced by this population. Early legislation allocated funding for the training of personnel to work with the handicapped and for the development of specific programming. Later public laws concerned the rights of parents and their handicapped children to participate in educational planning and encourage placement of children in the least restrictive environment. All this legislation paved the way for the most significant law with regard to the handicapped, the Education of the Handicapped Act (short title).

Education of the Handicapped Act (EHA)/Individuals with Disabilities Education Act (IDEA)

General Provisions (From Part A of EHA/IDEA)

Preparatory to stating the purpose of the EHA/IDEA in the official document, several facts related to the development of the law were presented. Section 1400 stated that more than eight million children with disabilities were living in the United States and that the needs of these children were not being met. Further, the majority of these individuals were not receiving appropriate education, and one million children were excluded entirely from education with their peers. The document also stated that many children had unidentified disabilities that limited their success in school, and some children with detected disabilities were forced to receive services from outside agencies because their needs could not be met in the public school setting. Assuming that, given appropriate financial assistance, local and state educational agencies could provide services to children with disabilities and that it was the responsibility of these agencies to provide such services, the federal government concluded that it was in the best interest of the nation to provide financial assistance to state and local educational agencies so that they could implement programs for children with disabilities and assure such individuals equal protection under the law. The purpose, then, of EHA/IDEA was presented as follows:

> *It is the purpose of this chapter to assure that all children with disabilities have available to them . . . a free appropriate public education which emphasizes special education and related services designed to meet their unique needs, to assure that the rights of children with disabilities and their parents or guardians are protected, to assist States and localities to provide for the education of all children with disabilities, and to assess and assure the effectiveness of efforts to educate children with disabilities (13).*

Definitions (From Part A of EHA/IDEA)

In order to identify the target population and the types of services that must be provided, Section 1401 included definitions of disabilities covered by the law. Among the children identified as disabled were those who are hearing impaired, deaf, or speech or language impaired. The Code of Federal Regulations (34 CFR 300) defines "deaf" as an impairment that prevents the child from processing linguistic information and, as a result, affects educational performance. A "hard of hearing" student has an impairment that also negatively affects educational achievement but is not categorized as deaf. "Speech impaired" students demonstrate communicative disorders in the areas of fluency, articulation, voice, or language; to be considered disabled, these disabilities must adversely affect educational performance. The EHA/IDEA defines specific learning disability as a disorder involving the understanding or usage of spoken or written language, including conditions such as perceptual problems, brain damage, dyslexia, and developmental aphasia. Sensory or motor disabilities are not included, nor are retardation, emotional disorders, or deprivation.

With regard to "special education," it is defined as classroom, physical education, and home instruction, and education in hospitals and institutions designed to meet the unique needs of the individual child. These services must be provided at no cost to the guardians or parents. Speech pathology services may be included when individual states consider these services to be special education and when they meet these criteria. Related services include transportation and supportive services (including speech intervention and audiology) required by each child in order to benefit from the special education services (an interpretation of this aspect of the law is presented later in the chapter). Medical services for diagnostic purposes are also designated as supportive. Another important requirement defined by the law is the individualized education program (IEP). Although Chapter 5 addresses IEPs at length, the following definition should provide a preliminary understanding of the intent of this requirement.

The term "individualized education program" means a written statement for each child with a disability developed in any meeting by a representative of the local educational agency or an intermediate educational unit who shall be qualified to provide, or supervise the provision of, specially designed instruction to meet the unique needs of children with disabilities, the teacher, the parents or guardians of such child, and whenever appropriate, such child, which statement shall include (A) a statement of the present levels of educational performance of such child, (B) a statement of annual goals, including short-term instructional objectives, (C) a statement of the specific educational services to be provided to such child, and the extent to which such child will be able to participate in regular educational programs, (D) a statement of the needed transition services for students beginning no later than age 16 and annually thereafter (and, when determined appropriate for the individual, beginning at age 14 or younger), including, when appropriate, a statement of the interagency responsibilities[2] or linkages (or both) before the student leaves the school setting, (E) the projected date for initiation and anticipated duration of such services, and (F) appropriate objective criteria and evaluation procedures and schedules for determining, on at least an annual basis, whether instructional objectives are being achieved (13).

Entitlements and Allocations (From Part B of EHA/IDEA Assistance for Education of All Handicapped Children)

Although a lengthy discussion of entitlements and allocations is not appropriate in a text of this kind, some aspects of this portion of the law require attention. Essentially, the law allocates funds to each state based on the number of children with disabilities between the ages of 3 and 21 who are receiving special education and related services. An average of the number of individuals receiving such services on specific dates each year determines the official count. The funding formula is based on a percentage of the excess cost of educating a disabled student in terms of average per pupil expenditure. In 1978, the law authorized 5 percent of the expenditure multiplied by the total number of children with disabilities receiving services; that percentage was to increase to 10 percent in 1979, 20 percent in 1980, and 30 percent in 1981. Beginning in 1982, and continuing each year thereafter, 40 percent of the average per pupil expenditure

---

[2]So in original. Probably should be "responsibilities".

was to be authorized. In reality, federal support has never exceeded 12 percent, and appropriations for both FY 1990 and 1991 were 9 percent (14).

Eligibility (From Part B of EHA/IDEA)

In order to be eligible for federal assistance, the state was required to show that it had a policy that "assures all children with disabilities the right to a free appropriate public education" (13). Further, each state was required to develop a plan designed to provide complete educational opportunities to all children with disabilities, which included a timetable for achieving that goal and a description of the necessary facilities, personnel, and services. Educational programming was required for all handicapped children between the ages of 3 and 21 by September 1980 unless "the application of such requirements would be inconsistent with State law or practice" (13). Further, the state was obligated to develop procedures for locating and evaluating children in need of special programming. The plan also had to conform to priorities specified by the law for providing special education to children with disabilities. The initial priority was to children with disabilities who were not receiving an education, with the second priority being to those children who were not receiving an adequate education. Additional eligibility requirements were that (1) the local education agency maintain IEPs for each child with a disability, (2) children with disabilities be educated with non-disabled children whenever possible, and (3) evaluative procedures be nonbiased with respect to race or culture. Regarding the final requirement, it was mandated that the procedures be provided in the child's native language; further, more than one evaluative instrument or procedure must be utilized. "The provision, in effect, orders that assessment procedures be multi-factored, multi-sourced, and carried out by qualified personnel" (15).

Procedural Safeguards (From Part B of EHA/IDEA)

Section 1415 of the EHA/IDEA required that all states and local educational agencies receiving assistance assure that children with disabilities and their parents are "guaranteed procedural safeguards with respect to the provision of free appropriate public education" (13). The agencies are required to permit parents or guardians of children with disabilities to have access to all relevant records "with respect to the identification, evaluation, and educational placement of the child" (13). They must also have the opportunity to request an independent evaluation of the child. Surrogates must be appointed to represent the child whose parents or guardians are unknown or unavailable. Additional safeguards require that parents be informed in writing whenever a change in their child's program is proposed or when the agency refuses to initiate a change in that program. Parents must also be given an opportunity to object to any aspect of the child's educational management.

If parents question the educational opportunities available to their child, they must have access to an impartial due process hearing to be conducted by the local, intermediate, or state educational agency. When the hearing is held at the local or intermediate level, appeals may be made to the state educational agency; subsequent appeals may be taken to the state or federal courts.

With regard to the hearing itself, all parties must be allowed to be accompanied and advised by counsel or individuals knowledgeable in the area of children with disabilities. Any party may present evidence, cross-examine, or request the attendance of witnesses. Written or electronic records of the proceedings, findings, and decision of the hearing must be made available to all parties.

Infants and Toddlers with Disabilities (From Part H of EHA/IDEA: PL 99-457)

Although legislation covered children with disabilities from age 3 to 18, with provision made for youths up to 21, a need was recognized to include infants and toddlers who required early intervention. The areas of concern were cognitive, physical, communicative, or psychosocial development, as well as self-help skills; children with diagnosed conditions that might result in developmental delays were also included. The early intervention services provided to infants and toddlers must be at no cost to families (except when covered by other federal or state laws), under public supervision, and individualized to meet the infant's or toddler's needs. An important stipulation of Part H (Sec. 1472) is that services must be provided by qualified personnel, including SLPs. Further, the services must conform to the individualized family service plan (IFSP).

Similar to the IEP requirements, the IFSP mandates that, following a multidisciplinary assessment of needs and specification of services, a program must be developed that includes

1. *A statement of the infant's or toddler's present levels of physical development, cognitive development, language and speech development, psychosocial development, and self-help skills, based on acceptable objective criteria,*
2. *A statement of the family's strengths and needs relating to enhancing the development of the family's infant or toddler with a disability,*
3. *A statement of the major outcomes expected to be achieved for the infant or toddler and the family, and the criteria, procedures, and timelines used to determine the degree to which progress toward achieving the outcomes are being made and whether modifications or revisions of the outcomes or services are necessary,*
4. *A statement of specific early intervention services necessary to meet*

> *the unique needs of the infant or toddler and the family, including the frequency, intensity, and the method of delivering services,*
> 5. *The projected dates for initiation of services, and the anticipated duration of such services,*
> 6. *The name of the case manager from the profession most immediately relevant to the infant's or toddler's or family's needs who will be responsible for the implementation of the plan and coordination with other agencies and persons, and*
> 7. *The steps to be taken supporting the transition of the toddler with a disability to services provided under subchapter II of this chapter to the extent such services are considered appropriate (13).*

Although the law is not specific about the length of time that may elapse between assessment and plan development ("within a reasonable time"), review of the plans is required at six-month intervals or more frequently if needed.

The discussion of the EHA/IDEA was not intended to be all-inclusive. Other parts of the law consider centers and services designed to meet the needs of individuals with disabilities, grants for training personnel, research opportunities, and instructional media and materials for persons with disabilities. Next the implementation of the EHA is considered. All of the cases cited occurred before the title was changed; hence, the consistent reference to EHA.

Legal Implementation of the EHA

SLPs must be cognizant of litigation involving various professionals as a result of EHA regulations and, in some cases, violation of these regulations. *The Education for the Handicapped Law Report* publications document several cases in which SLPs have been involved. Representative cases from mid-June 1989 and early 1990 follow (16).

The first case involved a 14-year-old (B. P.) whose handicapping condition included mental retardation, seizures, and tuberous sclerosis (16-EHLR 60). The parents contended that B. P. required an extended school year (ESY) and should receive individual speech-language services; at that time, the student received in-class therapy from her teacher in consultation with the SLP. The consultation plan was developed because individual therapy (fifteen minutes, three times per week) had yielded no positive results. The consultation model required the SLP to consult with the classroom teacher on a weekly basis, with the therapy goals implemented by the teacher within the classroom.

According to the school SLP, B. P.'s receptive language ability was at the 10- to 11-month level, with her expressive skills at the 5- to 6-month level. B. P.'s communication skills were minimal, and the SLP testified that the student would probably not develop any additional language system. However, B. P.'s father (who was also an SLP) testified that her language skills were in the 3- to 6-year range although he felt that no test could accurately assess

B. P.'s communication skills. Mr. P. further asserted that B. P. would regress without direct services.

The findings supported the district hearing officer's position that intervention could be implemented effectively using the consultative model. The classroom teacher, SLP, and SLP coordinator concurred that this was appropriate. Incidentally, the parent's desire for an ESY was denied since evidence of regression had not been presented.

The West Virginia Supreme Court of Appeals considered the case of two hearing-impaired siblings (16-EHLR 145). The board of education had recommended residential placement for the youths and had accepted IEPs that included minimal language intervention. The parents complained that the board of education was discriminating against their children on the basis of their handicaps.

The question of placement of one student was considered moot since he exceeded the maximum age for education. However, in reviewing the case of the other student, it was found that she had received counseling and language therapy two to three times each week for half-day periods. The district could not afford to fund an appropriate education for her; hence, the recommendation for institutional placement. The father would not consent to that placement. Eventually, the commission determined that the district had failed to provide an appropriate education in the least restrictive environment (LRE). The circuit court upheld the LRE recommendation, and this was upheld by the supreme court of appeals. Finally, it was determined that procedural violations had occurred but not discrimination.

In another case involving a hearing-impaired student, the parents alleged discrimination against their son because the district employed a special education teacher (with a specialization in the hearing impaired) to provide speech/language services (16-EHLR 119). The district contended that the teacher of the hearing-impaired was qualified to work with the student. It further stated that the student's IEP did not specify that the service provider be certified, just qualified. No discrimination was found by the OCR who received the complaints.

The prompt initiation and continuation of services were at issue in a complaint lodged against a California district (16-EHLR 253). The complainant held that direct speech/language services were not available for four weeks at the beginning of the school year; these delays were the result of testing and IEP development. In addition, services were not provided during the last week of the school year. The district investigated this complaint and determined that a ten-day delay did not constitute a deprivation of services but that the four-week delay was a technical violation of state law. California revised procedures require that services begin on the eleventh day of the school year, and this was to be specified in IEPs. Because of this procedural revision, action by the OCR was not required.

Compliance with the IEP specifications regarding service provision was also questioned in a Texas complaint (16-EHLR 299). The complainants alleged that their child's IEP specified five, twenty-five-minute speech-language sessions per week. However, the SLP missed twenty sessions during the year because of illness and other obligations. The parents complained that their child was discriminated against by the district, which failed to provide prescribed services. The OCR concurred with the complaint and recommended that SLPs not cancel therapy for other duties; in the case of absences, approved substitute SLPs must be employed. The district in question complied with these recommendations.

A Missouri case illustrated both the shortening of the school day and noncompliance with the IEP (16-EHLR 467). Because of transportation scheduling, this hearing-impaired student received thirty minutes less of education each day. In addition, speech-language services were not provided during the first six weeks of school. Discrimination based on handicapping condition was charged in the complaint. The OCR concluded that handicapped students were leaving thirty minutes earlier than nonhandicapped students, and this situation was rectified by the district. The district also acknowledged that speech-language services had been delayed six weeks and corrected this violation.

An unwritten policy of the Chicago Public Schools (District #299) not to provide speech-language services to deaf and hearing-impaired students was challenged in 1989 (16-EHLR 319). The district felt that those students who could benefit from such services should receive them from a teacher of the hearing impaired rather than an SLP. This, according to the complainant, was a case of discrimination based on handicapping condition. Further, it was contended that the district was not meeting the educational needs of hearing-impaired and deaf students. After receiving all evidence, the OCR found the district to be in violation of Section 504 of the Rehabilitation Act. The district, in response, presented written assurance that it would rectify the situation.

Failure to provide consistent resource room services and to reevaluate a speech-language impaired student on schedule was the complaint lodged against a West Virginia public school district (16-EHLR 471). The parents alleged that the resource room teacher was absent on seven occasions and that the services of a substitute teacher were not offered. Further, the district did not reevaluate the student on the required three-year schedule. OCR investigated the complaint and found the district to be at fault on these two charges. The district then implemented formal procedures for documenting reevaluation schedules. Further, the district generated a plan to have a substitute teacher present whenever the resource room teacher was absent.

A California case involved a hearing-, speech-, and language-disordered child who was allegedly misdiagnosed and placed in a classroom for the mentally retarded (16-EHLR 383). Following ear surgery, reevaluation was requested by the parents but not conducted by the school district in which the child resided. The parents, therefore, sent the child to live with the grandparents in another district. The second district adopted the original IEP and refused to reconsider the child's placement or other placement options. The grandparents charged that the education being provided to the child was inappropriate. The OCR agreed that the new district had failed to investigate a less restrictive placement for the child. The district responded to this violation by instituting revised procedures for assessing and placing transfer students.

In another case, a 9-year-old student was originally diagosed as speech and language impaired (16-EHLR 89-38). At a later point, the district modified the diagnosis to educable mentally retarded; the parents were not notified in writing of this change. This failure to notify the parents constituted the basis for the complaint. The hearing officer found for the parents. It was determined that the district's failure to notify the parents of the change in classification and not include them in the IEP development constituted procedural violations. Further, the officer determined that the classification was in error, as was the child's educational placement. As a result, it was ordered that the student's IEP be modified and that the child be placed in a language classroom, taught by an SLP. Finally, the officer ordered that the assessment team evaluate procedures, goals, and objectives every six weeks for one academic year.

A final case involved a 15-year-old who had suffered organic encephalopathy as the result of a bicycle accident when she was five (16-EHLR 685). Because the student continued to score in the low normal range on IQ tests during the next ten years, the school district would not consider special education placement. This was despite the fact that the student displayed communicative disorders and was health impaired. The district held that the student's placement in regular education was appropriate since an extreme discrepancy between her age and school level did not exist. The parents, dissatisfied with the district's position, had an independent evaluation done by a neuropsychologist (with a background in speech pathology and language/learning disabilities). The neuropsychologist, following assessment of the student, concluded that special education was required. The presiding judge concurred with the independent evaluator and ordered that the district execute an IEP in keeping with the independent evaluator's recommendation.

Concerns Regarding Federal Legislation

Although the passage of legislation at the state and federal levels should have been greeted with enthusiasm by all professionals involved with handicapped children, there is little doubt that difficulties in interpretation have tempered this enthusiasm. A perusal of the early literature revealed one offering entitled "Staying Out of Jail," an article dealing with the IEP requirements of PL 94-142 (17). This may have reflected the attitude with which some professionals approached the regulations. Most SLPs, however, realized that much of what was required by the law had always been done by conscientious professionals. Additionally, they realized that state and local requirements regarding the law were sometimes more involved than the federal law itself. Nevertheless, some concerns involving the laws have been raised, and some continue to exist.

PL 93-380, Section 513, has received much attention in professional literature (11). Referred to previously as the Buckley Amendment, this section of the law is known as the Family Educational Rights and Privacy Act of 1974. Enactment of this law allowed students and their parents the right to inspect information contained in all relevant official records concerning the students. In addition, it required schools to obtain the written permission of parents before student records could be released to any outside source. The law also limited the release of "any personally identifiable data on students and their families on the grounds that such actions constitute a violation of the right to privacy and confidentiality" (11).

Initial concerns created by the law included the impact of the regulations on research. It was projected that research efforts might be hindered by the inaccessibility of such information. As the former chair of an internal review board overseeing the participation of human subjects in research, the author concurs that some research efforts have been complicated by the Buckley Amendment. It should be pointed out, however, that researchers obtaining informed consent from the subject or their parents (in the case of minors) continue to be able to conduct sensitive and pertinent studies without violating Section 513. In retrospect, then, this concern proved to be unnecessary.

Another issue raised involved the inclusiveness of the term *official records*. Healey questioned whether this included information collected by the speech-language pathologist (18). Pickering addressed the Buckley Amendment and the potential effect it might have on the records maintained by professionals in this area (19). She commented on the fact that speech-language pathologists have enjoyed the luxury of a closed system of record keeping. With the advent of the amendment, objectivity and accuracy in reporting are even more essential since parents and students have access to this information. She concluded,

> We must now ask ourselves to examine what we write as well as how well we write it. If we are not willing to let our clients and their parents see our records, perhaps we ought not be saying certain things at all (19).

Although some inconveniences may have resulted from enactment of the Buckley Amendment, there is little doubt that it is serving a necessary function. SLPs involved in research should not be inhibited by the requirements of Section 513. Those investigators desiring to collect personal data for research purposes should be able to obtain informed consent if the project's objectives and procedures are presented to potential subjects (or their parents) in a reasonable manner.

With regard to accessibility of records, SLPs should maintain objective information on the clients they serve. The professional who declares that a child is "language disordered" without verifying objective data is suspect, whereas the SLP who bases such a diagnosis on analysis of a language sample and the results of standardized language tests will have no concern about making these records accessible to parents. Therefore, this provision of the law should present no problem to the professional SLP.

Questions regarding the impact of PL 94-142 were raised and answered by Dublinske and Healey (20). Following presentation of the general principles of the law, the authors discussed terms relevant to the speech-language pathologist. In defining "deaf," "hard of hearing," and "speech impaired," the law specifies that the disorder "adversely affects educational performance." Does that mean that it must be demonstrated that a child with a vocal disorder—hypernasality, for example—is not performing well academically as a result of this problem before he or she qualifies as being communicatively handicapped? According to Dublinske and Healey, the answer to this question is negative.

> *Educational performance is not defined in the law or the regulation. However, educational performance has been interpreted broadly to include not only academic performance but also a child's social and emotional performance, and interpersonal relationships (20).*

This interpretation allows for children with fluency or vocal disorders to receive services even though their communicative disorders may not affect academic performance.

Although it appeared that this concern had been resolved, such was not the case. Dublinske reported that questions still are raised at the local level by SLPs where superiors do not allow services to be provided to students who do not have concomitant deficits in academic achievement (21). Other SLPs report that they are required to document how the communicative disorder negatively influences academic achievement. The Department of Education interpretation suggests that, in both instances, policies are being violated. According to department interpretation, a communicative disorder that is severe enough to require services will adversely affect academic achievement. Further, it states that appropriate tests of speech and language (as opposed to achievement tests) administered by a qualified SLP should be the basis for deciding what impact the communicative disorder has on educational performance. Therefore, a district cannot withhold speech-language services to students on the basis of the absence of academic achievement problems.

Earlier in the chapter, the nature of the service provided by SLPs was presented. It appears that the EHA/IDEA includes speech pathology and audiology as related services rather than special education services. The latter term is defined as "specially designed instruction, at no cost to the parent, designed to meet the unique needs of a child with a disability (13). Included are classroom instruction, instruction in physical education, home instruction, and instruction in hospitals and institutions. According to Dublinske and Healey:

The regulations indicate that the term includes speech-language pathology and many other services if they consist of specially designed instruction provided at no cost to the parents to meet the unique needs of a handicapped child and if considered "special education" rather than a "related service" under state standards (20).

Included as "related services" under the law are transportation and other supporting services, including speech pathology and audiology. According to the law, children must be receiving special education services rather than related services in order to quality for EHA funding. It would appear, then, that children with isolated communicative disorders would not be considered eligible for funding. Interpretation of the law does not confirm this, however. According to Dublinske and Healey, these definitions permit the inclusion of speech-language pathology and audiology services as both special education and related services. To the child whose primary disability is in speech and language, special education in speech-language pathology is provided. Related services in speech-language pathology are appropriate for the child whose primary handicap is in an area such as mental retardation. Interpretation of the law suggests that the SLP may provide either special education services or related services to communicatively disordered children; both types of services qualify for funding under PL 94-142. Because some local districts considered moving speech-language pathology from special education to related services, the implications of this reclassification were explored by Dublinske (22).

A child who is handicapped (in the language of the article) requires special education; he or she may also require related services in order to benefit from the special education. If the child is not receiving special education, then, according to the law, he or she is not handicapped, and related services are not covered.

With regard to reclassification of speech-language services from special education to related services, Dublinske cautions that such a move would preclude reimbursement for children who presented isolated speech-language impairment. In dollars and cents, this reclassification would have cost districts approximately $267,517,440 during the 1983–1984 school year. In general, about 26 percent of EHA funding would be cut. Dublinske concluded that appropriate service to children with speech-language disorders is best assured when such services are classified as both special education and related.

Although Chapter 3 considers the assessment of communicatively disordered children in depth, some discussion of the impact of the EHA/IDEA on evaluative procedures is appropriate. First, the law mandates that a child must be assessed before he or she may be placed in any type of special program. Further, the testing procedures must be nonbiased with regard to race or culture, must be administered in the child's native language or "mode of communication" by a qualified professional, must test what it purports to test, and must take into account any disabilities that the child may have. There is little doubt that some of these qualifications might pose problems to SLPs. For example, many tests are considered to be racially and culturally biased. Further, some tests available to SLPs have questionable pertinence with regard to functional communicative ability; should this be taken into account in analyzing the results of such testing? In short, the assessment procedures recommended by the EHA/IDEA may be troublesome, but necessary.

Although the SLP determines what evaluative tools and procedures should be utilized, it is necessary that a diagnosis be made on the results of more than one test. The child with an articulatory disorder would not be diagnosed as having such a problem on the basis of a conversational speech sample only; it would also be necessary to administer a standardized test of articulation. Similarly, a child could not be diagnosed as language disordered on the basis of the results of a vocabulary test.

It should be noted that parental consent is required before such an assessment is undertaken; the exception to this rule is when parents fail to respond to a request to consent to an evaluation. In this case, several options may be available, including

1. Compel the parents to respond through the due process hearing or court action.
2. Initiate the assessment after giving prior notice.
3. Retain the child in the present placement until consent is obtained.
4. Refuse placement of any kind until the issue is resolved (20).

SLPs must be cognizant of the requirements regarding evaluation, as well as steps which may be appropriate if the parents fail to agree to such an assessment.

One of the outstanding features of the EHA/IDEA is the mandate that children with disabilities must be placed in the least restrictive environment (LRE). With regard to communicatively impaired children, this has been the case for years. Most children remained in the regular classroom and were seen intermittently for speech-language intervention. This early day "mainstreaming" was not the result of farsightedness on the part of SLPs but rather due to lack of placement opportunities for communicatively disordered children. Such a therapy schedule might have been effective with children with isolated articulatory defects but did not meet the needs of children with serious language disorders. Today, it is mandated that a continuum of management alternatives be made available for all children with disabilities. For students with language disorders, this might include placement in a special language classroom for the entire day, placement in such a class for a portion of the day, placement in the regular classroom with hour-long sessions in the resource room daily, placement in the regular classroom with collaborative intervention, or individual or group services.

The LRE has received criticism as it relates to at least one group of communicatively disordered students: the deaf and hearing impaired. As reported in *Asha,* the Commission on the Education of the Deaf is dissatisfied with the manner in which hearing impaired students are educated (23). Among other shortcomings identified by the commission is the inappropriate placement of students by disability rather than ability. According to the report, "placement has been stressed over educational content" (23). It is recommended that the child's IEP should be emphasized rather than the LRE.

In a similar finding, Domico reviewed the LRE as it related to deaf and hearing-impaired students (24). As the reader became aware earlier in this chapter, a great deal of litigation has resulted from inappropriate services to this population. Domico cites additional cases (*Hendrick Hudson School District* v. *Rowley, Springdale School District,* v. *Grace,* and *Bonadonna* v. *Cooperman*) in which educational placement and approach were disputed. In general, the question arises whether the LRE is also the most appropriate, and this must continue to be judged on an individual basis.

Considerable attention has been focused on the Individualized Education Program (IEP) requirement of the EHA/IDEA. SLPs should have little difficulty complying with this stipulation of the law since professionals have been employing modified versions of IEPs for years. Specific information concerning the development and execution of IEPs is presented in Chapter 4.

Another aspect of the EHA/IDEA should be mentioned. A previous discussion of the funding schedule indicated that states in compliance would be eligible for up to 40 percent reimbursement of excess cost expenditures for handicapped children in 1982 and each year thereafter. The critical factor is that states must be in compliance; they must indeed be meeting all requirements of the law. According to Dublinske and Healey, if parent or advocacy group feels that a district or state receiving PL 94-142 funding is not in compliance, they may notify the state superintendent or commissioner of education, regional compliance officers, or a variety of other officials. "If the laws are going to be enforced, parents and advocacy organizations, such as speech and hearing associations, are going to have to alert authorities when noncompliance is observed" (20). Whether this method of notifying officials if districts are not in compliance is effective or not is questionable. Several years ago, the author had a conversation with an SLP working in a major midwestern city. It was reported by the professional that special educators in her district had not developed IEPs for the 1979–1980 year. It seemed that during the summer of 1979, the chief administrative officer of the special education program had decided to revise the IEP format; he had not completed the revision by September, and so there was an initial delay in distributing the information. At some later point, the revised and printed forms were misplaced in a warehouse. Although many superintendents and other school officials searched the warehouse for the missing IEP forms, they were unsuccessful. As the final third of the school year approached, the special educators were told that if they felt uncomfortable without IEPs, they should not work with the handicapped children. In an attempt to initiate action to rectify the situation, the SLP contacted the state consultant and an official of ASHA. In both instances, she was given sympathy but no hope of intervention. A similar situation was encountered when an SLP attempted to inform parents of their rights to due process. As the story goes, it was a building principal who reprimanded the SLP for providing too much information to the parents. Clearly, noncompliance on the part of the local education agency was reflected in both situations. Currently, local districts are going to great lengths to assure that they have documentation of the fact that parents have had rights explained to them. Parents are asked to sign a form saying that they have received and understand rights.

PL 99-457 (EHA/IDEA, Part H) has raised some questions regarding funding and the qualifications of the service provider. Originally, it appeared to some that the act reduced the financial obligations of states or changed eligibility under certain parts of the Social Security Act. Instead, this act was intended to augment that funding (25). Such assurance by the states applying for funding is now required.

A second problem occurring as a result of PL 99-457 is that of "qualified provider." According to Dublinske, the intent was that the highest professional requirement (for either certification or licensure) be applied (26). This meant the master's degree in all jurisdictions except four. Some states have attempted to avoid the qualified provider requirement by suggesting that this does not apply to PL 94-142 or indicating that there is insufficient personnel to meet the standards.

Dublinske suggests that these reasons are not valid. More recently, the Department of Education has mandated that states not employing personnel with a master's degree specify how they will retrain current personnel or what plans they have for hiring individuals with that degree (27).

There is also some question as to the actual preparedness of "qualified providers" to deal with this younger population (28). In a survey of randomly selected ESB accredited programs, the authors found variations in coverage of infancy-related content, as well as practicum experience. With regard to the former, the most detailed content coverage was in the areas of phonological development, assessment, and intervention. In most instances, practicum experiences were offered but not required of students. Few programs offered an infant tract in the curriculum. The question must be asked, then, if the qualified providers of today and tomorrow are really qualified.

Summary

This chapter has attempted to provide an overview of legislation influencing the school SLP. From the landmark decision of *PARC* v. *the Commonwealth of Pennsylvania* through a variety of public laws and finally the original PL 94-142, legislation has been focused on providing all children with disabilities with the most appropriate public education in the least restrictive environment at no cost to their parents or guardians. Volumes have recounted litigation involving the implementation of the law, with selected cases from 1989–1990 being presented in this chapter.

Concerns still exist about some aspects of the law, including the effect of communicative disorders on academic achievement: How is this to be interpreted? Although the answer seems clear, the question continues to arise. The same situation is seen with the special education versus related services issue. Of great concern is the implementation of the LRE concept: Is the most appropriate academic setting always in the least restrictive environment and vice versa? Finally, the question of qualified provider is pursued. Given the educational preparation of past and current students, are they really qualified? These continue to be areas of concern for SLPs with regard to the law; let's hope that future interpretations will provide solutions to these concerns and put the finishing touches on the quiet revolution on behalf of handicapped individuals of all ages.

Endnotes

1. J. M. Caccamo, "Speech, Language, and Audiological Services — an Inalienable Right," *Language, Speech, and Hearing Services in Schools* 5(1974): pp. 173–175.

2. J. W. Melcher, "Law, Litigation, and Handicapped Children," *Exceptional Children* 43(1976): pp. 126–130.

3. T. K. Gilhool, "Education: An Inalienable Right," *Exceptional Children* 39(1973): pp. 597–609.

4. P. Kuriloff, R. True, D. Kirp, and W. Buss, "Legal Reform and Education Change: The Pennsylvania Case," *Exceptional Children* 41(1974): pp. 35–42.

5. A. Abeson and J. Zettel, "The End of the Quiet Revolution: The Education for All Handicapped Children Act of 1975," *Exceptional Children* 44(1977): pp. 114–128.

6. Public Law 88-164. Mental Retardation Facilities and Community Health Centers Construction Act of 1963.

7. R. Hagerty and T. Howard, *How to Make Federal Mandatory Special Education Work for You* (Springfield: Charles C. Thomas, 1978).

8. Public Law 89-10. Elementary and Secondary Education Act of 1965.

9. Public Law 89-750. Elementary and Secondary Education Amendments of 1966.

10. Public Law 91-230. An Extension of the Elementary and Secondary Education Act of 1965.

11. Public Law 93-380. Education Amendments of 1974.

12. Public Law 93-112. The Rehabilitation Act of 1973.

13. Individuals with Disabilities Education Act (amended). *Education for the Handicapped Law Report* (Horsham, PA: LRP Publications, 1990).

14. S. Dublinske, "Third Party Reimbursement for Speech-Language Pathology Services Provided in the Schools: The History." (Prepared for the ASHA Committee on Government Affairs, July 1990).

15. J. Ballard and J. Zettel. "Public Law 94-142 and Section 504: What They Say About Rights and Protections." *Exceptional Children* 44(1977): pp. 177–185.

16. *Education for the Handicapped Law Report,* volume 16 (Horsham, PA: LRP Publications, 1990).

17. M. C. Reynolds, "Staying Out of Jail," *Teaching Exceptional Children* 10(1978): pp. 60–62.

18. W. C. Healey, "Notes from the Associate Secretary for School Affairs. Buck-

ley Amendment Sparks Controversy: Parents and Students Gain Access to School Files," *Language, Speech, and Hearing Services in Schools* 6(1975): pp. 115–116.

19. M. Pickering, "The Speech Clinician and the Family Educational Rights and Privacy Act of 1974, *Language, Speech and Hearing Services in Schools* 7(1976): pp. 131–133.

20. S. Dublinske and W. C. Healey, "Questions and Answers for the Speech-Language Pathologist and Audiologist," *Asha* 20(1978): pp. 188–205.

21. S. Dublinske, "Action: School Services," *Language, Speech and Hearing Services in Schools* 20(1989): pp. 108–109.

22. S. Dublinske, "Action: School Services," *Language, Speech and Hearing Services in Schools* 16(1985): pp. 142–143.

23. "Deaf Education Commission Flunks Schools," *Asha* 30(1988): p. 9.

24. W. D. Domico, "The 1986 Education of the Handicapped Act and Judicial Decisions Relating to the Child Who Is Hearing Impaired," *Asha* 31(1989): pp. 91–95.

25. "PL 99-457 Clarifies Sharing of Costs," *Asha* 29(1987): p. 8.

26. "News," *Asha* 29(1987): pp. 7–8.

27. "At Press Time," *Asha* 31(1989): p. 7.

28. E. Crais and C. Leonard, "PL 99-457: Are Speech-Language Pathologists Prepared for the Challenge?" *Asha* 32(1990): pp. 57–61.

3

Identification and Assessment of Communicatively Disordered Children

Introduction

Before the actual class work is begun, there is still one more thing to be done. The teacher must meet each of the children who are to compose her speech classes and give to each a thorough examination (1).

Walter Swift writing in the *Quarterly Journal of Speech Education* in 1919 had this advice for "speech correctionists" initiating programs for the communicatively handicapped in the schools. The procedures advocated by Swift began with persuading school officials that a need existed for speech services; this was established through questionnaires sent to teachers in the district. The teachers were to indicate the names and addresses of all children thought to have speech disorders. According to Swift, this information was most convincing to educators. He said that 300 children with speech disorders would probably be located in school systems employing 100 teachers. Next, principals were asked to provide specific information about the students referred by the teachers. This was followed by a comprehensive evaluation of each child by the speech correctionists, and if indicated, therapy was initiated. Teacher and parental participation in the therapeutic process was encouraged.

Although many years have intervened since Swift wrote about the beginning of speech correction programs in the schools, some similarities between procedures he advocated in 1919 and those still employed today are apparent. Seldom is it necessary for SLPs to convince administrators that communicatively disordered children exist. That services should be provided to these children must not be questioned. In order to qualify for federal assistance under the EHA/IDEA, districts must meet the needs of these students. Swift suggested using questionnaires to locate communicatively impaired children; today, SLPs employ teacher referral and screening techniques to identify speech- and language-impaired individuals. Finally, Swift stated that a thorough evaluation must be completed before intervention was initiated; the EHA/IDEA requires that evaluative procedures confirm the presence and nature of communicative disorders.

Contemporary SLPs, then, have many of the same responsibilities as their 1919 counterparts did. They must identify and evaluate communicatively disordered children in the most efficient manner possible and plan and execute intervention based on their findings. This chapter considers identification and assessment procedures in an established speech-language therapy program. It is assumed that compliance with state and federal legislation makes it unnecessary to discuss the initiation of such programs.

Following a review of the legal mandates for assessment and definitions of pertinent terms, attention shifts to those techniques that may be employed in the identification and assessment of communicatively disordered infants, children, and adolescents. Although certain procedural biases may be detected by the reader, no conscious attempt is made to advocate one tool or technique over another.

Legal Requirements

In order to be eligible for EHA/IDEA funding, individual states are required to develop plans that meet certain federal guidelines. Section 1412 of Part B of the EHA/IDEA mandates that states must demonstrate that specific conditions must be met, including

> *all children residing in the State who are disabled, regardless of the severity of their disability, and who are in need of special education and related services are identified, located, and evaluated (2).*

Later in this section, it is stated that

> *procedures to assure that testing and evaluation materials and procedures utilized for the purposes of evaluation and placement of children with disabilities will be selected and administered so as not to be racially or culturally discriminatory. Such materials or procedures shall be provided and administered in the child's native language or mode of communication, unless it clearly is not feasible to do so, and no single procedure*

shall be the sole criterion for determining an appropriate educational program for a child (2).

It is apparent, then, that procedures had to be devised by individual states to identify children with potential communicative disorders and locate unbiased assessment tools. Finally, Section 1412 mandates that SLPs employ at least two methods of assessment to determine if communicative disorders exist in a given child.

Part H (Infants and Toddlers with Disabilities), Section 1476, identifies the minimal components of early intervention as including

a timely, comprehensive, multidisciplinary evaluation of the functioning of each infant and toddler with a disability in the State and the needs of the families to appropriately assist in the development of the infant or toddler with a disability (2).

Further, in Section 1477, it is stated that each infant or toddler "shall receive a multidisciplinary assessment of unique needs and identification of services appropriate to meet such needs" (2). The cross-disciplinary aspects of assessment, then, are stressed in Part H.

The major problem facing SLPs in attempting to meet the mandate of the law is not in utilizing multiple methods of assessment or in interacting with other professionals in a multidisciplinary effort; the problem is in locating assessment tools that are not biased. The profession has dealt at length with the question of language disorders versus language differences as it relates to social dialects. ASHA's position on such dialects was addressed in 1983 and resulted in a position paper. Cole, in clarifying the implication of this paper on SLPs, addressed unbiased assessment (3). She suggested that there were alternatives to standardized testing and included the development of local norms, the utilization of different scoring procedures, and clinical judgments as options.

Vaughn-Cooke elaborated on methods of assessing the language of minority students (4). She acknowledged that dialectal variations are not considered disorders; however, many tests are not sensitive to these variations, especially variations in black language. She suggested that it might be feasible to standardize commercial tests on "non-mainstream English speakers"; this method would not be workable, however, if the test "had been constructed to asses only one dialect of English" (4). Including minority children in the standardization population would be a partial solution only if social class were controlled. Modification of existing tests is a possibility if the persons making the adaptation are familiar with the dialect. Perhaps the best solution, and maybe the only ethical one, is to develop new instruments appropriate to nonmainstream children. Thus far, the majority of test designers appear to be opting for alternative scoring procedures.

Closely associated with the problems of unbiased assessment of children with social dialects is that of unbiased assessment of bilingual students. It should be noted that some would include black speakers in the latter category.

Increasing numbers of children are entering schools for whom English is a second language. As position descriptions suggest, a large number of these students speak Spanish, and bilingual SLPs are in demand in some parts of the country to meet the needs of such students. Although the following discussion centers on problems associated with Spanish-speaking students, many of the suggestions pertain to any bilingual population.

Langdon considered factors that must be included when attempting to determine if a Spanish-speaking child is language disordered or presents language differences (5). She suggested that SLPs must determine the child's exposure to English through a study of the student's length of residence in an English-speaking community, school attendance patterns, his or her language usage, and the methodologies employed in the classrooms in which the child has been. The SLP should also compare the student in question with his or her peers and determine how the child is perceived by the parents or caregiver. Finally, the child's development and medical history must be reviewed. Langdon also outlined a model protocol for the actual assessment of the bilingual student, which included language testing and sampling in both languages and a comparison between the languages in different areas. Need and eligibility decisions, then, may be made based on review of the background information and direct assessment.

Kayser also considered the issue of Spanish–English bilingualism and the difficulties encountered in the assessment of bilingual students (6). She pointed out that many bilingual students have a language dominance (that is, one language that is stronger) and that frequently assessment is delayed until that dominant language is identified. It should be recognized that the dominance is usually determined by the area of language being assessed and will, therefore, vary according to those parameters. To determine the child's language status, Kayser recommends directed observation of the child in a variety of settings over a period of time. Informant questionnaires may be utilized to supplement information obtained through observation. All these data should be available prior to assessment.

Acknowledging that no commercial tests are appropriate for all bilingual students, Kayser does not recommend the use of tools standardized on an English population. Specifically, she states "the use of a standardized test should not be a part of the diagnostic process" (6). Like others, Kayser suggests that bilingual children be tested in both languages, not just the one judged to be dominant. And, when using standardized tests, the test protocols should be modified to be relevant to the child. Kayser also recommends language-sampling techniques and provides examples of Spanish-influenced English to assist SLPs in evaluating the language sample.

It is apparent, then, that SLPs working in the schools are struggling with the mandate for unbiased assessment procedures. This issue will undoubtedly continue to be a concern as cultural and language diversity in the schools increases. The wise SLP will remain abreast of current test protocols and study standardization data carefully before assessing students with social dialects and those who are bilingual.

Definitions

When considering the various communicative disorders, SLPs classify clients according to the presenting deviant communicative behaviors or according to the etiology of such behaviors. An individual with an articulatory disorder presents difficulty in the production and use of speech sounds. Such a problem might be related to a single cause or may result from a combination of etiological factors. Although the cause of the problem will affect treatment options, it is critical that the overt behavior be accurately identified before etiology is considered. The professional who knows that a child is cerebral palsied may anticipate difficulty with language, phonation, hearing, rate of speech, or articulation. However, if the child distorts /r/, is that deviation necessarily related to his or her neuromuscular condition? Or, if the child has a language disorder, is it the result of brain damage or could it be due to overprotectiveness on the part of the parents? In short, although etiology is significant in treatment, an accurate description of the specific communicative problems presented by the child is perhaps more informative. For the purposes of this text, a descriptive classification is employed.

Three terms require explanation: case findings, case selection, and caseload. *Case finding* or *screening* refers to the procedure whereby communicatively disordered children are identified. Evaluative procedures are then employed to confirm the presence of a specific problem and its severity. Traditionally, the techniques used to identify communicative disorders in children are direct screening and referral. Direct screening involves a short conversation with each child in order to assess voice, fluency, language, and articulation in contextual speech; screening tests of language or articulation may also be administered. This procedure is intended to distinguish those children with possible communicative disorders from those whose communicative abilities are within the normal range. Teacher referral relies on the classroom teacher's identification of children with possible problems and subsequent referral of those students to the SLP for evaluation. Parent referral is also encouraged. A more complete discussion of case finding appears later in this chapter. *Case selection,* the second term that required definition, refers to the process of determining if the child is eligible to receive services. Finally, *caseload* refers to the actual number of students being serviced by the SLP. These two procedures are discussed in a later chapter.

Case Finding

Students with suspected communicative disorders may be identified through mass screening or individual screening by the SLP or through teacher referral. The population to be considered is determined by the state, with districts devising plans to comply with these regulations. In Illinois, for example, the state requires annual screenings of children between the ages of 3 and 5 and speech-language screenings of all students enrolling in an Illinois school for the first time (7). Mass screenings are allowed, but districts are also encouraged to provide inservices to parents and teachers so that they can participate in the case finding through referrals. The state of Indiana requires local education agencies to have written procedures for identifying children between birth and 21 years who may have handicapping conditions (8). Indiana guidelines indicate that local agencies inform the public through the various media on the procedures to follow for making referrals. Missouri differentiates between periodic screenings, which include formal screenings (presumably conducted by the SLP), and continuous procedures, which are done through teacher and parental observation; the latter process assumes that the parents and teachers have been trained to recognize potential communicative disorders (9). Reportedly, continuous screening is being employed with increasing frequency in that state.

When mass or periodic screenings are employed, the SLP may choose to employ a standardized tool or rely on clinical judgments based on interactions with the child. The *Fluharty Preschool Speech and Language Screening Test* is an example of a tool that may be used with children from 2 to 6 years of age (10). Based on the psycholinguistic theory of language, the Fluharty requires object identification, nonverbal responses, and sentence repetition. There are thirty-five test items, and the administrative time is approximately six minutes. Another screening tool, the *Joliet 3-Minute Speech and Language Screen,* may be utilized with children in kindergarten, second grade, and fifth grade (11). This tool also tests receptive vocabulary and requires sentence repetition. Both tests are designed to assess articulation, and both allow for dialectal differences in the scoring protocols.

Some SLPs prefer to identify children with potential communicative disorders through informal methods. To be efficient, the SLP should elicit a speech and language sample that is sufficient to allow for assessment of articulation (in single words and contextual speech) and analysis of the child's linguistic competence. Clinical judgments of vocal and rhythmic attributes and hearing acuity must also be made. Frequently, SLPs are able to elicit this information in a conversation with the child, but they must also be prepared to utilize conversation stimulating pictures or objects. When the SLP suspects that a vocal or fluency problem may be present, it is important that the SLP observe the child on more than one occasion and in additional settings.

Identification of children with communicative disorders may be done, then, by the SLP during mass screening, periodic screenings, or when the students enter the district for the first time. Both informal and formal screening methods may be employed. Another method of locating these children is through teacher referral, and that technique is considered next.

Teacher referral has long been considered a viable method of identifying children with possible deviations of speech, language, and hearing. When using the teacher referral method, teachers must receive inservice training, ideally through a series of sessions conducted by the school SLP. These meetings are designed to familiarize the teachers with the nature and characteristics of communicative disorders. This could be part of a total inservice program that would not only consider identification of children with speech, language, and hearing deviations but would also describe the classroom teachers' roles in intervention. The information given to the teachers should include material on the various disorders and examples of each. The teachers are then asked to refer to the SLP any children in their classrooms who may present speech, language, or hearing problems. The teacher referral method may delay the assessment process since it may be several weeks into the school year before the teachers have had sufficient opportunity to listen to the children and to make judgments regarding their communicative skills.

From the author's experience with teacher referral, several observations should be shared. First, the SLP should clearly differentiate misarticulations from mispronunciations. Stuttering should also be defined carefully so that teachers do not confuse so-called normal dysfluencies with those associated with stuttering. One would expect a paucity of voice referrals unless such problems were very obvious; SLPs may experience similar difficulties in identifying children with vocal disorders. Teachers would be expected to locate children with language problems with some ease since such difficulties would affect their classroom performance. Finally, teachers tend to be sensitive to children with hearing and processing problems and would be likely to make prompt referrals.

In summary, the SLP is one of many professionals responsible for identifying children with possible handicapping conditions. The screening process may not require parental consent and may be accomplished through direct contact with the child or through teacher referral. The population targeted for screening and the preferred methods for case finding differ from state to state and within districts in each state. Although some states allow for an intermediate process of attempting to implement classroom procedures to modify the communicative behaviors of those identified as having disorders, the next logical step in the process is the assessment of children with suspected problems. That process is considered next.

Evaluation of the Communicatively Disordered Child

Following the location of children with suspected communicative disorders, the SLP must evaluate each child so identified. First, the parents are informed that the child has been seen and that the results of the screening suggest that further testing is warranted. The parents must consent to an evaluation before it is initiated. Once consent has been obtained, the SLP must plan for the evaluation. The EHA/IDEA mandates that at least two methods must be utilized in making a diagnosis. This means, for example, that a child may not be diagnosed as having an articulatory disorder on the basis of a single test. It would be necessary for the SLP to administer a formal test of articulation and to supplement that with an analysis of contextual speech. In addition, a case history is desirable. Numerous forms are available for eliciting the case history, either prior to the assessment or through informant interview. Regardless of the methods used for obtaining the information, a complete case history should include: identifying information about the child and family members; the caregiver's description of the problem, including cause, development, and management; information regarding the child's development, with birth history; medical history; speech, language, and hearing history; and a description of the child's general behavior including his or her relationships with others. In a school setting, it is likely that a standard case history is recommended; however, the SLP should be certain to elicit additional information if it is not included on the standard form.

Following preparation of the case history, the SLP must determine which diagnostic tools and techniques should be employed in the evaluation. Although the following discussion does not purport to be exhaustive, some indication of techniques appropriately utilized in the school setting appears necessary. Only the section on assessing language skills is divided into age groups, as well as according to the aspect of communication to be evaluated.

Assessment of Articulatory Skills

The initial identification of an articulatory disorder is usually made during conversation. A formal test of articulation should provide additional information about that defect. Numerous commercial tests are available. They differ in ease of administration and scoring, format, and administrative time required, as well as in test philosophy. Such tests may be designed to analyze articulation in terms of distinctive features (*Fisher-Logemann Test of Articulation Competence*) or developmental norms (*Templin-Darley Diagnostic Tests of Articulation*), to assess according to the frequency of occurrence of various phonemes in American English (*The Arizona Articulation Proficiency Scale*), to obtain multiple response (*Goldman-Fristoe Test of Articulation*), or to analyze articulatory skills in terms of phonological processing (*The Assessment of Phonological Processes*).

Ease of administration, time required to administer the test, and ease of scoring were mentioned as criteria for test selection. The first factor might be individually determined; certainly practice in using a specific tool would improve efficiency in administration. Also, the clarity of the stimulus pictures or objects would be a factor. Tests with fewer stimulus items may not necessarily require less time to administer if the items are ambiguous and require prompting to elicit the desired response.

With regard to ease of scoring, preferences may again be related to experience with the tool. The *Goldman-Fristoe,* for example, was considered by many to be difficult to score. Similar observations have been made by those using phonological process analysis. However, once the examiner becomes familiar with the system, scoring is facilitated. Moreover, if the examiner has access to software designed to analyze test results, time required to score the tests is reduced.

It is often assumed that all tests of articulation measure what they purport to test. Schissel and James conducted a study that makes this assumption questionable (12). Comparing the responses of twenty-nine children to both the *Arizona Articulation Proficiency Scale* and the *McDonald Deep Test,* the researchers found the former to be less sensitive. The results indicated that the Arizona failed to detect some children who made consistent articulatory errors on relatively few sounds. Therefore, the SLP should be judicious in test selection with regard to the validity of the tool.

Many of the tests alluded to in the previous discussion involve picture-naming tasks. It was suggested that such tests should be supplemented by analysis of contextual speech. DuBois and Bernthal compared the efficiency of these two methods, as well as what they termed "modeled continuous speech" (13). The "continuous speech task" involved the child telling a story about various stimulus pictures. The "modeled continuous speech task" required the child to include specific stimulus words in phrases or sentences. The "spontaneous picture-naming task" required the child to name stimulus pictures. Not surprisingly, the researchers found that more errors were heard during the continuous speaking task; the fewest errors were elicited during picture naming. This finding should reaffirm the necessity for obtaining and analyzing a spontaneous speech sample.

Another aspect of assessing articulatory skills is the determination of whether the child can be stimulated to produce the error sound correctly. Some commercial tests include stimulability in their protocols; when this is not the case, SLPs should augment assessment procedures with stimulability testing.

Assessment of the articulatory skills of children, then, should include administration of a formal test of articulation, analysis of a contextual speech sample, and evaluation of stimulability. Audiometric testing is required, and supplementary tests of auditory discrimination and memory span may be administered. Finally, an assessment of the structure and function of the speech mechanism is indicated.

Assessment of Fluency

When the child presents a fluency disorder, a speech sample should be obtained and analyzed, but additional observations of the child's speech in different situations should also be made. The reader is well aware that stuttering varies significantly from individual to individual and fluctuates within each individual who stutters. The child may display severe dysfluencies in the classroom and be reasonably fluent at home; the reverse may also be true. It behooves the SLP to obtain several samples of the child's speech prior to making a firm diagnosis.

In assessing stuttering behavior, the nature of the dysfluencies should be noted. For example, the presence and consistency of repetitions, prolongations, or interjections should be recorded. The SLP should also attempt to identify any associated behaviors, including tension, gaze aversion, and other secondary characteristics. The variations in stuttering in different situations should also be noted.

Checklists, self-inventories, and scales for rating the severity of stuttering arc available to the SLP. Among these are *Riley's Stuttering Severity Instrument for Children and Adults,* the *Iowa Scale of Stuttering Severity,* and *Cooper's Chronicity Prediction Checklist.* Although a case history is an important part of any evaluation, its significance in assessing a young stutterer cannot be overemphasized. Therefore, a comprehensive evaluation should include direct and indirect observation of the child in a variety of situations, careful attention to the types of dysfluencies and related behaviors, and a meticulous case history. Only after all information has been analyzed can a diagnosis of stuttering be made.

Assessment of Voice

In the absence of sophisticated instrumentation, it is the ear of the SLP that is critical in the assessment of children with possible vocal disorders. Judgments concerning the adequacy of a child's voice should be made on a number of occasions. The child who is hoarse, for example, may be susceptible to allergies. A child may have a cold at the time of the initial screening and may not present a chronic vocal disorder. Therefore, the SLP must make several observations before proceeding.

Several checklists are available for assessing vocal attributes, as are procedural guides for conducting a voice evaluation. Boone and McFarlane and Aronson guide the reader through clinical examination for voice disorders, including supplementary case history information (14, 15). Although some of the procedures described by these authors are beyond the expertise of the SLP, the reader is referred to these sources for valuable guidelines. The reader is advised also to heed this message from Hutchinson et al., who said, "We can supply guidelines and specific procedures but recognition of the occurrence of harmful pitch, tensions or defects of loudness or qualities cannot be developed by reading a book" (16).

The case history is very important in the evaluation of a child with a suspected vocal disorder. Since medical clearance should be sought in cases in which a pathology may be present, early referral is imperative. It is the responsibility of the SLP to identify such problems and to obtain a confirming diagnosis from an otolaryngologist prior to initiating services.

Assessment of Hearing

The identification of children with hearing impairment may or may not be the responsibility of the SLP, depending upon the regulations of the school district. In some systems, hearing screenings are conducted by public health offi-cials or the school nurse. Those children identified as hearing impaired are referred to an audiologist for complete evaluation. SLPs may be responsible for screening the hearing of children in their caseloads. Since these individuals are not permitted to perform sophisticated assessments, it is necessary to refer children failing the screening to certified audiologists.

Assessment of Language

The assessment of language has taken on increasing importance as researchers have learned more about its development and intricacies. Also, members of the profession have developed more sophistication in generating tests that are sen-sitive to the various parameters of language. Because language expectations differ according to age, it seems prudent to discuss assessment procedures with respect to age groups. In the following section, assessment of infants and tod-dlers is considered.

Infants and Toddlers

The passage of PL 99-457 has caused practicing SLPs to review their language and child development notes and has encouraged students in training to attend more closely to lectures on those topics. Now, in addition to being cognizant of the evolving skills of 3-year-olds (through adolescents), SLPs must be prepared to assess the adequacy of the developing abilities of infants and toddlers, par-ticularly those considered at risk.

Rossetti made an important contribution to an understanding of the po-tential problems presented by high-risk infants (17). He also addressed the need to assess infants accurately so that appropriate intervention strategies may be implemented. Acknowledging the limited value of some infant assessment tools, particularly as they relate to prognosis, Rossetti suggests that periodic di-rected observations may be of more assistance than formal tests. He also rec-ommends that observations be descriptive and come from a variety of sources, including the parents.

It is obvious that most at-risk infants will require the attention of numer-ous professionals although the specific personnel involved with a given infant will vary from case to case. Certainly the services of an SLP will be required in many instances. Although assessment of these infants may take place in a vari-ety of settings, the home setting might produce the most reliable information. Among the tools available to the SLP for infant assessment are the *Battelle De-velopmental Inventory,* which considers communication development, along with personal/social, cognitive, adaptive, and motor; and *Bayley Scales of In-fant Development,* which includes communication as part of the mental scale section; the *Denver Developmental Screening Test,* which targets language as well as three other developmental skills; the *Receptive-Expressive Emergent Language Scale,* an informant test suitable for infants from birth to three years; and the *Sequenced Inventory of Communication Development,* which assesses both receptive and expressive abilities (17).

Other tools that may be used to assess at-risk infants and toddlers are *Assessment in Infancy: Ordinal Scales of Psychological Development,* the *Brigance Diagnostic Inventory of Early Development, Collier-Agusa Scale: G-Edition, Merrill-Palmer Scale,* and *Normative Adaptive Behavior Checklist.*

As noted earlier, observation of the infant is a critical component of an accurate assessment; similarly, reports from the observations of others must receive attention. It goes without saying that the SLP should always have access to the infant's case history. In short, assessment of the infant requires knowledge of what is considered to be within normal developmental limits and the skills and insight to identify what is not. The public school SLP may need to retool in order to prepare to meet the assessment needs of the infant-toddler population.

Preschool Children

Most students in training obtain experience with preschool children during their college practicum experiences; this population appears to be well represented in university speech, language, and hearing centers. However, as more schools provide services to preschoolers, accurate and efficient methods of assessment applicable to the school setting are required. Guidelines for assessment of the language of preschoolers are presented in this section.

A growing number of tools are available for assessing the language skills of preschool children. They differ in their theoretical basis, the language skills tapped, and the relevance of the information that is yielded. Using the categories outlined by Lahey, the information available from the various tests may be classified as general information about language performance, content/form, content-related, and use. Within these categories may be measures of expressive or receptive skills (19).

In the category of general performance fall several tests that may be utilized with the preschool population. The *Preschool Language Scale,* appropriate for children up to 7-years-old, assesses both auditory comprehension and verbal ability. Items appear in six-month increments from 1 year to 5 years. A language age and language quotient are derived. The *Bankson Language Screening Test,* appropriate for children from 4 to 8 years of age, assesses expressive and receptive information regarding semantic knowledge and morphological rules; only expressive responses are used for scoring purposes. Approximately twenty-five minutes are required for administration. The scores yield a language profile. The *Receptive-Expressive Emergent Language Scale* and the *Sequenced Inventory of Communication Development* may also be used to assess the general language skills of preschoolers.

Lahey identifies the *Test for Auditory Comprehension of Language* as a measurement of receptive lexicon and syntax in the content/form category. It may be utilized with children, ages 3 to 7. This test, which requires no speech, is a measurement of the comprehension of language structure. The test requires approximately 10 minutes. (There is a revised form that includes more items and may be used with children up to 10 years of age).

Tests that assess receptive comprehension of lexicon include the *Peabody Picture Vocabulary Test — Revised* (*PPVT-R*) and the *Boehm Test of Basic Concepts — Preschool Version*. The former tool was one of the earliest tests available to SLPs and continues to be widely used. The PPVT-R is a test of hearing vocabulary appropriate for children as young as $2^1/2$ years; speech is not required. The Boehm Test of Basic Concepts — Preschool Version, purports to assess the receptive language concepts needed by children to succeed in school. This test represents a downward extension of the original Boehm and is appropriately utilized with children from 3 to 5 years. The Preschool Version requires about fifteen minutes to administer. A fifty-two-item test, the Boehm assesses concepts such as "all," "after," and "tallest," together with their respective antonyms. A total score and a percentile equivalent may be calculated.

With regard to the expressive use of lexicon, the *Expressive One-Word Picture Vocabulary Test* is a unidimensional test that assesses vocabulary usage. The test requires ten to fifteen minutes to administer and tests general, abstract, and descriptive concepts and plurals. A mental age, intelligence quotient, and percentile may be figured from the test results.

Other measures of vocabulary are embedded in more comprehensive tests such as the *Test of Language Development* (*TOLD*), as well as single-purpose tools, including the *Receptive One-Word Picture Vocabulary Test*. Utilizing these two tests, along with the PPVT-R and Expressive One-Word Picture Vocabulary Test, Channell and Peek administered the four tests to thirty-six preschoolers (20). The researchers selected these instruments because of their similarities in representation and vocabulary. Because the correlations among the tests were only moderate, the researchers advised that several tests be used to determine the child's receptive and expressive lexical skills.

Lahey, in her identification of tests designed to assess the understanding of syntax, included the *Miller-Yoder Language Comprehension Test* (19). This test requires the child to point to the picture represented by the examiner's statement. There are eighty-four sentences, which form forty-two sentence pairs. The test yields age levels and developmental profiles. Expressive syntax used by the child is measured by the appropriate subtest of the *Test of Language Development — 2*. The *Northwestern Syntax Screening Test* also provides a measurement of expressive, as well as receptive, syntax usage.

Among the tools available to assess the preschooler's use of language is the *Test of Pragmatic Skills* (*TOPS*). Appropriate for children from 3 to 8, the TOPS employs natural and structured play to assess ten communication intentions. The child's responses to these interactions are rated in a 0–5 scale (5 being most complete). A mean composite score and a percentile rank may be obtained.

A recently developed tool for assessing pragmatic skills is the *Social Interactive Coding System* (*SICS*) (21). Acknowledging the importance of accurate assessment of pragmatic skills, the researchers state that "a major limitation for practitioners is that most of the available measurement systems are labor intensive, demand specialized training, and often require special equipment" (21). The researchers designed the SICS to measure the child's use of language in the classroom without the burdens outlined previously. After identifying and defining the various activities and interaction, the researchers prepared observation sheets to be utilized in the naturalistic classroom environment. Although Rice et al. recognize that some problems exist with the SICS, they see it as a "potential clinical tool for SLPs wishing to document a child's verbal initiations and responses in a natural classroom setting as a function of other environmental and child play variables" (21). This test appears to have promise as one method of assessing the pragmatic skills of preschoolers.

In summary, tools designed to measure the communicative skills of preschool children are increasing in number and level of sensitivity. SLPs must evaluate the tools in terms of assessment objectives and time effectiveness and analyze results as they compare with language-sampling techniques.

School-Aged Children

Many of the tools and procedures previously discussed apply to school-aged children; however, certain commercial tests have been targeted for this population or cut across the preschool and school-aged group. Among these are the *Clinical Evaluation of Language Fundamentals — Revised (CELF-R)*; the *CELF-R Screening, The Test of Early Language Development (TELD), The Test of Language Development — 2 Primary (TOLD-2 Primary)*, and *The Test of Language Development — 2 Intermediate (TOLD-2 Intermediate)*.

The CELF-R is purported to be a useful assessment tool for students from age 5 to 16. It should be emphasized that this is a measure of language skills as opposed to language function. Eleven different measures are tapped for analysis; these include linguistic concepts, word structure, sentence structure, oral directions, formulated sentences, recalling sentences, word classes, sentence assembly, semantic relationships, word associations, and listening to paragraphs. These subtests are designed to assess memory, syntax, and semantics. For students who are 8 and older, six of the subtests may be used. The time required to administer the CELF-R ranges from fifty-four to seventy-two minutes, with sixty-one minutes being the average length. The SLP should become thoroughly familiar with the testing and scoring procedures prior to administering the CELF-R; scoring is simplified for those who purchase the CELF-R Scoring Assistant software program.

The CELF-R Screening Test was designed to distinguish students between the ages of 5 and 16 years who have normal linguistic abilities from those who may have deficiencies and require in-depth evaluation. The test was generated by employing items from the CELF-R that had been most successful at identifying language deficits. A representative sample of 2,000 was utilized in researching the tool.

There are six sections of the CELF-R Screening Test. Morphological rules are screened in section 1, with section 2 tapping "the ability to interpret, recall, and execute oral directions that contain linguistic concepts" (brochure). Section 3 involves sentence repetition; relationships among word concepts are explored in section 4. Semantic relationships are screened in section 5, with the final section assessing the generation of appropriate sentences. Students ages 8 to 12 may omit section 1, and older students may be administered sections 3–6. With the latter group, screening is expected to require 16 minutes. A supplementary test of written expression may be employed, increasing the length of screening by eight and a half minutes.

The TELD is based on the form and content basis of the Lahey model; included are receptive and expressive tasks. Appropriate for children between the ages of 3 and 7-11, the TELD is a thirty-eight-item test that requires pointing, naming, repetition, gesturing, and the generation of information. The test yields a language quotient, a language age, and a percentile score.

The theoretical framework of the TOLD-2 Primary involves linguistic features (phonology, syntax, and semantics) and the linguistic systems of listening and speaking. It includes seven subtests that assess picture and oral vocabulary, sentence imitation, grammatic understanding and completion, word discrimination, and word articulation. It is appropriate for use with children between the ages of 4-0 and 8-11. Administration of the test requires thirty to sixty minutes, and results yield raw scores, percentile, standard scores, and quotients. A profile sheet provides a graphic representation of the students' strengths and weaknesses.

The TOLD-2 Intermediate follows the same basic framework as the TOLD-2 Primary and is appropriate for students between the ages of 8-6 and 12-11. Six subtests comprise the battery; included are sentence combining, vocabulary, word ordering, semantic and grammatic comprehension tasks. The last subtest assesses the student's ability to recognize absurdities in sentences due to the inclusion of similar sounding but incorrect words. The student must correct the error. Administration time varies from thirty to sixty minutes. As with the TOLD-2 Primary, raw scores, percentiles, standard scores, composite quotients, and a profile of the scores may be derived.

This summary of language tools appropriate for use in the school setting was not intended to be exhaustive. Many commercial tests are available, and most have strengths as well as limitations. It behooves SLPs to study the various protocols, their standardization data, and the language areas that each purports to test and make informed decisions based on the tool's application to specific populations.

Adolescents

In the mid-1960s, this author was contemplating a study of the communicative abilities of incarcerated male juvenile delinquents. A perusal of the tests available led to the realization that there were two from which to choose: the PPVT and the *Utah Test of Language Development* (*UTLD*). Both were utilized by default. These tests were augmented by conversational and narrative language samples.

Results from the PPVT were predictable but interesting. Most of the 119 subjects could identify the basic target words but broke down when presented with a word such as "casserole." However, these same youths knew "jurisprudence." Obviously, they were prepared environmentally and experientially for something other than a standard test of receptive vocabulary; it was not a true representation of their skills.

Even though the UTLD tapped a wider variety of linguistic abilities, it too presented procedural and scoring limitations. Again the different experiences of the youths both limited and, in some cases, enhanced their performances. There is little doubt that the majority of these youths displayed linguistic deficits; however, specificity in identifying these problems through formal testing was not possible.

The language-sampling technique was used primarily to identify deviations in articulation, voice, and fluency. The audiotaped samples were also used to verify linguistic differences and disorders. Given the paucity of information about adolescent language available at the time, in-depth analysis was not possible. Perhaps the most important and enlightening material came from the youths' response to the examiner's request to describe what they had done before they came to the training school (that is, the correctional facility). Included were "I beat up twelve old women and took their purses." "I didn't do nothing wrong." "All I ever did was run. I ran from home. I ran from Boys' Town. I never stole nothing—I just ran. I was trying to find my real dad." "I took some kid [sic] bike and they sent me here." The last response required 5 minutes to utter (or so it seemed) due to the youth's severe stuttering. Although these representative opening responses were interesting and remarkably accurate, our limited knowledge at the time allowed them to remain interesting and remarkably accurate and little more.

Today's SLP has the advantage of twenty-five additional years of adolescent language research. It may be that the years since the advent of PL 94-142 have been the most productive. During this time, tools designed specifically for use with adolescents have evolved; three such tests are described and compared in the next section. Methods of collecting and analyzing language samples are also presented.

In an attempt to design a tool for accurately assessing the linguistic skills of adolescents (ages 11–18), the Fullerton Union High School District, along with the California State University at Fullerton, developed a grant proposal to study this issue (18). The project was funded by the California State Department of Education for a period of five years. Following test development and field testing, the *Fullerton Language Test for Adolescents* (*FLTA*) emerged.

The test is administered individually in approximately forty-five minutes and consists of eight subtests; these include auditory synthesis, morphological competence, oral commands, convergent and divergent production, syllabications, grammatical competence, and idioms. Most of the subtests involve tasks required by other commercial tools.

Basal and ceilings are not utilized; each subtest is presented in its entirety. In addition, the items are not presented in an easy-to-difficult sequence. This type of presentation is considered to be motivating and nonfrustrating. Instead of attempting to specify the exact level at which an individual is functioning, each subtest identifies a general level of linguistic functioning. The three levels are competence (the skill is adequate), instruction (the skill is emerging), and frustration (the prerequisite skills are not present). This three-tier system is considered to be important in determining if intervention is necessary and in planning intervention.

The Fullerton is reportedly "user friendly" and may identify deficits that might otherwise be overlooked. The Fullerton should be used in conjunction with other tests and language-sampling procedures. Questions may arise about the demographic features of the experimental sample as well as the types of validity presented by the author. Nevertheless, the Fullerton Language Test for Adolescents should be useful in the school setting when employed cautiously by the SLP.

The Test of Adolescent Language—2 (TOAL-2) was another welcome tool for SLPs working with adolescents when it was revised in 1987. This norm-referenced test was intended to assist in determining which adolescents had significant linguistic deficits (in relation to their peers) and to identify specific strengths and weaknesses. The tool was also to be utilized in documenting progress.

The TOAL-2 was standardized on 2,628 adolescents between the ages of 12 and 18-5. The test model included form (spoken and written), system (receptive and expressive), and features (semantic and syntax). The subtests of the TOAL-2 include listening, speaking, reading, and writing tasks; vocabulary and grammar are tapped by the subtests. Although there are no time limitations, the test usually requires over an hour. The TOAL-2 yields an adolescent language quotient and a subtest profile.

The authors of the *Screening Test of Adolescent Language* (STAL), acknowledging the paucity of appropriate tools available to screen adolescents, sought to design and standardize a test that was easily and quickly administered, tested a variety of language abilities, was rapidly scored, and could be used to determine which students required additional assessment (23). Following preliminary study, the final version of the STAL consisted of a total of twenty-three items assessing vocabulary, memory span, processing, and the understanding of proverbs. According to the authors, administration requires 6 minutes; those familiar with the test do not encounter difficulty in scoring the STAL. Passing scores are based on grade level (6-8 and 9-12).

Liberman et al. compared the three language tests discussed previously and the CELF-R (24). The questions raised by the investigators were:

1. Do adolescent language tests measure the same language skills (content) in the same way (procedures)?
2. Do students perform in the same way on adolescent language tests? (24)

Following review of the four test manuals, the authors concluded that only the TOAL was based on a language model, upon which the subtests were based. The lack of a language framework precluded content analysis of the remaining three tests. The TOAL was also the only test that evaluated both the oral and graphic modalities; the others measured oral only. There was little consistency with measurement of the various language features among the tests; similar imbalance was noted when the researchers examined the receptive/expressive component of the four tools. Finally, variations in procedures were identified.

The authors, having reviewed the four tests, compared the performance of adolescents responding to the tools. Eight qualified examiners administered the tests to nine sixth-grade males and twenty-one sixth-grade females. The subjects were considered to be of lower-middle class socioeconomic status but did not differ appreciably from the expected norms in their performance on a standardized achievement test, the *California Achievement Test.*

The researchers found that the students performed rather consistently on the FLTA, TOAL, and CELF even though the tests differed in many ways. The STAL was not found to be a reliable screening device when STAL results were compared to the results of the other tools. Fewer students were identified as needing further evaluation according to STAL results than the results of the FLTA, TOAL, and CELF revealed. According to the authors, it may be that the STAL requires a lower level of performance than the other tools; conversely, the FLTA, TOAL, and CELF may just be more difficult.

It is apparent that, despite the valiant efforts of those who are engaged in the development of tests of adolescent language, there are some needs that must be met by other means. As was true with the assessment of young and school-aged children, the needs might best be met through language sample analysis. That topic is considered next.

Larson and McKinley made a major contribution to our understanding of adolescent language in 1987 (25). Among other things, the authors stressed the importance of eliciting language samples on a variety of occasions to augment formal testing so that a true picture of the adolescent's language may be obtained.

Initially, the authors discuss the need to obtain a complete case history. This, in itself, is not remarkable. However, Larson and McKinley suggest that the "feelings and attitudes of adolescents toward their current thinking, listening, and speaking abilities, and their willingness to modify these abilities" also be explored (25). This information is necessary for an understanding of the student's perspective regarding his or her communication. The SLP is also encouraged to assess the adolescent's learning style and cognitive functioning.

With regard to specific communicative abilities, the authors identify a variety of linguistic features and recommend that the SLP assess these in terms of comprehension and production. It is also important to evaluate discourse through the utilization of conversational and narrative samples. Copies of the Adolescent Conversational Analysis Profile and Narration Analysis also appear in their text. Finally, the authors recommend that nonverbal communication and survival language skills be assessed. Thankfully, Larson and McKinley offer suggestions to the SLP on how to go about collecting and analyzing the language sample, including microcomputer analysis.

An exhaustive discussion of the assessment of adolescent language is both inappropriate and impossible in a text such as this. There remains a paucity of information regarding this topic, but that void is beginning to be filled. The reader is encouraged to consult the Larson and McKinley publication and maintain professional currency through the various journals.

Referrals

An important part of the assessment process is determining which children should be referred for additional evaluation. The Code of Ethics of the American Speech-Language-Hearing Association prevents SLPs from becoming involved in areas in which they are not sufficiently trained. Although overreferral may become a problem, it is preferable to err on the side of overreferring children with possible medical or emotional problems than to underrefer. As pointed out earlier, children with vocal problems involving a suspected pathology must be referred for evaluation by an otolaryngologist. The child with a hearing impairment should be seen by an audiologist and an otologist. The child with a language disorder may or may not be referred to a psychometrist or psychologist; the same is true of a child who presents a fluency disturbance.

Most school districts now have teams of professional personnel who can perform a variety of evaluations. Some children seen by the SLP may require assessment by such a team. Frequently this evaluation is followed by development of a prescriptive intervention program and trial placement in a classroom that provides the services felt to be necessary.

It is important that the SLP be cognizant of the various resources available for placement of a child not only within the school district but within the community as well. There will be occasions when the services provided by the SLP will not be commensurate with the needs of the child. The needs of a severely language-delayed child, for example, might not be met by the itinerant SLP. In such a case, placement in a special language classroom would be preferable. It is also possible that the needs of that child might best be met in a facility outside the school district. The SLP must keep these sources of referral in mind when making decisions about children diagnosed as communicatively disordered.

Tests Employed by Other Professionals

The close interaction between SLPs, classroom teachers, and other specialists working in the school setting requires that SLPs have some knowledge of tests used by their colleagues. Bolton identifies some of these tools, their purposes, descriptions, and other identifying data (18). A selection of these tests is presented next.

Mental ability may be assessed using the *Columbia Mental Maturity Scale,* a tool that is appropriate for children 3½ to 10 years. A nonverbal test that also purports to assess mental ability is the *Goodenough-Harris Drawing*

Test, suitable for preschool children through adolescents. The *Merrill-Palmer Scale* may be used to measure mental ability in preschoolers. Finally, the *Wechsler Scales* may be employed to assess intelligence at all age levels.

Several tests are available that identify levels of achievement in various learning areas. The *Assessment of Basic Competencies,* for example, assesses language, processing, and ability to work mathematical problems. *The Brigance Inventories* also measure attainment in various academic skills areas; selected inventories are available for children and adolescents. The *Peabody Individual Achievement Test — Revised* may be employed with individuals 5 years and older. Others, such as the *Doren Diagnostic Reading Test of Word Recognition Skills* and the *Test of Early Reading Ability,* are specific to a single skill. And the *Detroit Tests of Learning Aptitude* measure both specific and general aptitudes of young children.

To verify that a multitude of commercial tests are available for use by educators, two catalogs were examined. There were twelve tools available to rate behavior and six to assess reading; sixteen achievement tests were also advertised. Once again, the SLP must make a concerted effort to learn which tools are being used in the local district, what they purport to assess, and how the results affect the SLP's intervention.

Summary

In summary, the initial obligations of the SLP are the identification and assessment of communicatively disordered children. In planning and executing these processes, the SLP must be aware that procedures must be nondiscriminatory. The identification of communicatively disordered children may be accomplished through direct screening procedures using informal or formal procedures or through parent or teacher referral; the latter requires that both groups of potential referrers be sufficiently educated to make such referrals. Following the identification of children with potential problems, the SLP must evaluate these students. Although all areas of assessment are discussed, the greatest emphasis is given to language assessment at various age levels. Both language-sampling techniques and formal testing are considered. The results of the evaluation may suggest that referral to another professional is necessary, and the SLP must be aware of appropriate referral sources. Finally, it is important that SLPs be somewhat familiar with other tests utilized in the educational setting, and limited attention is given to these tools.

Endnotes

1. W. B. Swift, "How to Begin Speech Correction in the Public Schools," *Language, Speech, and Hearing Services in Schools* 3(1972): pp. 51–56.
2. Individuals with Disabilities Education Act (amended). *Education for the Handicapped Law Report* (Horsham, PA: LRP Publications, 1990).

3. L. Cole, "Implications of the Position on Social Dialects," *Asha* 25(1983): pp. 25–27.

4. F. B. Vaughn-Cooke, "Improving Language Assessment in Minority Children," *Asha* 25(1983): pp. 29–34.

5. H. Langdon, "Language Disorder or Difference? Assessing the Language Skills of Hispanic Students," *Exceptional Children* 56(1984): pp. 160–167.

6. H. Kayser, "Speech and Language Assessment of Spanish-English Speaking Children," *Language, Speech, and Hearing Services in Schools* 20(1989): pp. 226–244.

7. *Illinois State Board of Education Piloting of the Comprehensive Plan for Speech-Language Service Delivery,* draft (1989).

8. *Proposed Rules, Regulations, and Policies,* Indiana Department of Education (1989).

9. *Special Considerations in Identification and Placement of Students with Speech and Language Disorders,* Missouri Department of Elementary and Secondary Education (1989).

10. N. Fluharty, *Fluharty Preschool Speech and Language Screening Test* (Hingham, MA: Teaching Resources Corporation, 1978).

11. M. Kinzler and C. Johnson, *Joliet 3-Minute Speech and Language Screen* (Tuscon: Communication Skill Builders, 1983).

12. R. J. Schissel and L. B. James, "A Comparison of Children's Performance on Two Tests of Articulation," *Journal of Speech and Hearing Disorders* 44(1979): pp. 363–372.

13. E. M. DuBois and J. E. Bernthal, "A Comparison of Three Methods for Obtaining Articulatory Responses," *Journal of Speech and Hearing Disorders* 43(1978): pp. 295–305.

14. D. R. Boone and S. C. McFarlane, *The Voice and Voice Therapy,* 4th ed. (Englewood Cliffs, NJ: Prentice Hall, 1988).

15. A. E. Aronson, *Clinical Voice Disorders,* 2nd ed. (New York: Thieme, 1985).

16. B. Hutchinson, M. L. Hanson, and M. J. Meeham, *Diagnostic Handbook of Speech Pathology* (Baltimore: The Williams and Wilkins Company, 1979).

17. L. Rossetti, *High-Risk Infants: Identification, Assessment, and Intervention* (Boston: Little, Brown and Company, 1986).

18. B. Bolton (ed.), *Special Education and Rehabilitation Testing* (Austin: Pro-Ed, 1988).

19. M. Lahey, *Language Disorders and Language Development* (New York: Macmillan Company, 1988): pp. 166–168.

20. R. W. Channell and M. S. Peek, "Four Measures of Vocabulary Ability Compared in Older Preschool Children," *Language, Speech, and Hearing Services in Schools* 20(1989): pp. 407–420.

21. M. L. Rice, M. A. Sell, and P. Hadley, "The Socially Interactive Coding System: The On-Line Clinically Relevant Descriptive Tool," *Language, Speech, and Hearing Services in Schools* 20(1989): pp. 2–14.

22. D. D. Hammill, V. L. Brown, S. C. Larsen, and J. L. Wiederholt, *Test of Adolescent Language* (Austin: Pro-Ed, 1987).

23. E. M. Prather, S. Brucher, M. L. Stafford, and E. Wallace, *Screening Test of Adolescent Language* (Seattle: University of Washington Press, 1980).

24. R. J. Liberman, A. M. Heffron, S. J. West, E. C. Hutchinson, and T. W. Swem, "A Comparison of Four Adolescent Language Tests," *Language, Speech, and Hearing Services in Schools* 18(1987): pp. 250–266.

25. V. Larson and N. McKinley, *Communication Assessment and Intervention Strategies for Adolescents* (Eau Claire, WI: Thinking Publications, 1987).

4

Case Selection, Service Delivery Options, and Scheduling Models

The most competent speech clinician in the schools cannot be considered effective if he is working with the wrong children. Said differently, all the best techniques and skills in the world are of no consequence if wasted on those not needing it and denied to those who do (1).

Prior to the implementation of the EHA/IDEA, SLPs in the schools screened the target population using techniques described in the previous chapter and then, using district, state, or personal guidelines, selected a predetermined number of students for inclusion in the active caseload. Decisions for including some children and eliminating others might have been based on the SLP's skill (or lack thereof) in managing specific kinds of disorders, the vehemence with which teachers and parents sought services for communicatively disordered children, the severity of the various problems, the age of the child, the number of children presenting problems, the teacher's willingness to release children from the classroom, or combinations of these factors. Those children who were not selected for direct intervention were conveniently placed on a "waiting list." Some matured sufficiently while on this list to be dismissed; others were assimilated into the active caseload when vacancies occurred. Today, districts that have waiting lists are not in compliance with the EHA/IDEA. Nevertheless, many SLPs are still responsible for more children than they can legally or ethically provide with appropriate services. Therefore, some alternative management plans are necessary. In this chapter, caseload is considered, and guidelines for case selection are presented. In addition, the management alternatives available to contemporary SLPs are discussed.

Caseload

When the author was a school SLP in the early 1960s, the state of Illinois had established 100 students as the maximum caseload, with 70 being the minimum. The method by which these numbers were selected was unknown, and justification for establishing such limitations would be difficult. Consider, for example, the SLP working with multiply handicapped children; could that person achieve effective results seeing seventy severely involved children each week? Assuming that the average school day does not exceed six hours, the SLP could conduct twelve half-hour sessions or eighteen twenty-minute sessions each day. It is obvious that the needs of these seventy students could not be met. The SLP assigned to several rural schools might also have difficulty maintaining an active caseload of seventy students because of the time lost in traveling between schools. Therefore, the establishment of specific maximum and minimum caseload figures seems inappropriate. It would appear that individual decisions based on the types and severity of the communicative disorders, the ages of the children presenting the problems, and the number of schools assigned would be a more justifiable means of determining the caseload. Nevertheless, caseload size continues to be mandated in some cases and must be a consideration for the SLP.

It is a positive trend that caseloads appear to be decreasing. A survey of over 1,400 public school SLPs in the late 1950s revealed that the mean caseload was approximately 130 children (2). At that time, West Coast and Northeast SLPs reported the highest caseloads, with the Southwest-Mountain-Hawaii region and the Midwest reporting fewer students. That same survey revealed that 25 percent of the SLPs had their caseloads limited by state law; an additional five percent reported local restrictions. Twenty-three percent of those responding to the survey reported that the number of children requiring services determined the caseload; apparently no minimum or maximum figures were utilized. Finally, 45 percent of the SLPs employed professional judgment in establishing caseloads.

In 1969, O'Toole and Zaslow described the changing roles of the SLP (3). Among the changes they noted was a substantial reduction in caseload size. In a school district, the following caseloads were identified: One SLP worked with thirty-seven children, many of whom were cerebral palsied; a second SLP had a caseload of forty-five; and three SLPs each worked with ten or fewer hearing impaired children. These figures are in contrast to the mean caseloads reported in the 1959 survey.

Hoopes and Dasovich, in their 1972 study, surveyed seventy-six public school SLPs (4). The majority (forty-seven) were employed in a county school district, with twenty-nine working in the city school district. Although the survey was multipurposed, one of the seventeen pieces of information obtained revealed differences between the SLPs employed by the city and those working in the county; that item dealt with caseload size. It was found that 52 percent of the city SLPs carried caseloads of 100, but none of the county had caseloads that high. Fifty-seven percent of the county SLPs reported caseloads between fifty-one and eighty. Only 7 percent of the city SLPs had comparable loads. Thirty-eight percent of both groups carried caseloads between eighty-one and ninety-nine.

Hahn surveyed sixty-one speech-language pathologists nationwide (5). Only one of the forty-eight professionals responding to the question on caseload reported carrying a caseload above ninety students; the majority (twenty-five) had fewer than forty-five students, whereas seventeen SLPs serviced forty-five to sixty-five students.

Contemporary school SLPs are providing services to fewer students than did the professional of the late 1950s. In part, this reduction may be the result of state recognition that effective therapy requires some degree of intensity. California, for example, does not permit a full-time SLP (or, in California terminology, a language, speech, and hearing specialist) to exceed an average of fifty-five students unless prior approval is obtained (6). If the SLP is providing services to preschoolers, the caseload limitation is forty. Illinois has drafted guidelines that would utilize "service delivery units" based on severity to determine caseload; a full-time caseload could not exceed 100 units (7).

Hypothetically, SLPs could service between forty and seventy-two students based on the severity of the communicative disorders presented by the students. Defining caseload as "the number of individualized education programs for which that person has implementation responsibility," proposed Indiana guidelines identify a caseload range from forty-five to eighty (8). If this sampling of state requirements on caseload is representative, it is apparent that some downsizing is occurring.

Case Selection

Case selection has always been a somewhat volatile issue among SLPs. Professionals have viewed the relative significance of the factors involved in this process from different perspectives. The type and severity of the disorder, the age of the child presenting the problem, the length of time the disorder has existed in its current state, the child's perception of the problem, and the social and educational implications of the disorder have all been considered. As noted previously, the law specifies that the communicative disorder must adversely affect classroom performance. In this section, the means by which four states have dealt with case selection through entry criteria are considered. As the reader reviews this information, it would be helpful to determine if the issues presented at the outset of this section are resolved.

In California, eligibility for speech-language services is described in the *California Code of Regulations, Title 5,* Section 3030 (6). With regard to articulatory disorders, the student eligible for services must misarticulate one or several age-expected sounds, and these misarticulations must reduce intelligibility, call attention to the student, and negatively affect academic achievement. Isolated tongue thrusting behavior or dialectal differences do not make the student eligible for services. Voice disorders must be chronic, inappropriate, and noticeable; medical clearance may be required. Students with fluency disorders who are eligible for services demonstrate rate and rhythm abnormalities that interfere with communication. To be eligible for intervention under the category of language disorder (language development), the results of two or more standardized tests should demonstrate that the child is "at least 1.5 standard deviations below the mean or below the seventh percentile on both standardized tests in at least one area of language development" (6). Expressive or receptive language disorders require the same criterion; in addition, the student must display linguistic incompetence as judged by analysis of a language sample. Again, dialectal differences are not considered disorders.

Preschool children and children for whom English is a second language (Limited-English-Proficient: LEP) are also considered in the California Code. Articulatory disorders are identified when the preschool child has developmental delays of at least six months. When a child is 25 percent below expectation in language, he or she is eligible for services. LEP students present particular problems in determining eligibility, and wisely, it is recommended that SLPs rely on professional judgment rather than test scores. A checklist for eligibility of LEP students and related California criteria materials appear in the appendix.

In a pilot program, the state of Illinois is testing eligibility criteria guidelines (7). Noting that other factors, including cultural differences and language proficiency, must be considered, the criteria are designed to establish severity levels. In turn, the severity rating helps to determine the amount of service required. The severity classifications include mild, moderate, severe, and profound. Mild disorders cause minimal interference in communication, whereas a moderate disorder limits communication. The guidelines suggest that a severe problem interferes with communication, and the child with a profound problem is unable to communicate appropriately. The guidelines stress that communication must be judged in response to the learning environment as well as in social situations.

A mild articulatory disorder is identified as the misarticulation of one or two unrelated sounds by a child who is eight years or younger. Students with developmental errors are excluded. Moderate disorders are characterized in the eight and younger group by the misarticulation of one to four unrelated sounds; children over eight must misarticulate one to two sounds. A child of any age who has four or more unrelated error sounds is considered to have a severe problem, and the child with a profound disorder is essentially unintelligible. The guidelines for determining severity of an articulatory disorder provide helpful definitions and stress stimulability.

Using the categories of form, use, and content, Illinois guidelines for language eligibility are determined by the child's performance on at least two standardized tests. A mild rating is applied to children whose performance is one to two standard deviations below the mean standard score; moderate disorders are two to three standard deviations below. When a student's performance is three standard deviations below the mean standard score, a severe rating is derived, and a profound disorder is identified when the child's scores are four or more standard deviations below the mean. The guidelines emphasize that observations by the SLP and others should be considered, as well as the results of language-sampling procedures.

With regard to fluency, the SLP is encouraged to elicit and analyze a tape recording of 100 words or more. Dysfluencies on 3 to 5 percent of the recorded utterances may place the child in the mild category; a child who is dysfluent on 6 to 12 percent of the 100-word sample and who displays secondary characteristics is considered to have a moderate problem. Severe ratings are applied if 13 to 25 percent of the words are characterized by dysfluency, and a profound rating is given to anything higher; secondary characteristics may also be present. The guidelines suggest that the child's age and his or her and other's perceptions of the problem must be considered as well as its impact on learning and social adjustment.

A tape-recorded sample is also analyzed to determine eligibility for intervention for a voice disorder. The level of concern demonstrated by the child and those in his or her environment assists the SLP in determining whether a voice difference is considered mild or moderate; obviously, the latter rating is employed when concern exists. When the voice is abnormal in terms of pitch, quality, or intensity and this abnormality is readily apparent, it is considered a severe disorder. When communication is seriously impaired because of vocal abnormalities, a profound severity rating is applied. In most cases, medical referral is indicated.

As indicated earlier, the Illinois guidelines may assist in case selection but are primarily designed to determine service delivery unit requirements. Using a formula that defines one unit as fifteen to thirty minutes of intervention weekly, the guidelines recommend one unit for mild disorders, two for moderate, three for severe, and five for profound problems.

Although this discussion is concerned with entry criteria and case selection, the Illinois guidelines consider exit criteria as well. It is suggested that services may be discontinued when the child is functioning at a level commensurate with his or her cognitive abilities, the problem is no longer handicapping to the student, the child lacks the motivation to continue, or other factors preclude additional progress.

The *Proposed Rule S-1 Revision* for Indiana also has some general guidelines for eligibility (8). The guidelines suggest that eligible students must have a nonmaturational condition, which may be organic or functional in nature. If an organic problem is suspected, a physician's statement is required as documentation. Although the guidelines state that disorders of communication may range in severity from mild to severe, criteria for making such judgments are not presented. Perhaps because of the ambiguity of the state guidelines, one Indiana co-op devised their own guidelines to assist in case selection and dismissal (9).

Articulatory and phonological disorders, according to these guidelines, should be identified based on developmental norms, stimulability, and error consistency. Students opposed to intervention should not be enrolled. With regard to language, students should be considered if they score two or more years below their chronological ages on language tests, if they demonstrate language gaps, or if their PPVT score is "moderately low" (9). If a dysfluent child has difficulty in his or her response in social or educational settings as the result of dysfluencies, he or she may be a candidate for intervention. Children with voice disorders are enrolled after physician referral. Exit criteria for the co-op include attainment of IEP goals, lack of progress over a three-year span, or a need for the student to have additional time available to work on other problems.

Eligibility for inclusion in language programs in Missouri is viewed in terms of proficiency in form, content, and use and differentiates language disorders from speech disorders (voice, articulation, and fluency) (10). In determining eligibility for language, the SLP must assess the child's language through language sampling and through the utilization of two standardized tests. A younger child (grades K–6) is considered to have language functioning significantly below his or her cognitive abilities if the scores are 1.0 standard deviations below his cognitive scores; a 1.5 standard deviation is considered significant in students in grades 7–12. In addition, it must be shown that this disorder negatively affects academic achievement.

An articulatory disorder is identified if the child has a "significant delay" in articulation when compared to developmental norms. "A significant delay is defined as more than one year beyond the upper limit of developmental age range for normal sound acquisition" (10). Further, the disorder must affect intelligibility and must not be the result of such causes as mental retardation or dialectal differences.

Both formal and informal tasks are utilized to determine whether a dysfluent child is in need of intervention. The specific criterion suggests that five dysfluencies per minute that interfere with communication may qualify a child for services. Students with voice disorders must present chronic deviations that are inconsistent with the norm and interfere with communication. Acknowledging that exit decisions are made by a team, the guidelines state that it is appropriate to dismiss a child when his or her goals have been met or when he or she has achieved maximal progress.

A question about case selection criteria that might be asked is whether SLPs feel that they need guidelines to assist them in case selection. This was one of many questions posed in a survey of sixty-one SLPs working in schools in the United States (5). The first area explored was determination of what persons or agencies made decisions regarding case selection. Of the sixty-one respondents, thirty-three SLPs reported professional judgment to be the sole criterion for case selection, with six reporting state regulations and two stating that district regulations governed the process. One respondent indicated that the speech-language supervisor was instrumental in the case selection procedure, and the remaining nineteen professionals reported that they were restricted by a combination of state and district regulations and professional judgment. Of the SLPs functioning under some degree of state-imposed restrictions regarding case selection, 47 percent found them to be adequate and helpful, with 31 percent indicating that the regulations were too specific. The remaining respondents reported that the regulations were too general to be helpful. When the group without state guidelines was asked whether such regulations were desirable, the overwhelming majority responded negatively; only 22 percent favored such guidelines.

Case selection or eligibility questions have been discussed for years, and the information presented here demonstrates that states are making valiant efforts to establish appropriate criteria. It is important to determine how a student performs in terms of speech-language proficiency and how the student compares with his or her peers. And, legally, it must be demonstrated that any speech or language deficit present interferes with educational performance. Documentation that these criteria exist is essential. There are, however, variables that are difficult to measure and more difficult to build into eligibility criteria. Children, their caregivers, teachers, and peers respond differently to communicative disorders. Some students with problems that would fit into the "mild" category are deeply distressed by these problems. Conversely, children who are unintelligible may be affected by their communicative disorders very little. Parents, too, will vary in their perceptions of, and responses to, children with communicative disorders. And some disorders, such as stuttering, may be perceived by others as communicable as well as communicative. These variables contribute significantly to the severity of a communicative disorder, and only sensitivity and clinical judgment make it possible for the SLP to determine how significantly.

Nevertheless, eligibility and case selection criteria are important aspects of the intervention process. To some extent, the service delivery systems or management alternatives available in any given area will influence eligibility for a specific option. These options are considered next.

Service Delivery Options

Once children with communicative disorders have been identified, assessed, and found to be eligible for intervention, the SLP, in a meeting with the parents, teacher, other professionals, and sometimes even the child formulates an Individualized Education Program (IEP). The preparation of that program is considered in Chapter 5. One section of the IEP requires a statement of which delivery system will best meet the needs of the individual student. In its recommendations on caseload size, ASHA also considered several delivery models. In this section, these selected intervention options are described, and the comprehensive service delivery plan of the state of California is presented; finally, model programs are discussed.

Service delivery may be seen as existing on a continuum based on the directness of the services provided (11). The services range from indirect (consultation) to direct, including itinerant, resource room, and self-contained classroom. The types of students served by the consultation model are those presenting mild to severe communicative disorders. The SLP in this model develops programs to be executed by others. (Because this intervention strategy is among the newest to SLPs, it is considered in more detail later.) SLPs are most familiar with the direct service management option delivered on an itinerant basis. This method of intervention is conducted on an individual or small group basis to students presenting all types of communicative disorders and all degrees of severity. The recommended caseload for itinerant services is twenty-five to forty. SLPs have had some experiences in resource rooms and in self-contained classrooms where students with moderate and severe communicative disorders receive individualized and intensive intervention. These, then, were AHSA recommendations.

The state of California also recognized that students require a variety of services to meet their individual needs and identified service delivery models that could be adapted and implemented to meet these needs. It should be noted that a combination of services may be delivered to a single student if required.

Traditional Pull-Out Model

This model is the most familiar to contemporary SLPs and, according to California guidelines, may be used in the schools or other settings with individuals from birth to 21. Employing this model, the SLP identifies, assesses, and establishes objectives and goals, and implements direct services to either individual children or children in small groups. SLPs are also involved in instructional inservices for parents and teachers. The SLP must allow time in scheduling for conferences, IEP meetings, and staffings. Scheduling models for a pull-out system are considered later.

Infant–Preschool Home-based or Center-based Model

Both direct services to infants and young children and instruction to parents and caregivers are provided through this model. Services may be delivered in the home or at a designated site. Specifically, these methods of intervention are encouraged:

1. *Instruction in primary language when possible*
2. *Information and stimulation techniques in language and speech development*
3. *Observation and evaluation of children*
4. *Focus on phonology and language development (6)*

Using this model, the SLP is expected to assist with referrals and to train parents and caregivers in language stimulation techniques. With regard to scheduling, the SLP spends one to two hours, "one to three times weekly at four week to eight week intervals" (6).

Transdisciplinary Team Model

This model is employed to provide educational services to children from birth to five years; both assessment and program implementation are included. The SLP serves as a consultant to team members and provides informational counseling to parents and caregivers. This is a team model, and all members share assessment and implementation responsibilities.

Classroom Intervention Model (Elementary)

This delivery system is based on the assumption that most members of a given class would benefit from speech-language stimulation. The classroom teacher and the SLP may both provide the instruction on a mutually agreed upon schedule. The model is appropriate for at-risk children enrolled in a regular classroom setting.

Activities that may be included in this model are those that emphasize oral language instruction, continuous consultation between the SLP and classroom teachers and other school personnel, inservice instruction, and service to the students. The SLP has assessment, programming, and monitoring responsibilities in addition to the consultation role.

Classroom Intervention Model (Secondary)

Team teaching is central to this type of service delivery, and students are taught to "generalize effective language strategies" (6). The SLP not only provides direct services to at-risk and handicapped students but also participates in curriculum development, inservice instruction, and consultation. The SLP may also be involved in identification and assessment of students, session plan development, modification of testing materials and strategies, and consultation.

Departmentalized Model (Secondary)

This system of service delivery requires the SLP to function as a teacher, applying core curriculum content "to the remediation of oral and written language disabilities" (6). Credit toward graduation is awarded to students whose counselors recommend placement in these classes. Within the classes, emphasis is placed on vocabulary, vocational skills, pragmatic skills, learning strategies, and functional writing skills. As in all classroom situations, the teacher (SLP) is responsible for behavior management. It is recommended that classes be conducted on a regular basis (five times weekly), with the class members having similar needs and IEP goals. Time must be scheduled for preparation and conferences.

Language Laboratory Model

Emphasis in the model is on all areas of oral and written language as it relates to the core curriculum, as well as critical thinking and decision making. The laboratory is under the direction and supervision of the SLP, and students are placed there as the result of a team recommendation; included in the decision making are the parents and other school personnel. The amount of time spent by individual students in the laboratory is not specified.

Paraprofessional Model

Qualified paraprofessionals, working under the supervision of an SLP, may also provide services to communicatively disordered children if it is so recommended in the IEP. The paraprofessional should have adequate communicative abilities, be sensitive to the needs of handicapped children, and be able to function with individual children or small groups. Paraprofessionals may also be employed with other models and may be used to perform clerical duties. It is important to note, however, that the SLPs caseload may not be increased when a paraprofessional is used. Additional issues regarding paraprofessionals are considered later.

Postsecondary Transitional Model

Services are provided to communicatively disordered older students through community colleges. Using self-referral procedures, students may seek assessment and intervention and obtain information about other services.

Language and Speech Consultative Model

California provides consultative services to a variety of persons in a variety of settings; through consultation the number of individuals to whom services can be provided is increased. Both at-risk individuals and those with exceptional needs may be serviced. "This model, which is intended to answer questions, provide information, present demonstrations, and facilitate access to resources, is emerging as a popular model for both the resource specialist teacher and the LSH (Language, Speech, and Hearing) specialist" (6). Nonverbal and bilingual populations may be served by this model, or the SLP may provide diagnostic consultation; SLPs also serve as consultants to community-based facilities and as mentor teacher consultants.

Consultant Services for a Nonverbal Population

In this role, the SLP may assess nonverbal students and recommend augmentative materials and techniques. In addition, the SLP should instruct teachers, parents, and school personnel in the utilization of these devices. Conferences with related professionals are also held by the SLP, and that person is responsible for reassessing the students' progress.

Diagnostic Consultant

According to the California plan, the SLP in this capacity serves as an advisor on multidisciplinary teams, performs assessments, and makes recommendations.

Community-Based Consultant

This innovative delivery system requires that the SLP accompany communicatively disordered students as the latter go into different settings. In so doing, the SLP assists the students in learning and utilizing pragmatic and social skills in these environments. Students are also helped to learn directions and how to seek information.

Mentor Teacher Consultant

SLPs in this capacity provide guidance to new and returning SLPs and teachers. They also assist the novices in developing plans, acquaint them with current procedures and laws, and provide them with access to contemporary literature.

School-Based Model

This model is intended to assure all students "an instructional program rich in curriculum content, as well as in problem-solving and critical-thinking activities" (6). Specifically, it is designed to provide student focus, as well as flexibility. Moreover, the school-based model attempts to make certain that handicapped students receive the full range of programs and instruction that they require.

This, then, is a summary of the rather comprehensive service delivery system available in the state of California. Other states undoubtedly have similar plans but with varying degrees of specificity. Most assuredly, the California plan offers the continuum of services advocated by ASHA. Reports of successful programs demonstrating different service delivery systems have been reported in the literature, and some of these are spotlighted next.

Model Programs

Jelinek described a program for young children who displayed communicative disorders as either a primary or related handicapping condition (12). The program was designed to accelerate development in eight areas: "(a) social-emotional, (b) gross motor, (c) fine motor, (d) adaptive reasoning, (e) receptive language, (f) expressive language, (g) feeding, and (h) dressing and simple hygiene" (12). Using an eclectic curriculum designed to meet the IEPs of the various children, the staff organized activities in each of the eight areas.

Potential subjects were identified through referrals and screenings; it was then determined which children required further assessment. Various professionals, including an SLP, psychologist, teachers, therapists (occupational and physical), and a social worker, administered tests appropriate to their disciplines. A thorough case history was also obtained on each candidate. Additionally, the children received otoscopic and physical examinations. Following the diagnostic process, staffings were held to determine which children required services, if referrals were required, or if a given child would benefit from the model program. Parents were included in the staffings and in IEP development.

Children received instruction either in the home or classroom setting. Each of the eight areas outlined above was targeted, with individual children receiving additional special services in accordance with their IEPs. A reassessment was done at the completion of the year, and placement recommendations were made.

Parental involvement was emphasized in this program. Not only were parents included in staffings and IEP conferences, their needs were also addressed and programs implemented to address these needs. The programming for parents was designed to provide support, exchange information, encourage participation, and facilitate child–parent interaction. Flexible scheduling was employed to meet the needs of the parents.

Of the forty-three children involved in the program, fifteen presented speech and language developmental delays as the primary handicapping condition; other primary handicaps included mental retardation, emotional disturbances, and orthopedic impairments. All but five of the total group were included in both pretest and posttest data. The latter revealed that significant gains were made by the children involved in this preschool program. Amazingly, these handicapped children demonstrated one month gains during each month of the program, and some two month gains during a single month were observed.

Since part of an SLP's function is the prevention of speech-language disorders, programs of this kind are very appropriate. As the author stated, as a result of this program "the future educational potential of this target group of children has been maximized" (12).

Some children, with or without the benefit of receiving services prior to entering school, present themselves as language-disordered kindergartners. For a number of years, the SLPs in the Capital Area Intermediate Unit of Pennsylvania have been involved in serving such children in self-contained language kindergartens (13). Candidates for the classroom are children of normal intelligence who have been diagnosed as communicatively disordered.

Children were referred for assessment by parents, preschools, and other agencies. The diagnostic evaluations were performed by an SLP, an audiologist, and a psychologist. Using a variety of assessment tools and procedures, the SLP evaluated receptive and expressive systems. Eligible students demonstrated expressive delays of one year or more, with varying levels of receptive competence from above average to a one year or greater delay. The majority of students who have been enrolled in the class demonstrated severe articulatory disorders.

The language class was designed to have curricular consistency with the regular kindergarten program. "The main and critical difference was that the language class developed many more steps to reach a particular goal and moving on to the next step was contingent on the student's demonstrated success" (13). The class, consisting of ten or fewer students, had programs designed to improve language, motor, auditory, self-help, and social skills; they met daily for complete days.

Although posttesting data were important, the success of the kindergarten language class may best be seen in placement recommendations. Over a nine-year period during which data were collected, 52 percent of the "graduates" went into regular educational placements, either kindergarten or first grade. An additional 25 percent entered the first grade language classroom. The placements were as follows: learning disabilities (4 percent), neurodevelopmentally delayed (14 percent), educable mentally retarded (1 percent), socially and emotionally disturbed (1 percent), and hearing impaired (3 percent). A three-year follow-up of the placement of eighty-five of these children revealed that almost half (47 percent) remained in regular education programs.

The author, in summarizing the results of language intervention in a classroom setting, stressed the desirability of this system of delivery. According to Mroczkowski, it is important to observe the child in situations in which meaningful communication occurs (the classroom) and to modify the delivery system to take advantage of these situations.

Christensen and Luckett described a combined service delivery system in which school-aged children received direct intervention one time per week and participated in "whole-class language" lessons for twenty to thirty minutes weekly (14). For this service delivery model to be appropriate, at least one child in the classroom must have an IEP targeting speech-language intervention. Then, the SLP "may design activities to enrich the entire classroom while targeting the specific objectives ascribed to the IEP-student" (14). The classroom activities emphasized vocabulary, listening, grammar, and reasoning (grades K–2), and supplemented the regular curriculum (grades 4–6). The authors emphasize that the whole language class concept requires the presence of both the teacher and the SLP and should not be regarded as a break for the classroom teacher. They also report that this delivery system has been well received by parents and teachers.

These examples of delivery models have demonstrated that a continuum of services is possible with younger and school-aged children. Adolescents may also benefit from alternative modes of intervention. Anderson and Nelson report on such a system being utilized with adolescents in an alternate language classroom (15). Acknowledging that traditional service delivery models do not always meet the language-based academic needs of students, a more intensive model was devised. It was designated the Alternate Adolescent Language Classroom (AALC). This model was offered as a regular class, meeting for one hour each day. "The Alternate Adolescent Language Classroom was to provide an academic setting that would focus on the total integration of language-related skills in an organized framework of learning" (15). The teacher was an SLP.

The program, which has been in existence since 1984, has had promising results. Between its inception and 1987, the AALC serviced five to seven students. Most of the students who have been involved in the program were mainstreamed; one student returned to the AALC at his own request, and another is receiving support services. The success of the AALC has led to expansion of the delivery model and the addition of an AALC at the third-grade level.

Thus far, discussion has centered on alternative management options and the effectiveness of some as viewed and reported by SLPs. One important ingredient is missing from these success stories: the perceptions of the consumer. Jenkins and Heinen attempted to fill this void when they assessed student preferences for service delivery (16). The 686 subjects included in this study were not classified as speech-language impaired but were those who received special assistance for learning difficulties. One may assume that many of the subjects experienced language problems as well.

Three service delivery models were utilized to provide remedial and special instruction to the students; they included pull-out programs and in-class and integrated programs. The pull-out system is familiar to SLPs and requires no explanation. The in-class format involves a specialist providing instruction to students in the classroom setting. "Remedial and special education teachers came to a special setting" (16). Finally, the integrated programs were conducted by the regular classroom teacher with an assistant; specialists were not involved.

The subjects involved in the study were interviewed and asked their preferences regarding the location of service delivery (in or outside the classroom) and the title of the service deliverer (specialist or regular classroom teacher). In general, students showed an inclination to prefer the service delivery location in which they were currently placed. Most students involved in pull-out programs preferred that placement. However, no such consensus was reached by students receiving services in the classroom. Further, older students preferred the pull-out model. "The results challenge the notion that children, generally, prefer to have specialists come to them rather than go to the specialists" (16).

When students were asked why they preferred the pull-out model, they cited the fact that they would get more assistance than in the classroom and that it would be less embarrassing. Some students thought that remaining in the classroom would be more convenient.

With regard to the preferred service provider, they expressed preference for the classroom teacher rather than a specialist. The younger students particularly felt that the classroom teacher understood their needs better than a specialist. Older students who preferred assistance from a specialist indicated that they would get more help than they could from the classroom teacher.

The results of this survey suggest that students do have preferences regarding service delivery models. In some instances, their ages and experiences influence their choices. Students also tend to believe that classroom teachers are capable of meeting their needs. According to the authors, students should be consulted about their service delivery preferences "because it is hazardous to assume that children necessarily 'see it our way' " (16).

What can be said about service delivery models in summary? Certainly, more opportunities for intervention packages are available to contemporary SLPs. It is difficult to know if school SLPs are taking full advantage of the continuum of service models or are just beginning to experiment; probably, the latter is accurate. Nevertheless, the possibilities exist, and the next section on scheduling attempts to allow for these possibilities.

Scheduling Models

In the days before the EHA/IDEA, scheduling for the SLP was a relatively simple matter. First, a plan was made for the year; several weeks at the beginning of the year were allocated for screenings and evaluations, and a week or two at the end were freed-up for year-end activities. Next, the SLP established weekly schedules that allowed time for evaluations, conferences, consultations, and other duties, as well as for direct intervention. At least one-half day per week was set aside for coordination purposes. Finally, students were fit into the schedule for individual sessions or placed in congenial small groups. The sessions were scheduled at fifteen-, twenty-, or thirty-minute intervals with time allowed for recesses and lunch. When travel between schools was necessary, that was also plugged into the schedule.

There were problems involved in scheduling, however. Teachers did not always agree with the therapy times established for their students, nor did they always remember to send the children for speech. Scheduling conflicts with art, music, and PE occurred. The "congenial" groups sometimes turned out to be less than congenial, and the SLP went back to the scheduling drawing board. However, the SLP spent the greater part of his or her day in direct therapy in whatever facilities were assigned and had infrequent contacts with parents and other professionals. That somewhat uncomplicated modus operandi has changed and will continue to change. The degree to which the changes have occurred is questionable, however. It may be that some districts continue to identify students through screening and provide direct services; for that reason, some consideration of traditional scheduling models is appropriate. It should be noted, however, that no scheduling model can be employed indiscriminately; the scheduling of services for a given child must be in compliance with his or her IEP. The following descriptions are intended only as models within which variations are possible.

Intermittent Scheduling

Two basic scheduling models and variations of these models have been utilized in the school setting; they include the intermittent model and intensive cycle scheduling. Intermittent scheduling involves the establishment of a yearly schedule wherein children are seen a specific number of times each week throughout the academic year. Although some children may be dismissed and others added to the schedule, the school assignments remain the same. Therapy times may be established according to the needs of the children and will vary to comply with IEP specification.

Two important variables related to intermittent scheduling are the number of schools assigned to the SLP and the distance between the schools. Tables 4-1 through 4-4 illustrate scheduling possibilities for one to four schools.

Intermittent scheduling, then, involves the establishment of a schedule that permits children to be seen at least twice weekly throughout the school year. If this scheduling is employed, students should be seen in a Monday-Thursday or Tuesday-Friday configuration. The initial screening and evaluation processes are not necessarily conducted according to the yearly schedule. In other words, the SLP would probably complete these activities at one school

TABLE 4-1 Intermittent Schedule for One School*

	Monday	*Tuesday*	*Wednesday*	*Thursday*	*Friday*
a.m.	Groups 1–6	Groups 13–18	Coordination	Groups 1–6	Groups 13–18
p.m.	Groups 7–12	Groups 19–24	Coordination	Groups 7–12	Groups 19–24

*This schedule assumes that sessions are 30 minutes in length. The "group" designation is not intended to preclude individual sessions.

TABLE 4-2 Intermittent Schedule for Two Schools

	Monday	*Tuesday*	*Wednesday*	*Thursday*	*Friday*
a.m.	School A	School B	Coordination	School A	School B
p.m.	School A	School B	Coordination	School A	School B

TABLE 4-3   Intermittent Schedule for Three Schools

	Monday	*Tuesday*	*Wednesday*	*Thursday*	*Friday*
a.m.	School A	School C	School B School C	School A	School C
p.m.	School B	School C	Coordination Office: School C	School B	School C

TABLE 4-4   Intermittent Schedule for Four Schools

	Monday	*Tuesday*	*Wednesday*	*Thursday*	*Friday*
a.m.	School A	School C	Coordination	School A	School C
p.m.	School B	School D	Coordination	School B	School D

before moving to another rather than adhere to the Monday-Thursday, Tuesday-Friday schedule.

Intensive Cycle Scheduling

Intensive cycle scheduling differs from the intermittent model in terms of the number of times per week children are seen and the number of weeks during the year they receive services. In general, on an intensive cycle schedule, students are seen four times each week for a period of at least six weeks and then are furloughed for a specific length of time. The number of blocks during the thirty-six-week school year depends upon state or district policies and the number of schools serviced by the individual speech-language pathologist.

Looking again at variations based on the number of schools, the SLP assigned to a single building would have the utmost flexibility. Screening, evaluations, and IEPs would be completed during the first three or four weeks of school. Assuming that a month was required at the beginning of the year and that two weeks were set aside for year-end activities, thirty weeks of intervention would be possible. If a strict intensive cycle schedule were employed, the thirty weeks could be divided into two eight-week blocks and two seven-week blocks. Since positive results occur early, the two eight-week blocks would probably occur first, followed by the seven-week sessions. The results would be the type of schedule illustrated in Table 4-5. One of the more positive aspects of this schedule is that it does not preclude the provision of intensive services throughout the year to those students with complex problems. Combinations of intermittent and intensive cycle service would also be possible.

The SLP assigned to two schools would enjoy similar flexibility. Both intensive and intermittent services could be provided according to the needs of

TABLE 4-5   Intensive Cycle Scheduling for One School

Pretherapy block (4 weeks)	Block 1 (8 weeks)	Block 2 (8 weeks)	Block 3 (7 weeks)	Block 4 (7 weeks)	Posttherapy block (2 weeks)
Screening, evaluations, IEP development and scheduling	Group 1 students	Group 2 students	Group 1 students	Group 2 students	Year-end duties

the children. One scheduling option would be to service School A in the mornings and School B in the afternoons, provided the schools were in proximity. In order to accommodate kindergarten students in both buildings, the schedule would be reversed during two of the four blocks. Such a schedule is presented in Table 4-6.

Another approach to intensive cycle scheduling would be to service School A students during Blocks 1 and 3 and School B children during Blocks 2 and 4. Table 4-7 illustrates that plan.

The SLP using intensive cycle schedules may not be able to complete screening prior to the initiation of therapy. The Department of Public Instruction of North Dakota, for example, presents a block model for four schools in which screening and evaluations for two schools are postponed until therapy is to be started (17). The allocation of time for this process is unclear. Table 4-8 represents that model.

The question of when testing should be scheduled in an intensive cycle model requires some attention. Medical and related referrals should be made expeditiously; in such cases, it is best if all testing and subsequent referrals be accomplished at the beginning of the school year rather than at the beginning of the block. On the other hand, some children with communicative disorders may improve without intervention, and the child presenting a problem in September may not have that same disorder in November. Nevertheless, in order

TABLE 4-6   Intensive Cycle Scheduling for Two Schools (Option 1)

	Pretherapy block (4 weeks)	Block 1 (8 weeks)	Block 2 (8 weeks)	Block 3 (7 weeks)	Block 4 (7 weeks)	Posttherapy block (2 weeks)
a.m. / p.m.	Screening, evaluations, IEP development and scheduling	School A — — — School B	School B — — — School A	School A — — — School B	School B — — — School A	Year-end duties

TABLE 4-7   Intensive Cycle Scheduling for Two Schools (Option 2)

Pretherapy block (4 weeks)	Block 1 (8 weeks)	Block 2 (8 weeks)	Block 3 (7 weeks)	Block 4 (7 weeks)	Posttherapy block (2 weeks)
Screening, evaluations, IEP development and scheduling	School A	School B	School A	School B	Year-end duties

TABLE 4-8   Block Scheduling for Four Schools

Testing Schools A and B	Block 1* Schools A and B	Testing Schools C and D	Block 2* Schools C and D	Block 3* Schools A and B	Block 4* Schools C and D

*8–9 weeks.
North Dakota Department of Public Instruction, 1977. Reprinted by permission.

for the SLP to plan efficiently for all children with disordered communication, it seems reasonable for all screening, evaluation, and IEPs to be completed prior to the initiation of any intervention.

As noted earlier, it is possible to provide a combination of intensive and intermittent services with some scheduling models. Option 1 of the intensive cycle plan for two schools (Table 4-6) allows for some students to be seen continuously, whereas others may be seen only during specific blocks; intervention for the former children may be either intermittent or intensive. The same flexibility is available when only one school is serviced.

Throughout the years, attempts have been made to determine which scheduling models were most appropriate. Early research seemed to show that children with articulatory disorders responded well to intensive cycle scheduling. However, this was not a consistent finding, nor was evidence obtained that suggested that intensive cycle scheduling was effective with children presenting other types of communicative disorders. In general, it appears that SLPs who use the pull-out system favor intermittent over intensive cycle scheduling. However, the decision must be made based on the needs of the students as specified in their IEPs.

General Considerations

The current trend toward diversity in service delivery models makes the development of arbitrary schedules less concise. No longer is it possible to create a schedule and plug students into available slots. Rather, the SLP must determine the needs of the students and generate a service delivery option that will meet those needs. This may require direct or indirect intervention.

For the SLP who feels most comfortable with structure, perhaps it is best to think of the school year in terms of minimal start-up and close-down time, that is, a short period of five to ten working days to commence direct services in the fall and a similar time frame at the end of the school year. In most instances, this would leave approximately a thirty-two-week school year during which intervention would be possible (assuming that the school year was thirty-six weeks). Since IEPs on the majority of the students should be in place, work with these children would not be delayed. For districts that require fall screenings (followed by assessment and IEP development) or employ teacher referral procedures for identification, the beginning date for direct intervention may be postponed; when this is the case, it must be documented on the IEP.

With regard to a weekly schedule, the SLP should build time into the schedule each week for evaluations; conferences with parents, teachers, and other professionals; and housekeeping chores. Although it would be ideal to think in terms of an entire day for accomplishing these tasks, it is more likely that a half-day will be allocated. As the intermittent schedules demonstrate, when the pull-out system is employed, sessions are best scheduled in a Monday-Thursday, Tuesday-Friday configuration; less time between sessions occurs using this plan. This would leave Wednesday, either partly or entirely for coordination. Therefore, the SLP would be involved in intervention four or four and a half days each week, with time on Wednesdays to fulfill other responsibilities.

Daily schedules are less easily devised because of the many intervention options available. Perhaps it is best to think of the day in terms of thirty-minute increments. In most districts, the teachers and, therefore, the SLP are required to be in the building at least thirty minutes before school starts. The SLP should use that time to prepare for the day. As the school day begins, it may be prudent to continue to plan in thirty-minute blocks, whether that time be used for pull-out purposes, for in-class activities, or consultative work. Many SLPs, like teachers, have breaks during the morning and again in the afternoon. If these breaks are confined to fifteen minutes, the thirty-minute configuration remains intact. The lunch hour for school personnel might better be considered a lunch half-hour, and this, too, would be consistent. Finally, the SLP should plan to remain at least thirty minutes after the students leave school in the afternoon to write progress notes and bring closure to the day. Table 4-9 displays a sample schedule; time is allowed for a wide variety of activities, and allowance is made for flexibility.

Summary

Today's SLP is doing more things, in more places, with more guidelines than ever before. Formerly, SLPs had vague guidelines concerning the numbers of students they could service and were undoubtedly encouraged to maintain high

TABLE 4-9　Sample Weekly Schedule for One School

Time	Monday	Tuesday	Wednesday	Thursday	Friday
8:00	Preparation	Preparation	Preparation	Preparation	Preparation
8:30	Pull-out 1	Pull-out 8	Evaluations	Pull-out 1	Pull-out 8
9:00	Pull-out 2	Pull-out 9	Evaluations	Pull-out 2	Pull-out 9
9:30	Pull-out 3	Pull-out 10	Report writing	Pull-out 3	Pull-out 10
10:00	Break	Break	Break	Break	Break
10:15	In-class 1	In-class 3	Teacher consultation	In-class 5	In-class 7
10:30	In-class 1	In-class 3	Parent conference	In-class 5	In-class 7
11:00	Pull-out 4	Pull-out 11	Parent conference	Pull-out 4	Pull-out 11
11:30	Pull-out 4	Pull-out 11	Parent conference	Pull-out 4	Pull-out 11
12:00	Lunch	Lunch	Lunch	Lunch	Lunch
12:30	Pull-out 5	Pull-out 12	Consultation	Pull-out 5	Pull-out 12
1:00	Pull-out 5	Pull-out 12	Consultation	Pull-out 5	Pull-out 12
1:30	Pull-out 6	Pull-out 13	Consultation	Pull-out 6	Pull-out 13
2:00	Pull-out 7	Pull-out 13	Consultation	Pull-out 7	Pull-out 13
2:30	Break	Break	Break	Break	Break
2:45	In-class 2	In-class 4	Consultation	In-class 6	In-class 8
3:30	Dismissal	Dismissal	Dismissal	Dismissal	Dismissal

caseloads. Now states are recognizing the fact that caseloads must be limited to meet IEP criteria and, further, that a shotgun approach in intervention is neither ethical nor effective. Hence, caseloads are decreasing.

Entry criteria are also being proposed in many states to assist SLPs in determining which students meet eligibility requirements. Although the severity of the communicative disorder and its impact on academic achievement are logical considerations, it is important to note that some variables are difficult to objectify. Therefore, some measure of clinical judgment must be built into case selection decisions.

A continuum of services is available to contemporary SLPs. Where once the SLP saw students individually or in small groups in the speech room, now the SLPs are moving into other settings and performing in different capacities. In this chapter, the California plan was highlighted, but other states are devising plans that encourage the SLP to become more involved in consultative work, as well as actual classroom teaching. Some examples of different patterns of intervention at the preschool, elementary, and secondary levels were presented to illustrate this diversity.

Finally, consideration was given to scheduling models. Since the profession is experiencing a metamorphosis, it was necessary to consider scheduling as it was (and may still be), as it is (and may be changing), and as it will be (and maybe is). Attention was given to two models (intermittent and intensive cycle) with the admonition that variations within both were desirable. Recognizing that SLPs are probably making transitions between the traditional methods of service delivery and those requiring greater interaction with teachers and in the classroom, a sample weekly schedule was provided. Once again, it must be noted that scheduling decisions are driven by IEP recommendations, and it is the development of that document that is considered next.

Endnotes

1. R. K. Sommers, "Case Finding, Case Selection, and Case Load." R. J. Van Hattum (ed.), *Clinical Speech in the Schools* (Springfield, IL: Charles C. Thomas, 1969), pp. 232–276.

2. D. S. Bingham, R. J. Van Hattum, M. E. Faulk, and E. Toussig, "Program Organization and Management," *Journal of Speech and Hearing Disorders Monograph* 8(1961): pp. 33–49.

3. T. J. O'Toole and E. L. Zaslow, "Public Schools Speech and Hearing Programs: Things are Changing," *Asha* 11(1969): pp. 499–501.

4. M. Hoopes and M. O. Dasovich, "Parent Counseling: A Survey of Use by the Public School Speech Clinician," *Journal of the Missouri Speech and Hearing Association* 5(1972): pp. 9–13.

5. C. Hahn, "An Investigation into Current Procedures of Case Finding, Case Selection and Scheduling in the Schools," master's thesis, Southern Illinois University at Edwardsville (1980).

6. *Program Guidelines for Language, Speech and Hearing Specialists Providing Designated Instruction and Services,* California State Department of Education (1989).

7. *Illinois State Board of Education Piloting of the Comprehensive Plan for Speech-Language Service Delivery,* draft (1989).

8. *Proposed Rules, Regulations, and Policies,* Indiana Department of Education (1989).

9. "General Guidelines for Speech and Language," Daviess-Martin Special Education Cooperative (1990).

10. "Special Considerations in Identification and Placement of Students with Speech and Language Disorders," Missouri Department of Elementary and Secondary Education (1989).

11. "Recommended Service Delivery Models and Caseload Sizes for Speech-Language Pathology Services in the Schools," *Asha* 25(1983): pp. 65–70.

12. J. A. Jelinek, "A Model of Services for Young Handicapped Children," *Language, Speech, and Hearing Services in Schools* 16(1985): pp. 158–170.

13. M. M. Mroczkowski, "Self-Contained Language Classes for Kindergartners—Nine Years of Data," *Seminars in Speech and Language* 9(1988): pp. 329–339.

14. S. S. Christensen and C. H. Luckett, "Clinical Exchange: Getting into the Classroom and Making It Work," *Language, Speech, and Hearing Services in Schools* 21(1990): pp. 110–113.

15. G. M. Anderson and N. W. Nelson, "Integrating Language Intervention and Education in an Alternate Adolescent Language Classroom," *Seminars in Speech and Language* 9(1988): pp. 341–353.

16. J. R. Jenkins and A. Heinen, "Students' Preferences for Service Delivery: Pull-Out, In-Class, or Integrated Models," *Exceptional Children* 55(1989): pp. 516–523.

17. *Special Education in North Dakota Guidelines III: Programs for Students with Language, Speech and Hearing Disorders in the Public Schools,* North Dakota Department of Public Instruction (1977).

5

Individualized
Education Programs

As we look for ways to comply with the IEP regulations, let us not forget that all educational personnel are equal partners in the enterprise and that we are accountable for our efforts not only to handicapped pupils, their parents, and the public, but to each other as well (1).

Consistent with the mandate of the EHA/IDEA the school SLP must prepare an Individualized Education Program (IEP) for each communicatively disordered child in the caseload. Although preprofessional and master's level students in speech-language pathology are required to write goals, objectives, and session plans using behavioral language, the IEP format may not be familiar. In this chapter, the IEP process is discussed, and IEP development is considered. Finally, issues regarding the IEP are presented.

Federal IEP Laws

Section 1401 of the EHA/IDEA defines an IEP as follows:

The term "individualized education program" means a written statement for each child with a disability developed in any meeting by a representative of the local educational agency or an intermediate educational unit who shall be qualified to provide, or supervise the provision of, specially designed instruction to meet the unique needs of children with disabilities, the teacher, the parents or guardian of such child, and, whenever appropriate, such child, which statement shall include (A) a statement of the present levels of educational performance of such child, (B) a statement of annual goals, including short-term instructional objectives, (C) a statement of the specific educational services to be provided to such child, and the extent to which such child will be able to participate in regular educational programs, (D) a statement of the needed transition services for students beginning no later than age 16 and annually thereafter (and, when determined appropriate for the individual, beginning at age 14 or younger), including, when appropriate, a statement of the interagency responsibilities[2] or linkages (or both) before the student leaves the school setting, (E) the projected date for initiation and anticipated duration of such services, and (F) appropriate objective criteria and evaluation procedures and schedules for determining on at least an annual basis, whether instructional objectives are being achieved. (2)

The law, then, requires the SLP to (1) describe the presenting problem, (2) project objectives and goals for the year, (3) determine which service delivery option will best meet the child's needs, (4) plan transitional services, (5) anticipate the length of time it will take the child to reach the goals, and (6) describe the methods by which progress will be measured. Although the legal language may appear to make the requirements more complex, the law demands little more than what the student in training is currently asked to do. The seemingly difficult requirement is the development of the IEP. This is a group project rather than one completed by the SLP working in isolation. Participants include the parents and may involve other professionals and the child. The major responsibility for program development resides with the professional, but parental participation should provide the SLP with additional insight into the individual child's abilities and disabilities. As an added benefit, involvement of the parents in IEP planning should increase their participation in program implementation. Similarly, when the child can take part in the IEP planning, his or her role in the habilitative effort is more clearly defined. All individuals involved in program development agree on the appropriateness of these goals and procedures and assume responsibility for the execution of the plan.

Shrybman discussed the various components of the IEP in some detail (3). The first requirement of the IEP is that the child's current level of performance be described. In completing a written description, it is noted that "the statement should accurately describe the effect of the handicap in any area of education that is affected" (3); both academic and nonacademic areas should be included. In addition, the description should contain objective and measurable data. If test scores are meaningful to the participants, they may be included; otherwise, some explanation of the results is required. "Whatever test results are used should reflect the impact of the handicap on the child's performance" (3). Finally, it is imperative that the statement of present level of performance relate to other parts of the IEP. In other words, if a language deficit is described, appropriate goals and objectives should appear in the IEP, along with services designed to reach those objectives.

---

[2]So in original. Probably should be "responsibilities".

Goals relate to gains the child may be expected to make in a twelve-month period and, along with objectives, constitute the second component of the IEP. The objectives are "measurable, intermediate steps between the present performance level and the annual goals that have been established" (3). According to Shrybman, there are three criteria to be considered when formulating short-term objectives. First, the objectives must be sound when viewed from a developmental perspective, and they should reflect small and logical progression toward a goal. A child who consistently misarticulates a specific phoneme would not be expected to produce the sound and then move directly into the maintenance phase. Second, parental priorities must be taken into consideration when developing objectives. If the parents consider it important that the child develop appropriate pragmatic skills and this is consistent with the child's needs, this may be targeted. Certainly, greater parental participation will occur if the parents support the objectives. Finally, the objectives should be consistent with progress toward a least restrictive environment (LRE) placement. Objectives that would lead a language-disordered child out of a self-contained class into the regular classroom for some part of the school day would be appropriate.

The third component of the IEP concerns the nature of the services to be provided to meet the individual child's needs. An important distinction with regard to the child with a communicative disorder is whether the problem is primary and requires special education services or if the disorder is considered to be related. If the child's primary problem is in the area of communication, speech-language services are considered to be "special education." "Related services" in speech-language pathology are appropriate for the child whose primary disability is in an area such as mental retardation. This part of the IEP must also designate the amount of time the child will be receiving special services and how much time the child will remain in the regular classroom.

Information regarding the continuum of speech-language services available to children with communicative disorders contained in the previous chapter should illustrate that important decisions must be made regarding placement. Students with severe language deficiencies may be placed appropriately in a language classroom while enjoying some activities with their peers in a regular classroom. These placements are rather easily determined. Questions arise with students who display mild to moderate disorders; would these students respond best to a pull-out delivery system or could they benefit more from a consultative model?

In addition, time specifications are required. All participants must be aware of the amount of time the child will be involved in intervention, regardless of its location. Some students may benefit from individual pull-out sessions totaling 60 minutes each week; others may require additional time but a less restrictive service delivery system. And in some cases, the participants (including the SLP) may miscalculate the effectiveness of the scheduled service delivery model, and a modification may be necessary. According to Shrybman, the type of service delivery may be modified without reconvening an IEP meeting as long as the amount of time remains stable. If the amount is decreased or increased, a meeting must be held.

In the current document, the next criteria are considered separate items; an earlier EHA combined the dates and duration of services with the criteria to be employed to determine if objectives are being met. With regard to initiation of services, they should begin as soon as possible after the IEP conference and are projected to be in effect for twelve months. "If it is expected that the pupil will need a particular service for more than one year, the duration could be projected beyond that time in the IEP" (3). Although the evaluation procedures may not be a separate entity in the IEP, they must be included. It is sensible for these procedures, criteria, and the schedule for assessment to be part of the objectives. (It should be noted that Shrybman's article predated IDEA and did not include transitional services. Sample IEP forms included in the Appendix also omit the new requirement.)

These, then, are the legal minima for the IEP document. This document is theoretically devised at a meeting attended by school personnel, the parents, and in some cases, the child. The IEP meeting is considered next.

IEP Meeting

The IEP meeting occurs after the child has been identified as having a possible disabling condition, after the parents have consented to assessment of the child, and after the results of the assessment have determined that the child is eligible for services. This meeting must be held within thirty days of the initial determination that services are required.

Preparatory to the IEP meeting, parents must be notified in writing of its time, place, and purpose. Parents, along with a representative of the public agency, the child's teacher, those who have assessed the child, and perhaps even the child, constitute the IEP meeting participants. Other participants designated by the parents or district may also be in attendance. The key elements in the IEP meeting are the parents and the child since, prior to the EHA/IDEA, staff members convened to discuss a given child's intervention plan. It is the inclusion of parents and children that distinguishes an IEP meeting from other types of staffings.

As noted previously, parents must be informed that the IEP meeting will take place; if the parents do not respond to documented attempts to communicate with them, the meeting may be held in their absence. At or prior to the meeting, the parents must be informed of their rights with regard to access to information, independent evaluation, confidentiality, and due process. Throughout the deliberations, it should be made clear that differences of opinion not resolvable in the meeting may be taken to due process. When parental agreement is obtained (as is the case in most instances), their signatures, along with those of the other participants, signify approval of the document.

In summary, the IEP is a document developed in a meeting that provides goals and intermediate objectives for a disabled child's educational program; each IEP is reviewed on at least an annual basis. Parents are considered an essential part of the IEP process, and at least one state has sought to inform parents of their rights through a comprehensive booklet. This and other state IEP compliance procedures are presented next; in this discussion, it is apparent that individual states have expanded on the legal requirements for IEPs.

State IEP Regulations

Illinois is one state that has provided guidelines for the development of IEPs and the IEP process (4). This process is illustrated in Figure 5-1. The initial responsibility of the local district, as illustrated in the flowchart, is public notification of the annual screening. It is required that all exceptional children between the ages of 3 and 21 be identified and that residents within the district be informed of the rights of exceptional children and of programming available for these students. The screening process includes assessment of preschool children as well as speech and language screening of all children entering public school programs. Following screening, or upon the recommendation of parents, agencies, or professional persons, children may be referred for case study evaluation. The school district determines whether a case study evaluation should be conducted or if outside services should be sought and notifies the parents of this decision. This written notification must be in the parents' native language and must include an explanation of procedural safeguards and a description of the proposed action. Before proceeding with the case study evaluation, written parental consent must be obtained. If the parents do not agree to such an evaluation, a due process hearing may be requested by the district. Figure 5-2 illustrates a formal request to evaluate a child.

Once parental consent is secured, the case study evaluation is planned. Children whose problems appear to be limited to speech and language must be screened for hearing sensitivity, and their medical and academic histories and current functioning must be reviewed. In addition, a certified SLP must interview each child and assess his or her speech and language competencies. Following the case study evaluation, the SLP determines the child's need and eligibility for services and convenes an IEP conference. Figure 5-3 illustrates notification to the parents of the time and date for the IEP meeting. After this meeting, recommendations are made to the local district superintendent or his or her representative regarding placement of the child, and the IEP is implemented.

Children presenting multiple disorders require a comprehensive case study evaluation. In addition to the information obtained on the child with a suspected speech or language disorder, the following must be done: consultation with parents, compilation of a social history, vision screening, assessment of the learning environment, and any special evaluations that may be necessary. The latter may include psychological assessment, medical examination, or

FIGURE 5-1 Individualized Education Program (IEP) Process

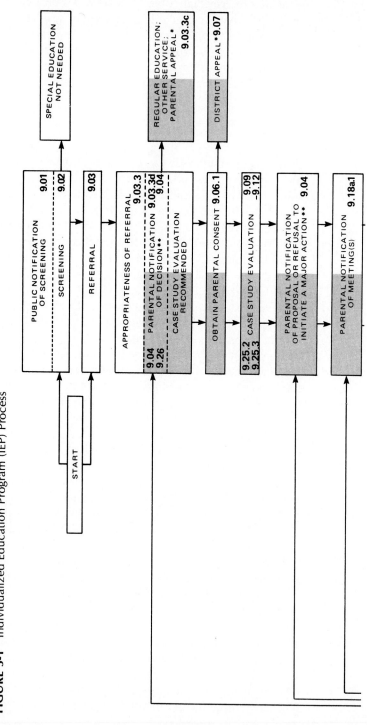

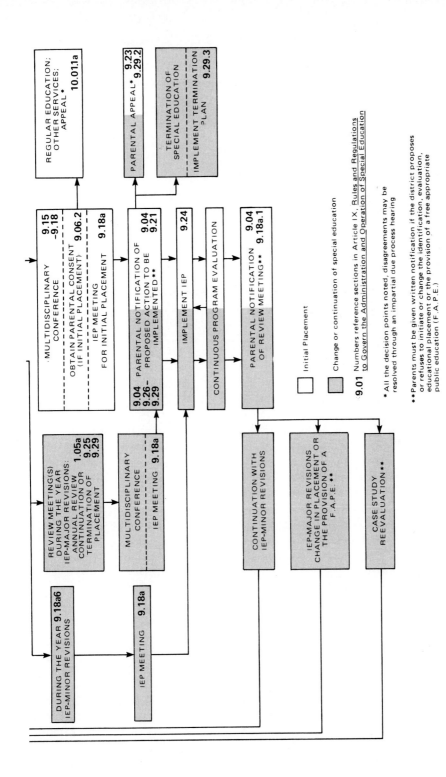

Redrawn from State Board of Education et al., 1979. Courtesy of Illinois Office of Education.

89

FIGURE 5-2 Peoria Public Schools, District 150, Special Services Division, Form S/L #2

_____
(Speech Pathologist)

SCHOOL:_____

DATE:_____

RE:_____

D.O.B.:_____

I.D.#:_____

Dear Parent:

On _____, _____ filed a referral requesting that your child be evaluated by this office. We intend to proceed with an individual Speech and Language case study evaluation of your child for the following reason(s):_____
_____
_____

With your permission, the evaluation procedures we may use with your child to assist us in planning an appropriate therapy program are as follows:

      An assessment of your child's speech and language.
      A review of your child's medical history and current health status.
      An interview with your child.
      A hearing screening.
      A review of your child's academic history and current educational functioning.
      A consultation with you if needed.

This evaluation and subsequent parent conference(s) will be completed within sixty (60) school days of the date of receipt of the signed permission. You will be informed in writing as to the date, time, and location of this conference. Your child will not receive speech and language therapy services without your knowledge.

Please be advised that according to the Rules and Regulations to Govern the Administration and Operation of Special Education (filed pursuant to Chapter 122, Article XIV, Illinois Revised Statutes, 1975) you have the right to object to the proposed evaluation of your child. If you object to the proposed evaluation of your child, we would like to discuss this with you within thirty (30) days. During this period you have the right to meet with the Department Supervisor, the school principal, your child's teacher, and myself to try to alleviate your objections. If after an informal conference we cannot come to a mutual acceptance of the proposed evaluation, you are advised that the Peoria Public Schools, District #150, may request an impartial due process hearing.

You are also advised that you have the right to review all records related to the reason for the evaluation, know the results of the evaluation, and participate in the conference(s) at which the speech and language therapy plan for your child will be developed. Additionally, you have the right to obtain an independent speech and language evaluation from a clinically certified speech pathologist.

Following is a Permission Form which is to be completed by you and returned to me within ten (10) school days. Should you have any questions please do not hesitate to call me. Return all copies of this form to me at _____ School.

                                      Sincerely,

                                            672-
                        (Speech Pathologist)   Phone

I am in receipt of the Intent and Procedures to conduct a Speech and Language evaluation of my child,_____. I have been informed of my rights and know that my child will not receive Speech and Language therapy services without my knowledge. I understand the reasons and the description of the evaluation process that you have provided and have checked the appropriate box below.

        YES ☐ Permission is given to conduct the Speech and Language evaluation.

        NO ☐ Permission is denied.

Parent/Guardian Signature:_____ Date:_____

D.O.C.: w/Master File, y/Sp. P., p/Parent, g/Sp. P.
Rev.: 04-80

Courtesy of Peoria Public Schools.

audiological testing. All evaluations must be done at the expense of the local school district; if the parents object to any part of the assessment, the district is financially obligated to cover the cost of an independent evaluation. Once the results of the case study evaluation have been reviewed, a multidisciplinary or IEP conference must be convened. Parents must be informed of this meeting and invited to attend and participate. During such conferences, the participants review their findings in order to establish a composite understanding of

FIGURE 5-3   Peoria Public Schools, District 150, Special Services Division, Form S/L #3

RE:_____

_____   D.O.B.:_____
(Speech Pathologist)   I.D.#:_____

DATE:_____

Dear Parent:

The speech and language evaluation of your child has been completed. As a result of this evaluation, it has been determined that your child would benefit from speech and language therapy. Before this support service can begin, it is important that you be informed of the results of the evaluation and to participate in the development of your child's Individual Educational (Therapy) Program (IEP). We would like to meet with you to discuss the evaluation and to assist in the preparation of the therapy program on:

_____, _____, at _____ at _____
(Day)   (Date)   (Time)   (School)

Check the appropriate box(s), sign and date below. Please return all copies to me within ten (10) school days. If you should have any questions, please call me.

Sincerely,

                                                   672-_____
                                    (Speech Pathologist)   Phone

----

YES ☐   I can keep this appointment.

NO ☐   I cannot keep this appointment, but

        YES ☐   I give my permission for my child to receive speech and language services
                and for you to develop my child's Individual Educational Program (IEP).
                By giving my permission without a conference, I understand that all
                papers relevant to the evaluation, including actual results of the assess-
                ment are available for my inspection, the records pertaining to this eval-
                uation are available to me for copying, and my child's IEP will be sent to me.

        NO ☐   I do not give my permission for my child to receive speech and language
                services and for you to develop my child's IEP.

Please be advised that according to the Rules and Regulation to Govern the Administration and Operation of Special Education (filed pursuant to Chapter 122, Article XIV, Illinois Revised Statutes, 1975) you have the right to object to the proposed support service which is being recommended for your child. If within ten (10) school days you object to the proposed support service we would like to meet with you sometime during the next 30 days. During this period you have the right to meet with us to try to resolve any differences. If we cannot resolve any disagreement informally you have the right to request a hearing before an impartial officer. If you decide to request a hearing you will need to write a letter to Mr. Harry F. Whitaker, Superintendent, Peoria Public Schools. This letter shall specifically request a District level hearing with an impartial hearing officer and shall describe the reason(s) the hearing is being requested and shall provide all other information pertinent to the request.

You are also advised that you have the right at your expense, to the following: to be represented by legal counsel, bring witnesses, request certain school personnel to be present, cross examine, obtain an independent evaluation, request an open hearing.

If the child has not reached the age of majority, you have the right to determine if the child shall attend the hearing, except on a finding by the hearing officer that attendance would be harmful to the welfare of the child. The child may then be excluded from all or part of the hearing. The burden of proof as to the adequacy and appropriateness of the proposed course of action shall be upon the school district. A tape recording or other verbatim record of the hearing shall be made and shall be controlled by the Illinois State Board of Education. You shall have the right to a copy of this record on request. At all stages of the hearing, interpretation for the deaf and interpreters in the primary language of the home (when other than English) shall be provided at public expense. During any period of disagreement over placement, your child will continue in his present educational placement.

If you do not grant permission and we cannot resolve any disagreement through an informal conference and you do not request a hearing, be advised that the Peoria Public Schools may proceed with the proposed support service(s).

Signature, Parent/Guardian: _____   Date:_____

D.O.C.: w/Master File, y/Sp.P., p/Parent, g/Sp.P.   Phone:_____
REV.: 04-80

Courtesy of Peoria Public Schools.

the child's behavior. In addition, the child's eligibility for services, his or her educational needs, and the most appropriate special placement are determined. Recommendations are then made regarding the child's placement in the least restrictive educational environment close to the child's home. A written report of the conference must be prepared and filed, and the parents must be informed that they may have access to this report.

In the event that the multidisciplinary and IEP conference are not combined, an additional meeting must be held to prepare the IEP. This conference should be convened within thirty days after the child's need for special services has been identified. Participants in this meeting should include a district representative, the child's teacher, the child's parents or guardians, and when appropriate, the child; other persons may be invited by the parents or local district officials. If the parents cannot attend the meeting, other opportunities for participation must be provided. During the IEP meeting, placement of the child in the appropriate environment is considered, short-term objectives and long-range goals are established, and evaluative criteria are outlined.

The child's parents must be notified in writing of the results of the case study evaluation, the proposed placement, and the services to be delivered ten calendar days before the child is to be placed in a special program. The parents must also be informed of their right to object to this proposal and notified that they have ten calendar days in which to appeal the placement. If no objection is made, the IEP is implemented as soon as possible or at least by the beginning of the next school semester. Interim services must be provided to the child awaiting placement.

Once the child has been placed in the appropriate educational environment, continuous evaluation of progress is recommended. Illinois rules and regulations mandate that an annual review of short-term objectives be completed, but this review should be supplemented by periodic monitoring of progress so that the appropriateness of the IEP may be evaluated. Although revisions in the IEP may be made at any time by convening an IEP meeting, formal annual reviews are required. Again, parents are notified of the review conference, and all professionals involved with the child are invited to participate. During this meeting, the child's current functioning is reviewed as it relates to the objectives set forth in the IEP. In some cases, additional evaluations may be recommended, and the IEP may be revised. When the child no longer requires services, special education is terminated. Again, a conference is held, and parental participation is encouraged.

As is apparent in Figure 5-1, multiple options are available for the entry IEP meetings. Similarly, opportunities for parental and district appeal, revisions of the IEP, and reevaluation of the child are provided throughout the IEP process. In this discussion, only the general sequence of the process recommended by the state of Illinois has been presented. California guidelines present information similar to those in the *Illinois Primer* but include questions (and answers) that may be raised regarding IEP development and meetings (5).

For example, the necessity of having an administrator present at the IEP meeting might be questioned. The presence of such a person is needed because he or she has the authority to make decisions and is able to commit necessary resources. The administrator (or a designee) also serves in a problem-solving capacity and can "accept ownership of special education programs" (5).

It might also be asked if the classroom teacher must be present at the IEP meeting if the child's primary problem is in the area of speech. The response is negative since, in this instance, the SLP is regarded as the teacher. The question of who chairs the IEP meeting might be raised; the logical choice is the administrator or designee. In some cases, speech-language sessions may need to be canceled because of the absence of the child or the SLP; when this happens, what should be done? In this instance, the SLP should document absences carefully and maintain the evidence in the student's file. The utilization of computerized IEPs might be questioned. According to California guidelines, they are acceptable if they are individualized and meet legal requirements. Finally, there are those who might ask how frequently IEP meetings should be held and how long they are required to be. The obvious answer to the first part of the question is annually or more frequently if needed. The meetings themselves should be long enough to allow for meaningful participation, but no specific length is required. There is no doubt that professionals may have other concerns about IEPs, and some were addressed in *NICHCY* publication, and those questions are considered next (6).

SLPs have been accustomed to reevaluating students during the fall prior to implementing services. Is this required by the IEP? The answer is that IEPs must be in effect in the fall but may be reviewed at any point during the year. If an IEP meeting is needed prior to the annual review, who may initiate such a meeting? Although it is normally the public agency that initiates IEP meetings, the latter may also be requested by the parents. Some children require a variety of services; if these services are prescribed in the IEP, is the public agency responsible for the provision of all recommended forms of intervention? In order to be in compliance with the EHA/IDEA, the answer is yes. All service must be provided free of charge. It may be convenient and time-effective to prepare IEPs prior to the meeting, but it is not permissible. The regulations clearly state that the IEP is to be developed during the meeting; however, it is advisable that participants come prepared with progress notes, results from testing, and recommendations but only with the understanding that this information is open for discussion and revision. Since IEPs are purported to ensure accountability, a final question that might be posed relates to the IEP as a performance contract. That is, what are the implications for the SLP if the child does not achieve the IEP objectives? Although it is binding that the services provided to the child be consistent with the IEP, the SLP is not held accountable if the child does not meet the criteria specified in that document.

Although SLPs may have additional questions about IEP development and content, it is conceivable that parents have even more concerns. One state has attempted to anticipate these concerns by issuing a parents' guide. That material is considered next.

Guidelines for Parents

It is important that consumers understand what the EHA/IDEA means with regard to their rights and the rights of their children, and the Illinois State Department of Education provides this information to parents (7). In this pamphlet, guardians and parents are made aware of eligibility requirements and of the fact that the child need not live at home to receive necessary services. Children in private and parochial schools, as well as those in institutions and hospitals, are eligible for special education services. Parents and caregivers are guided through the screening and referral processes and informed of the timelines that must be met. The various components of a case study evaluation are described, along with special evaluations that may be required. Parents are also informed of their right to request an independent evaluation if they disagree with the findings of the public agency's assessment.

The three types of meetings that are held are also explained in the pamphlet. The Multidisciplinary Conference (MDC) is held to consider assessment findings, to determine type of eligibility, the required services, and the most appropriate placement. Such consideration as the least restrictive environment, an extended school year placement, and transportation needs are included in MDC discussions. Parents are also informed that they must have a written report made available to them after the MDC.

The second meeting described in the Parents' Guide is the IEP meeting. The components of the IEP are explained, and disclaimers are placed on its contents so that parents understand that it is not a lesson plan, nor is it a legally binding contract. The cast of participants is also presented. Parents are informed that modifications in the IEP are possible at any time but that annual reviews (the third meeting) are required. A timeline for the implementation of services is presented in Figure 5-4.

Pursuant with federal and state regulations, parents are informed that they may examine their child's school records. The guidelines delineate parent rights with regard to confidentiality, obtaining copies, and releasing information. The release of information when divorced parents are involved is also considered.

As presented in Chapter 2, public agency representatives and parents do not always agree on the appropriate course of action for a particular child. Therefore, conflict resolution is necessary. In part V of the guidelines, the procedures for filing a complaint are explained, and mediation is discussed. The two levels of due process hearings are also considered. Either a local district or the parents may request a Level I hearing if disagreements occur. A hearing officer from the State Department of Special Education reviews the case after hearing from both participants. The hearing officer's decision is binding. Grounds for parents to request a Level I review are enumerated in the guidelines. In addition, parents are informed of their rights regarding the language employed during the hearing (interpreters must be present if necessary), the presentation of testimony, and records of the hearing. Within ten calendar days after the hearing, the written decision must be sent to the participants by certified mail. If either side disputes the hearing officer's decision, a Level II review may be requested, and if the parents disagree at that level, they "may bring civil action in any circuit court of competent jurisdiction" (7). A summary of parents' rights is illustrated in Figure 5-5.

FIGURE 5-4   Timelines for Services to Handicapped Students

Action	Person Responsible	Number of Days to Complete Action/ Frequency of Action	From
Screening for referral for case study evaluation	Teacher, school nurse, diagnostician, principal pupil personnel services staff, appropriate professionals	Ongoing	
Case study evaluation	Multidisciplinary diagnostic team	60 school days	Date of referral
Development of IEP	The IEP meeting participants	30 school days	Date of MDC and prior to implementation of placement
Notification of placement (written)	Local district to designate placement	10 calendar days prior to actual placement	
Implementation of placement	Teacher and others pursuant to IEP	As soon as possible but not later than next semester	
Review of placement and IEP	Local district to designate	Annually	
Reevaluation	Multidisciplinary diagnostic team	Every three years	

A Parents' Guide: The Educational Rights of Handicapped Children. Courtesy of the Illinois State Board of Education.

Issues Surrounding IEPs

Since IEPs became mandatory, many issues regarding their development and implementation have surfaced. The National Association of State Directors of Special Education, for example, published a summary of research findings on individualized education programs (8). The first project, entitled the "Connecticut Study," dealt with the participation of team members in the IEP process. A total of 1,478 persons involved in 230 planning teams (PTs) was surveyed. The researchers were specifically interested in the levels of participation and satisfaction of PT members, PT members' understanding of their roles, and their decision-making styles, as well as the roles played by parents in the IEP process.

FIGURE 5-5   Parent Rights in Brief

As the parents of a child who may or will receive special education benefits, you have certain rights which are safeguarded by state and federal statute. You have the right to request a copy of the special education rules (23 II Adm. Code 226) from your local district. The rights to which you are entitled are listed below in abbreviated form under nine headings.

Student Records:

1) Right to inspect and review records;
2) Right to obtain copies of records at cost or at no cost, depending on ability to pay;
3) Right to be informed of all types and locations of records being collected, maintained or used by the agency;
4) Right to ask for an explanation of any item in the records;
5) Right to ask for an amendment of any record on the grounds it is found inaccurate, misleading or in violation of privacy rights;
6) Right to a hearing if the agency refuses to make the requested amendment.

Confidentiality of Information:

1) Right to restrict access to your child's records by withholding consent to disclose records;
2) Right to be informed before information in your child's file is to be destroyed;
3) Right to be told to whom information has been disclosed.

Notice:

1) Right to notice before the agency initiates or changes (or refuses to initiate or change) the identification, evaluation or placement of your child;
2) Right to have that notice in writing, in your native language, or other principal mode of communication, at a level understandable to the general public;
3) Right to have the notice describe the proposed action, explain why it is proposed, describe the options considered and explain why those other options were rejected;
4) Right to be notified of each evaluation procedure, test, record or report the agency will use as a basis for any proposed action.

Consent:

1) Right to give consent before an evaluation is conducted and before initial placement is made in special education;
2) Right to revoke consent at any time.

Evaluation Procedures:

1) Right to have a case study evaluation of your child's educational needs completed within 60 school days of referral;
2) Right to have more than one criterion used in determining an appropriate educational program for your child;
3) Right to have the evaluation performed by a multidisciplinary team;
4) Right to obtain a copy of the multidisciplinary conference report;
5) Right to have your child assessed in all areas related to the suspected disability;
6) Right to have a reevaluation every three years or more frequently if conditions warrant or if you or your child's teacher request it.

Independent Evaluation:

1) Right to an independent educational evaluation;
2) Right to have the district pay for the independent evaluation if it is determined through a due process hearing that the district's evaluation is not appropriate;
3) Right to be informed of the procedures for obtaining an independent evaluation at public expense;
4) Right to have an independent evaluation considered when

placement and program decisions are made.

Least Restrictive Environment:

1) Right to have your child educated with nonhandicapped children to the maximum extent possible;
2) Right to have your child removed from the regular educational environment only after supplementary aids and services were tried and found unsatisfactory;
3) Right to have placement in the school your child would attend if nonhandicapped unless the individualized education plan requires some other arrangement;
4) Right of your child to participate with nonhandicapped children in nonacademic and extracurricular services and activities, such as meals, recess, counseling, clubs, athletics, and special interest groups.

Complaint Resolution and Mediation:

1) Complaints alleging violations of parent and special education rights can be referred to the local building administrator.
2) Complaints alleging violations of parent and special education student rights can be referred to the Department of Special Education, Illinois State Board of Education for review, investigation and action within sixty days.
3) Illinois' mediation service, designed as an alternative to the Due Process Hearing, is a means of resolving disagreements regarding the appropriateness of the provision of special education and related services. This service is administered and supervised by the Illinois State Board of Education and is provided upon request at no cost to the parties. Parents and/or local school districts who wish to request mediation services or to know more about the State Board of Education complaint resolution system may contact the Department of Special Education, Illinois State Board of Education, at 217/782-6601.

Hearing:

1) Right to request an impartial due process hearing to question the district's identification, evaluation, or placement of your child or to question the district's provision of a free, appropriate public education (The request should state the reasons the hearing is being requested and should be sent to your district superintendent.);
2) Right to be informed of the procedures to follow to make a request for an impartial due process hearing (i.e., to whom, how, what to include in the request, timeliness, etc.);
3) Right to be informed of any free or low-cost legal and other relevant services available (e.g., expert on handicapping conditions that may be a witness at the hearing);
4) Right to have the hearing chaired by a person not employed by a public agency involved in the education of your child or otherwise having any personal or professional interest in the hearing;
5) Right to see a statement of the qualifications of the hearing officer;
6) Right to be advised and accompanied at the hearing by counsel and to be accompanied by individuals with special knowledge or training in problems of the handicapped;
7) Right to have your child present at the hearing;
8) Right to having the hearing open to the public;
9) Right to present evidence and confront, cross-examine and compel the attendance of witnesses;
10) Right to prohibit the introduction of any evidence at the hearing that has not been disclosed at least five days before the hearing;
11) Right to have a record of the hearing;
12) Right to obtain written findings of fact and a written decision within 45 days after the initial request for the hearing;
13) Right to appeal to the Illinois State

Continued

FIGURE 5-5 *Continued*

Board of Education and receive a decision within 30 days of the filing of an appeal;

14) Right to have a hearing and an appeal set at a time reasonably convenient to the parent;

15) Right to appeal a decision from the Illinois State Board of Education in court;

16) Right to have your child remain in his or her present educational placement during the pendency of

the administrative proceeding, unless the parent and district agree otherwise;

17) Right to recover reasonable attorney's fees if you, the parent, prevail in a hearing or court action. Prior to proceeding to a hearing, you should thoroughly discuss with an attorney the question of cost and the applicability of the *Handicapped Children's Protection Act of 1986.*

Among the findings of the survey was that because communication was oral rather than written, it was sometimes inadequate. The researchers also found that PT conferences were usually dominated by administrators and appraisal personnel, whereas teachers played rather passive roles. This was attributed to the presence of building principals at the meetings. Because personal satisfaction seemed to be directly related to degree of participation, teachers were disenchanted with the conferences. With regard to role understanding, the participants were not cognizant of the purposes and scope of committee activities, and teachers seemed to be the least well informed. Moreover, the researchers found that decisions were being made by one or two PT members rather than by the entire group. Finally, the parents' role in planning was not well defined. Although they provided information to the PT, parents were not expected to participate in decision making.

Marver and David analyzed 150 IEPs and interviewed 200 parents, teachers, and administrators between October 1976 and September 1977 (8). Regarding preplacement preparation, the researchers found that early parent notification was beneficial but that parents were not included in the preplanning meetings. Assessment of children with potential problems was inefficient. Frequently, examiners were not trained, the process was incomplete, and assessment guidelines were not available. The researchers found that at IEP meetings, committee size ranged from three to fifteen members. They also found that because meetings were held before or after school, or at noon, the teachers' unions were displeased. Although parents participated in 60 to 90 percent of the cases, their contribution in meetings was inconsequential. Child participation was found to be nonexistent.

Marver and David's review of IEPs revealed that emphasis was on special education rather than on special and regular educational programming. Although compliance with state IEP regulations was apparent, the quality of IEPs differed from district to district. Confusion between goals and objectives was revealed, and staff members agreed that they needed training in the IEP process and development. Finally, even though the staff were aware that the IEP was not legally binding, they seemed to be fearful of their accountability as it related to IEP content. With regard to placement, the researchers found that the time span from identification to placement ranged from two weeks to six months; six weeks was the average. On a positive note, the researchers reported that children with disabilities were being identified more frequently and that the services provided to these children were improving.

Among the issues studied by Morrissey and Hafer was the parental role in the IEP process (8). The researchers interviewed 1,000 persons in four states, including representatives of state education agencies, school personnel, parents of exceptional children, and members of advocacy groups. Both parents and school personnel expressed concern about parents' capacity for participation in the IEP process. Representatives from the schools felt that parents were unprepared to participate in educational program development. Although parents concurred with this reservation, they did feel that they could provide useful information to the planning team and should participate in the IEP review.

Some concern related to the costs of parental participation when compared to the benefits derived from such involvement. It was noted that conferences were sometimes held after school or in the evenings, and home visits were occasionally necessary to obtain parental consent. Formal notification and consent procedures resulted in some delays in initiating services.

The role of the teacher in the IEP process was also explored. Teachers expressed concern about the time consumed by noninstructional activities and by activities for which they were not trained. The teachers further appeared to view the IEP mandate of PL 94-142 as "an expression of lack of faith in the ability of our nation's teachers to effectively educate handicapped children" (8).

There were positive reports from the teachers. Many considered the IEP process helpful in their teaching. The methods of measuring progress not only assisted the teachers but also served to motivate and involve students. In general, however, the teachers felt that they needed additional training in order to execute their responsibilities in the IEP process effectively.

The importance of seeking assistance from allied professionals and working with the parents of nonhandicapped children was stressed by Reynolds (1). He suggested that special educators could learn from sociologists about family interactions and that psychologists could help educators develop clinical skills for IEP conferences. For example, in order to function adequately in IEP meetings, educators must learn to listen to parents and must be willing to share different perspectives about children with others. Reynolds also indicated that special educators were obligated to inform parents of nonhandicapped children about PL 94-142 and the impact of that legislation on their children. The latter children must be taught to deal with the handicapped children in their classrooms, and it is the teacher's responsibility to create a supportive and cooperative social environment within that room. In short, Reynolds states that the IEP process should be a cooperative, sharing effort among professionals, parents, and children.

Parental participation in IEP meetings was investigated by Turnbull and

Hughes (9). Recognizing that parents appeared to be somewhat passive during IEP conferences, the authors attempted to objectify these observations. Specifically, they sought information regarding the communicative interaction among the participants. In addition, participation of the parents and their evaluations, along with the SLPs, were examined.

Four SLPs in rural Michigan each tape-recorded two IEP conferences and submitted the tapes for analysis. Telephone interviews with the parents and SLPs were also reviewed by the researchers. The latter conversations concerned the child's program, the interaction between the parents and SLP, and evaluative feedback.

The data obtained from the eight tape recordings were categorized into communication units (CUs) and coded for pragmatic content. The thirteen topic areas included such items as objectives, performance, and procedures, as well as rights and responsibilities. Also collected were descriptive data, including the location of the conference, its participants, and its duration.

With regard to analysis of the descriptive data, it was found that six of the conferences were for initial placement, and two were annual reviews. The participants included the SLP, the classroom teacher (in seven cases), and at least one parent. No conference had an administrator in attendance. The topic most frequently discussed was the child's performance, with parental responsibility for intervention considered least frequently. Statements were made with greatest frequency (92 percent), with questions posed infrequently, primarily by the SLP. "The overall communicative interaction for all conferences was predominately one-way, with clinicians providing information to other participants" (9). With regard to the follow-up telephone conversations, the parents' assessments of the conference were more positive than the SLPs.

In discussing the results of the study, Turnbull and Hughes expressed pleasure that classroom teachers participated in the majority of conferences. Conversely, they found the absence of an administrator to be "noteworthy" (9). Neither the parents nor the SLP thought that this void negatively affected the conference, however. With regard to topics discussed in the conference, the emphasis was on the child's present performance rather than on ways in which the performance could be modified. The fact that parental involvement in intervention was unstressed appeared to be troublesome to the researchers. Finally, the lack of interaction was discussed; the researchers suggested that this aspect of the conference might be improved if SLPs allowed for silence and asked open-ended questions. Since the involvement of parents is thought to be desirable, perhaps SLPs need to study strategies to encourage such participation.

Simpson considered the issues involved in conferring with parents of handicapped children (10). A perusal of the table of contents illustrates broad consideration of the child's family (including minority and single-parent families), the skills needed for conferencing (including the importance of listening), and the conferences themselves. IEP meetings fall within the last category. After reviewing parental rights, Simpson discusses strategies that include, rather than exclude, parental participation in the IEP process. One important need is that of trust; parents and professionals must share that trust before meaningful interaction can occur. Further, the parents must know that their participation is expected and considered. Bureaucratic restraints also confuse parents. Although school personnel may recognize the need for specific services to be outlined in the IEP, parents should not be expected to be knowledgeable. The language used during IEP conferences may also be unfamiliar to the layperson. "Parents may be somewhat reluctant to reveal their lack of understanding and, in some instances, may actually employ terms and phrases for which they have little comprehension" (10). SLPs, particularly, should understand the need to use meaningful terminology during IEP meetings so that they actually communicate with parents and other professionals.

An important prerequisite in encouraging parental participation in IEP conferences is that the meeting be perceived by the parents as nonthreatening. It is understandable that a parent may feel intimidated when placed in a situation with a group of professionals. In addition, the parent may be unfamiliar with these people and uninformed about the conduct of the meeting. Simpson identifies procedures that may assist in alleviating parental apprehension. One is to limit the number of participants; he says that individuals with marginal involvement should not be allowed to attend. He further suggests that a warm and friendly atmosphere be created so that parents feel welcome and comfortable. In order to reduce the isolation that a parent might feel, that person should be encouraged to bring a friend to the meeting; it is particularly helpful if this friend is knowledgeable about the IEP process. Finally, it is important that at least one of the participants be known to the parent; it would appear that this should be a "given." Simpson reported that one mother entered her son's IEP meeting with the same apprehension she experienced when she went to the dentist. Surely, professionals can create a better atmosphere than that.

The current author's most recent experiences with IEP meetings were in an observational rather than a participatory capacity as an administrative consultant to a private school for behaviorally disordered students. These students also presented concomitant disabilities, including speech-language problems. The IEP meetings were held in a somewhat luxurious conference room containing a large table around which up to sixteen people could be seated. The room was resplendent with overstuffed furniture and a piano. In short, the conference room provided a comfortable setting for the IEP meetings.

The cast of characters in attendance at the conferences changed with each meeting, as did the chair. In many instances, the school's principal or associate principal presided. Since students are bused to the facility from a variety of districts, representatives from these districts attended; building teachers and specialists were also present. With less regularity, parents and caregivers attended.

For annual IEP review meeting 1, the participants convened and awaited the arrival of the student's mother. Fifteen minutes after the meeting was scheduled to begin, the mother arrived. It was a warm day and no one was surprised when the mother requested a glass of ice water. Meanwhile, as a soon-to-retire psychologist read the local newspaper, the chair reviewed the purpose of the meeting, and the professionals involved in the student's program began to present progress information and proposed objectives for the next year. When the SLP began her report, the mother appeared to become interested in the proceedings and watched the SLP carefully. (It later became apparent that the mother was watching the clock above the SLP's head.) At some point, the mother reached for facial tissues and proceeded to dip them in ice water and stuff them down the front of her dress; this action was accompanied by an audible sigh of relief. Needless to say, the participants attempted to ignore the mother's behavior, but it was highly distracting. It is to the credit of the professionals that the annual review continued and was concluded with a modicum of disruption. It is doubtful that the mother contributed or gained much from the proceedings.

A second IEP meeting involved a student who had left the facility and was being considered for readmission. Mindy (the child), accompanied by both parents, attended the meeting. Even the disinterested observer quickly became aware that the 10-year-old candidate for readmission was the dominant member in the family. It was also apparent that she had intellectual resources that exceeded those of her parents.

Serving as her own advocate, Mindy told the group that she was not experiencing problems in her current public school setting; rather, it was the teacher and the other children who were at fault. Apparently, Mindy was quite adept at playing her parents against school personnel and vice-versa. When, during the meeting, the father attempted to clarify a point, Mindy shook her finger at him and declared, "One more word out of you . . ." The father, upon her admonition, moved away from the table. At that point, the meeting chair felt the need to reestablish control of the meeting and explained to the child that she was just that, a child. Mindy was not, explained the chair, the decision maker. The meeting continued, Mindy was readmitted, an IEP was written, and Mindy proceeded to run the classroom for the remainder of the school year.

There were also poignant moments during IEP reviews. One involved a 17-year-old female (Jamie) who was moderately retarded but whose behavior had become more appropriate. She, along with her diminutive mother, attended the meeting. The professionals reporting during the conference felt that Jamie was ready to be placed in a less restrictive environment for mentally retarded youth. When this consensus was reached, Jamie's mother fought back tears as she told the staff that one of her relatives had been placed in the proposed facility and "bad things had happened." Although it was not clear what these bad things were, the participants acquiesced, and Jamie remained at the private school where she will probably stay until she is 21.

Success stories do occur. Joe entered the school at the age of 15, after being released from a psychiatric hospital. For three years, he responded well to the structured environment and progressed academically. Joe represented himself at his annual IEP review and listened as the professionals reported that he had met all of his goals and objectives, including academic requirements for high school graduation. It was a touching moment for all participants and must have reaffirmed the dedication of the school staff to their mission.

Not all IEP conferences will be as diverse as those described above. When the child's only problem is in the area of speech or language, the IEP meetings may include only the parent, teacher and SLP or only the parent and SLP. Some SLPs use the telephone to conduct IEP meetings and mail the documents to the parents for signatures. Regardless of the forum employed, SLPs must keep several important points in mind. They must communicate respect to the parents, caregivers, and other professionals — respect for them as people and respect for their opinions. SLPs must listen and question, not just inform and instruct. Finally, as experts in the area of communication, SLPs must use meaningful language and terminology and not attempt to impress their colleagues or parents with their professional jargon.

Summary

In this chapter, the issues of IEP development, content, and conferences were addressed. With regard to content, the EHA/IDEA is quite specific. It is necessary to describe present levels of functioning, project goals, and objectives; identify the most appropriate service delivery option; identify transitional services, if necessary; project a time frame for these services; and determine what methods will be used to measure progress. The law also specifies that the IEP be developed in a meeting called for that purpose. The fact that all professionals providing services to the child are included in the meetings is not novel; that parents are invited, is.

Attention has been given to the extent to which parents actually participate in the IEP process. Because it appears that parental input is minimal, professionals are studying ways to make their participation more meaningful. Professionals, including the SLP, should strive to conduct IEP conferences in an informal, nonthreatening manner; they should engage in active listening and employ language that is meaningful to lay participants.

IEP conferences, themselves, may be very educational. Although highlights from four such meetings were presented, not included was an instance when an irate parent threatened bodily harm to the school psychologist, or a situation when a parent pulled, not a rabbit, but a puppy out of a bag. The puppy's role in the meeting was not clear; maybe he was there to prove that happiness is. . . .

Endnotes

1. M. C. Reynolds, "Staying out of Jail," *Teaching Exceptional Children* 10(1978): pp. 60–62.
2. Individuals with Disabilities Education Act (amended). *Education for the Handicapped Law Report* (Horsham, PA: LRP Publications, 1990).
3. J. A. Shrybman, *Due Process in Special Education* (Rockville, MD: Aspen Systems Corporation, 1982).

4. *The Illinois Primer on Individualized Education Programs,* State Board of Education (1979).

5. *Program Guidelines for Language, Speech, and Hearing Specialists Providing Designated Instruction and Services,* California State Department of Education (1989).

6. "Individualized Education Programs," *NICHCY: National Information Center for Children and Youth with Handicaps,* reprint (2/90).

7. *A Parents' Guide: The Educational Rights of Handicapped Children,* Illinois State Board of Education (1987).

8. *Summary of Research Findings on Individualized Education Programs,* National Association of State Directors of Special Education (undated).

9. K. K. Turnbull and D. L. Hughes, "A Pragmatic Analysis of Speech and Language IEP Conferences," *Language, Speech, and Hearing Services in Schools* 18(1987): pp. 275–286.

10. R. L. Simpson, *Conferencing Parents of Exceptional Children* (Rockville, MD: Aspen Systems Corporation, 1982).

6

The School SLP's Competencies and Roles

Introduction

It is now the rule rather than the exception that school clinicians take pride in their work, use highly efficient methods of organization and management of their programs, and possess clinical skills at least equal to those of their colleagues in other employment environments (1).

Throughout the years, the attributes and responsibilities of competent public school SLPs have received consideration from a number of sources. Black described the "speech therapist's" responsibilities in terms of direct services; professional relationships with administrators, classroom teachers, guidance personnel, and colleagues; and involvement with parents (2). The "speech clinician's" roles as professional person, educational team member, consultant, counselor, and researcher have also been explored (3). With the advent of state and federal legislation, the responsibilities of the school SLP have expanded; among those responsibilities are the identification and diagnosis of children with communicative disorders. In addition to providing services to those students found to be eligible, the SLP is also responsible for making referrals and counseling with parents, children, and teachers. One state has added another responsibility, that of "coordination of speech and language services with an individual's regular and special education program" (4). In this way, the SLP's role as an active member of the educational team has been recognized.

With such diversity of responsibilities, it may be difficult for one individual to function effectively while carrying out each of these roles. Many years ago, Powers presented a method for evaluating the competencies of the public school "speech therapist" (5). The efficiency of the professional in the areas described in the following outline was to be rated as excellent, satisfactory, or un-satisfactory:

- Program organization, including case finding, case selection, scheduling, and maintenance of records
- Evaluative procedures, including knowledge of appropriate tools and of their diagnostic reliability
- Direct intervention, including skills in managing students, planning and executing therapy, and evaluating therapy results
- Relationships with colleagues within the school system, including building principals, classroom teachers, administrators, and other school personnel; and with parents and other professional persons and groups within the community
- Personal characteristics, including appearance, communicative ability, personality, intellectual functioning, and cultural attainment
- Professional ethics and attitudes, including attitudes toward clients, their families, and colleagues, and dedication to the profession

According to Powers, the effective SLP rates high in all these areas, and utilization of this outline by SLPs, their supervisors, and school administrators should assist in assessing efficiency in specific roles.

North Carolina provides performance expectations that might be employed in evaluating "speech-language specialists" (6). The guidelines list the responsibilities of the SLP ("Conducts speech language and hearing screening"), as well as "sample evidence" that the SLP is, indeed, carrying out this responsibility efficiently ("uses appropriate screening instruments") (6). The major areas assessed are student identification, including identification, evaluation, and referral; service planning, including IEP development and cooperative planning; service delivery; program management, including timely reporting, supervision of interns and paraprofessionals, and efficient use of resources; liaison, which is concerned with consultation, interpersonal relations, and coordination of services; and, professional growth and ethics. The latter criterion specifies that the individual adhere to ethical standards, engage in continuing education, cooperate with other members of the educational team, and comply with regulations and laws. A performance appraisal rating scale is also provided by North Carolina. SLPs are judged as performing in a superior fashion, exceeding expectations, performing satisfactorily, needing improvement, or performing in an unsatisfactory manner.

Thus, it can be seen that the SLP is not only doing more things in more places but is also being appraised more carefully in the pursuit of these expanded responsibilities. Have this diversity and scrutiny in the pursuit of the schools SLP's duties improved their status in the profession? This topic is considered next.

The School SLP's Status and Roles

SLPs have frequently reported that their education and experience are inappropriate and inadequate for entry into the school setting. The effective SLP must be knowledgeable in program management, as well as informed about appropriate intervention strategies for individuals from birth to 21 years of age presenting a variety of communicative disorders. The school SLP is expected to consult, intervene, refer, confer, and work with a variety of team members. Frequently these expectations are to be met in the face of inadequate materials, limited financial support, and little experience. By contrast, students in training are accustomed to working with individual clients, under fairly ideal conditions, with appropriate materials and equipment. Further, although college courses in education are required by many states for certification, few graduates report that these courses prepared them for the realities of the school settings. Therefore, the SLP entering the school may feel inadequately prepared and inappropriately educated. And once they are employed in that setting, they ce additional problems.

One such dilemma concerns the status school SLPs have enjoyed (or not enjoyed) in the profession (7). In the past, professionals in the schools tended to believe that neither their professional colleagues nor university training programs had respect for them. This latter view was reinforced by the statement of an individual from a training program who said, "I question that they [public school SLPs] are engaged in a clinical practice oriented to an individual and his unique disability. Those I have known are not suited by training, education, or inclination to be that kind of a clinician" (7). Statements such as this certainly gave the school SLP cause to be defensive and were professionally unethical.

Although Van Hattum discussed roles already described by others, he did address an issue that still confronts the profession today. Has the school-based SLP been one rung down on the professional ladder from those working in hospitals, community centers, or university clinics? In order to determine how school SLPs would answer that and other questions, Weaver conducted a survey of 318 professionals employed in the schools (8). A total of 192 responses to the mailed questionnaire were returned. The respondents' mean age was 34 years, and their years of school experience ranged from one to forty-one years, with the mean a little over eight years. Only 14 percent of the respondents were male.

One of the tasks requested in the questionnaire was a ranking of the following professionals in order of importance: classroom teacher, public school SLP, special education teacher, SLP employed in a setting other than the schools, and college instructor. Of the respondents, 89 percent completed the ranking and rated the classroom teacher well ahead of the other professionals. The school SLP was ranked second, followed by college instructor, SLP working outside the schools, and special education teacher. If these results may be generalized, it would appear that public school SLPs did not regard themselves as second-class citizens when compared with colleagues engaged in other settings.

The respondents were also asked to assign a level of importance to the work of the school SLP. Of the respondents, 41 percent considered that work to be of "highest importance," and 52 percent assigned a ranking of "significant importance." Only 1.5 percent considered intervention in the school setting to be of "average importance," and less than 1 percent assigned a ranking of "less than average importance" or "not very important."

When asked whether public school therapy was of primary or secondary importance, 76 percent chose "primary," 18 percent selected "secondary," and 6 percent did not respond. Additionally, 93 percent answered that they would choose public school work if they had to do it over again, 5 percent stated that they would not, and 2 percent were uncertain.

Weaver also sought to determine if school SLPs felt that national, state, and local professional organizations were representing them well. Of the respondents with master's degrees, only 38 percent felt that ASHA represented their needs; 28 percent of the bachelor's level respondents agreed. The remainder of the respondents felt that they were not well represented. With regard to the representation of interests, 23 percent felt that ASHA was the organization that best represented public school SLPs, whereas 44 percent indicated that their particular state organizations were more effective. The remaining respondents either chose not to respond or identified other organizations.

The results of Weaver's investigation suggest that public school SLPs have a positive image of themselves and a good attitude toward their positions in the schools. This seems to contradict Van Hattum's belief that public school persons regard themselves as second-class professionals. The respondents were less positive when questioned about the effectiveness of the national organization (ASHA) in representing them and their interests.

In recognition of the needs of public school SLPs, ASHA created the position of Associate Secretary for School-Clinic Affairs in 1969 (9). A mailing list of 12,500 SLPs who worked in the schools or had an interest in school programs was developed. In addition, in April 1970, the first edition of *Speech and Hearing Services in Schools* (later, *Language, Speech and Hearing Services in Schools*) was distributed to all persons on the mailing list. This journal has been instrumental in helping school SLPs maintain professional currency and in keeping them informed about pertinent developments specifically related to the public school setting. The journal's establishment was a positive acknowledgement by ASHA of the unique needs of public school SLPs.

Bown, when considering the expanding responsibilities of the SLP, questioned whether ASHA should be involved in defining the role that the professional should play or whether this task could be carried out more effectively by the school SLPs themselves or their administrators or superiors (10). Although no conclusions were drawn, the author did reflect on the new roles that SLPs might play. One such role would be as a resource teacher based in a single building. As another possibility, school SLPs might begin to concentrate their efforts on children with complex communicative disorders, while paraprofessionals worked with children with mild articulatory defects. Increased attention to the total needs of language-disordered children was also predicted by Bown. Finally, the school SLP must recognize the need to function cooperatively with other professionals and to define his or her role as a team member.

Van Hattum, after alluding to his previous article regarding the "defensive" SLP in the schools, discussed progress that had been made and projected role modifications for the future. Acknowledging the establishment of the Associate Secretary for School Affairs by ASHA and the publication of *Language, Speech and Hearing Services in Schools,* Van Hattum also noted that school SLPs had higher regard for themselves than previously. In order that this progress be maintained and additional strides made, Van Hattum suggested that school SLPs might need to adjust their professional roles.

Greater efficiency in service delivery might result from the utilization of altered delivery systems. Both communication aides and tape-recorded articulation programs could reduce the number of children being serviced directly by the SLP, allowing that professional to provide more intensive therapy to students with complicated communicative disorders. Van Hattum also discussed increased participation in service delivery to children who have linguistic disorders and learning disabilities and who are mentally retarded. The author emphasizes that the SLP's responsibility to the retarded child is the same as it is to the student with normal intelligence and may be consultative or direct. In addition, the area of prevention is one to be entered more vigorously. Early childhood screenings and intervention, when necessary, may prevent the development of handicapping conditions. Finally, Van Hattum suggested that school SLPs might want to reexamine their lack of training in the teaching of reading and writing. By acquiring such skills, SLPs might incorporate these areas into their therapy, thus increasing their potential value to the total educational program.

In the past, some have referred to a participant–separatist dichotomy in school SLPs. Participants are active in the child's total educational experience; separatists, on the other hand, exclude themselves from activities not directly related to speech-language intervention. Van Hattum suggested that the separatist position was inconsistent with appropriate therapeutic management in the school setting. The future, he said, may depend on a reevaluation of the role played by the school SLP. Professionals in the schools must be prepared to modify their delivery systems and to expand into the area of the total communicative and education processes.

Falck emphasized the importance of the SLP's role in integrating speech and language services into the educational program and in consulting with parents and teachers. Calling attention to the participant role, Falck discussed ways in which the SLP can work with teachers and parents to meet the needs of communicatively disordered children. The SLP's expertise in facilitating interaction in IEP meetings and teacher and parent conferences was also stressed.

An opportunity for involvement of the SLP with nonhandicapped children was discussed by Dublinske (12). Pursuant to PL 95-156, the Education Amendments of 1978, SLPs may participate in basic skill improvement programming for students whose oral communicative skills are not impaired but could be improved. Such involvement will permit increased interaction of the SLP with teachers, greater input into the curriculum, and expansion of career possibilities.

Has the passage of time improved the status of school SLPs and have the prophecies of Van Hattum and the others become a reality? The answer to both questions appears to be yes. In 1986 and again in 1989, *Asha* volumes highlighted public school SLPs and their activities. More than 40 percent of ASHA's members were reported to be school SLPs, and one article described this group as a "devoted corps . . . whose energy, enthusiasm, and creativity have resulted in innovative, high quality speech-language-hearing programs in public schools across the country" (13). Described were unique school programs for children who stutter, who are hearing impaired, who reside in rural settings, or who present phonological disorders, as well as for those who are preschoolers or adolescents. Certainly both a positive status and a broadening of the SLPs responsibilities were reflected in this article, aptly titled "A Class Act" (13).

The January 1989 issue of *Asha* focused on services in the schools with the hope of addressing "issues that are common to at least a large portion of the approximately 45% of our members who work in school settings" (14). Included were descriptions of an interdiscplinary program for infants and toddlers in Maryland (15), a bilingual program for Connecticut children (16), and a collaborative program in Ohio (17). Dubinske also speaks to the role of the professional in the regular education initiative (18). The January issue also contained a guest editorial, "Working in the Public Schools and Loving It" (19). In it, Kohler discusses her attitudes toward the profession and the peaks and valleys of her career in the schools. After realizing eight years ago that the fulfillment that she had once obtained from the profession was no longer there, Kohler rededicated herself. She took additional coursework, became more active in ASHA, initiated some research projects, and experimented with creative service delivery models. As Kohler noted, an individual SLP cannot change "poor opinions about teachers . . . and biases regarding the professionalism of the public school clinician"; however, each one can do something to improve his or her "own corner of the world" (19).

Has the status of school SLPs improved? The evidence suggests that it has. Increasing recognition of the role of the SLP in professional literature, as well as the positive attitudes reflected by these professionals have improved the stature of school SLPs in the profession. As Kohler stated, "I choose to be a school clinician because I like it" (19). And have the roles of the SLP in the schools expanded? That answer, also, is affirmative. SLPs are doing more than assessment and direct intervention; they are counseling, supervising, and collaborating. The SLP as a counselor and supervisor is considered next; collaboration is discussed in Chapter 7.

The SLP as a Counselor

Many, if not most, students in training and practicing SLPs may respond with some fear to the prospect of counseling students with communicative disorders or their parents. They may feel unprepared academically and experientially and may protest that they are SLPs, not counselors. However, is it possible to separate the two activities? Both involve interaction and communication; both involve a reasonably sound person (the SLP) and one who is seeking assistance; both involve a speaker (the client) and a listener; and both involve a holistic approach. It would appear that it would be more difficult to exclude counseling from speech-language intervention than to include it as a sometimes necessary component. Since counseling will be one of the many functions an SLP is required to fulfill, it is important to be prepared for this role. In the following sections, the qualifications of an effective counselor, approaches to counseling, and physical settings are discussed. Finally, the application of counseling with students and their parents is considered.

Qualifications of the SLP Counselor

In Chapter 1, consideration was given to the personal qualifications of an effective SLP. The following characteristics were cited: modesty, humility, honesty, patience, imagination, creativity, originality, resourcefulness, dependability, responsibility, empathy, and sensitivity. Competent SLPs are also nonjudgmental, open to cultural differences, and active listeners. Very few of these traits do not apply to an effective counselor. However, if one were to select the ones most critical to successful counseling, they would include patience, honesty, empathy, and sensitivity. At the top of the list would be the abilities to be nonjudgmental, to be open to cultural differences, and to listen actively.

Nonjudgmental SLPs possess the ability to view children and parents whose attitudes, philosophies of life, and cultural heritages are quite dissimilar to the professionals without passing judgment on these differences. Consider the child who presents himself in a nonhygenic manner, slouches in his or her desk, and communicates primarily through four-letter words; are SLPs apt to make judgments about the child, his or her parents, and his or her environment? Should they? An effective SLP may make some assumptions about the child and his or her background but not commit the child to some stereotypic category. This is being nonjudgmental.

Sue addresses the need for counselors to be aware of cultural differences and responsive to these differences (20). He classified the differences in three categories: variables in language; variations in such class-bound values as structure and adherence to schedules; and cultural values, including expressiveness and openness, as well as distinctions between physical and mental health. For example, Asian Americans may present a bilingual language background (language) and an action orientation with immediate goals requiring a concrete approach (class). By virtue of their cultural heritage, they may be very private and define physical and mental health quite differently. The naive SLP could misinterpret the behavior of an Asian American student quite easily were he or she not aware of these potential differences.

It is equally important for the SLP to be aware of variations in nonverbal communication. Many cultures dictate less personal space between speakers than that with which Anglos are comfortable. Eye contact variations also occur and must be understood. Even differences in conversational conventions, including the meaning of silence, occur. The SLP who is effective in counseling culturally different students will be knowledgeable about these differences and open to them.

Finally, the competent SLP and effective counselor must be an active listener. Wolvin and Coakley identified five types of listening, including discriminative, comprehensive, critical, appreciative, and therapeutic (21); although the SLP engages in all these listening activities in the execution of his or her professional duties, it is therapeutic listening that is of concern here. The purpose of therapeutic listening is "to provide a troubled sender with the opportunity to talk through a problem" (21). Five specific skills are required in therapeutic listening; these include "focusing attention, demonstrating attending behaviors, developing a supportive communication climate, listening with empathy, and responding appropriately" (21). In addition, "the listener must posses the willingness to listen, the capacity to care, and the desire to understand" (21). These are traits that should characterize the competent SLP, as well as the effective therapeutic listener. Therefore, is not the SLP qualified to serve as a counselor? According to Clark, "It is quite appropriate for . . . speech-language pathologists to extend their professional responsibilities to encompass the emotional/support needs of their clients. This counseling is precisely within their domain" (22).

Counseling Approaches

SLPs should be aware of the general theories behind three counseling approaches; these approaches are considered appropriate when working with functional clients who may be experiencing occasional problems or who may require support. (Students who are thought to be dysfunctional should be referred to mental health experts for assessment and intervention.) Included in the three well-patient theories are the behavioral, rational-emotive, and client-centered approaches.

SLPs who have used behavior modification are cognizant of Skinner's behavioral model. He "contends that human behavior is shaped by the environment that 'operates' on it; that is, if a particular behavior is rewarded—reinforced—by the environment, then that particular behavior will be reinforced" (23). Such conditioning has been found to be very useful in speech-language intervention programs. When used as a counseling technique,

"Behavioral counseling is a directive approach, with the client working in concert with the counselor to achieve environmental conditions that may help produce positive behavioral change" (22).

The rational-emotive theory is also directive and assumes that irrational views or perceptions lead to emotional distress. If, for example, an individual who is using slow speech to control stuttering believes that this technique may cause discomfort in his or her listener, the individual may abandon this strategy. "The goal of rational-emotive counseling is not to change clients' beliefs for them, but to teach clients the skills needed to identify and modify their own self-defeating thoughts or beliefs" (22). With regard to the example given previously, the goal would be to help the individual who used slow speech to recognize that it was absurd to believe that it was offensive. Then, the person would be able to adapt more positive beliefs.

Rogers is the central person behind the next theory, client-centered counseling. The basic tenet involved in this strategy is that the client has the capacity to recognize his or her own problems and to work to resolve them. It is a nondirective approach, which may be less time effective than a more direct technique; however, cilent-centered counseling may be the most appropriate for the SLP.

Rollin suggests that these three theories of counseling may share more similarities than differences and that SLPs may be eclectic in their approach (24). In so doing, the SLP must be aware of the various theories and techniques and select those that would be most applicable to a given client. According to Rollin, "Counseling is too complex a process to be conducted in a hodgepodge fashion or to be treated unidimensionally from one rigid viewpoint" (24).

Physical Settings for Counseling

In the first edition of this book, considerable attention was given to the physical environment of the SLP. Described were the ideal conditions in terms of room size, decoration, and furniture, as well as the real-world conditions. The former included rooms containing 150–250 square feet, with natural and artificial lighting and with an adjacent office (25). Minimally, the room should be acoustically treated; drapes and carpeting were considered ideal. With regard to furniture, an office desk, at least two adult chairs, an adjustable table, a variety of children's chairs, and an equipment stand were recommended. Storage facilities included a locked file, locked storage space, and a book case. In addition, the ideal speech room should be private, quiet, and accessible. Unfortunately, this ideal situation was not achieved in many instances.

When the author was a public school SLP, her assigned speech rooms were clearly inadequate. In one building, the speech room was located adjacent to the patrol boy's equipment storage area. In fact, access to the room was through this storage area. The 8-by-10-foot room contained an adult-size table, four large chairs, and one movable locked storage unit. A reversible blackboard-mirror unit was also provided. One light located on a high ceiling provided inadequate lighting, but this was compensated for (on sunny days) by natural light coming through a single window. The room was relatively quiet since it was located on the second floor of the building and well removed from the noisy primary classrooms. This serene environment was disrupted at the beginning of the school day and at lunch time, however, when the patrol boys collected their equipment.

In another school, the physical facilities were new and cheerful. Located in a recently constructed building, the speech room was well lighted and well ventilated. Two large mounted blackboards, along with a small table and chairs, an office desk and chair, the usual movable storage unit, and reversible blackboard-mirror were provided. Unfortunately, the speech room also served as the health and teacher preparation room. A duplicating machine, sink, and first-aid cabinet were also in the speech room, and teachers sometimes disrupted therapy by duplicating materials during sessions. Injured students also appeared frequently to have their wounds bandaged, their temperatures taken, and their major and minor illnesses diagnosed. Since the school nurse was not in the building daily, the author foolishly attended to some of the less serious physical problems at the expense of therapy time (and also at the risk of a malpractice suit).

In the other three schools serviced by the author over a five-year period, the situations were not appreciably better. One room doubled as the art supply room; needless to say, this was a helpful source of tagboard, colored paper, and other therapy-related materials. (All acquisitions, of course, were made with the knowledge of the building principal!) Another room was rather large and, when properly decorated, it evolved into a rather comfortable facility. Unfortunately, it was too large, too attractive, and too comfortable; thus it was quickly transformed into a resource area for the entire school. The fifth speech room was also large; it accommodated two office desks and chairs, a children's table and chairs, the movable storage unit, and the reversible blackboard-mirror quite nicely. Two mounted blackboards and a bulletin board covered three walls, and windows occupied the other wall. Although the artificial illumination was inadequate, natural lighting compensated to a great extent. The major problem here was the room's location within the building. This school, which accommodated approximately 1,000 students, had three distinctive sections. The speech room was located in the oldest section of the building, on an upward extension of the second floor. An addition connected the original building to the most recently constructed primary wing. The reader will understand why so many young children arrived late for therapy or missed sessions altogether as a result of "losing their way."

The author has also supervised students working under certified school SLPs in teachers' rooms, furnace rooms, and "coat closets." Speech rooms were also located adjacent to lavatories, music rooms, and gymnasiums. Flushing toilets, off-key musicians, and yelling athletes do not provide suitable acoustic environments for perfecting articulatory, linguistic, fluency, or vocal skills. The overwhelming majority of speech rooms had architectural barriers that would preclude the servicing of nonambulatory children. In fact, at least one room was so small that the student clinician could not be supervised unless the supervisor sat outside in the hall. Recently, an experienced school SLP confided to the author that her current speech room has only a table and chairs and that she keeps her session plans and IEPs in a cardboard box!

The fact that SLPs are moving out of the speech room and into the classroom to deliver services may make the sometimes dismal condition of the former less critical. However, the fact remains that counseling most often takes place in the speech room or SLP's office; thus, it is important that this setting be appropriate.

In general, the physical setting should be comfortable and private. Comfort is attained by providing suitable chairs (for a variety of child sizes), attractive decorations, and appropriate lighting. Overhead lighting is not conducive to comfort; rather, natural lighting or lamps should be used. Although some suggest that an illusion of privacy must be provided, it is undoubtedly preferable to provide actual privacy. A small room with the door closed is ideal. Auditory and visual distractions should be minimal. If a telephone is present in the room and it is possible to reroute calls, that should be done. A box of tissues should be displayed in a prominent place in the event that they are needed. Barriers, such as desks, should not separate the SLP/counselor from the client although the directive counselor may wish to retain such a barrier.

It is probable that many SLPs will not be able to provide counseling in a physical setting meeting all these criteria, but it is important to create an inviting, warm, and private atmosphere. Just as a perfectly designed and well-equipped speech room does not guarantee excellent intervention, an appropriate setting does not assure competent counseling. Nevertheless, the SLP should strive to make the speech room as conducive to both endeavors as possible.

Counseling with Children

In the past, much of the literature on counseling with communicatively disordered individuals has dealt with older children presenting fluency, vocal, hearing, and linguistic problems. Rollin, for example, considers these populations, plus those with congenital disorders (24). Is it not possible for children with articulatory deviations to have concomitant emotional needs? Experience suggests that it is not uncommon. Nevertheless, this discussion is limited to two groups of communicatively disordered students who may be in need of the most support: those who stutter and those who are hearing impaired.

Travis offered one of the most graphic and vivid expositions of the emotional problems experienced by some persons who stutter (26). In his discussion of the unspeakable feelings of these people, he presented transcriptions of audiotapes made by several individuals who stuttered. Anger, hostility, repression, and antisocial feelings are revealed in the utterances. Not all individuals who stutter present such blatant distress as those quoted by Travis; however, the SLP must be prepared to provide counseling to children and adolescents who stutter and who require counseling support.

One such client encountered by this author was a 14-year-old male named Timmy. Timmy's twin brother was a good student, a good athlete, and was well liked by teachers and peers alike. Timmy was a year behind his classmates academically, was slightly built, and had few friends; teachers were not at all fond of him. Timmy stuttered severely; his stuttering pattern was characterized by all types of dysfluencies, including repetitions, blocks, and prolongations, and he presented obvious struggle behaviors. His stuttering was at its worst in the classroom except when he was engaged in abusive language of the four-letter variety; he was fluent while swearing.

Timmy was seen on an individual basis and, after only a few sessions, became secure enough to verbalize his resentments. He resented his successful brother, he resented the teachers, and he resented the father that he did not see; most of all, he resented the fact that he stuttered. The counseling strategy employed with Timmy was exclusively active, nonjudgmental listening. Traditional symptomatic intervention was successful in the speech room, but carryover was nonexistent. Although it could have been predicted that Timmy would experience more fluency with younger children, it was quite by accident that such a situation arose. During a session turnover (Timmy was preparing to return to the classroom, and three first graders were arriving for their session), the author was called out of the room. Timmy was left in charge. When the emergency was over and the author returned to the speech room, she observed three little ones responding attentively to a totally fluent peer clinician. Timmy was quite proud of himself, and since his teacher was content to have him out of the classroom, he continued to serve as a peer paraprofessional for short periods each day.

This story has a poor beginning, a happy middle, and an uncertain ending. Timmy moved on to junior high school, and the author left the area the following year. Although it would be nice to believe that Timmy's release of negative feelings combined with his positive experiences as a therapy assistant were sufficient to compensate for thirteen years of failure, this is doubtful. However, if Timmy had received counseling earlier, the prognosis might have been better.

The central counseling strategy employed with Timmy was active, nonjudgmental listening. Although an attempt was made to include Timmy's mother in the process, she, herself, presented a plethora of pathologies that extended beyond the author's expertise. A veiled referral to a mental health agency received no follow-through. Rollin suggests that in some cases a family systems approach in counseling is appropriate (24). This approach is appropriate when there is evidence of a dysfunctional family or of excessive parental pressure. The child should be no more than moderately involved with regard to secondary characteristics. Finally, the family should express a desire to participate in the process, and no evidence of a psychopathology in either the child or other family members should exist. Because of the severity of Timmy's stuttering and his mother's poor mental health, the family systems approach would have been inappropriate.

Rollin also proposes the utilization of client-centered techniques. When a secure and trusting relationship has been established between the child and the SLP, the former will be able to verbalize his or her feelings about the stuttering and "the shame, guilt, anxiety, preoccupation, and low self-esteem associated with the stuttering behavior can be resolved" (24). Parent counseling may also be employed. Although this strategy is considered at some length later in the chapter, it is important to emphasize its utilization with parents of children who stutter. First of all, parents need information about the disorder; perhaps no other communicative problem has more myths and misinformation related to it. They also need to know how to deal with their child at home; this, too, is in the realm of informational counseling. Of equal importance in parental counseling is information seeking. The SLP must seek specific information, as well as provide open-ended opportunities for the parents to express their concerns. Finally, the SLP must be prepared to provide support for the parents, recognizing that many will harbor feelings of guilt, impatience, resentment, and grief that must be resolved.

Parent counseling is also significant in dealing with children who are hearing impaired. According to Matkin, "The belief that successful habilitation of young hearing-impaired children requires the support and involvement of their parents is widely accepted" (27). Parents, as well as the audiologist (and by extension, the SLP) must work to help the child become as independent as possible. Before that independence is reached, however, parents must accept the fact that the child is hearing impaired. Some parents are relieved at first because their greater concern was that the child was mentally retarded. After this may come the grieving process; the SLP must be very supportive during this period. Finally, if the child is fitted with aids, the first visible sign of his or her disability becomes apparent to others. Both parents and the child must be assisted through this sometimes trying process as well.

Matkin suggests that six premises may serve as the basis of an appropriate management program for parents. First, parents should understand and practice good parenting skills; to acquire this information, it may be necessary for parents to enroll in parenting classes. Next, three kinds of assistance should be made available to parents, including education, guidance, and counseling. Premise three involves the continuous support of the family; according to Matkin, the literature indicates that most support programs are discontinued after the preschool years. Because of fiscal and time constraints, the SLP must be creative in using a variety of educational materials and resources; group meetings may be effective. The final two premises deal with the family constitution and variations in family systems; it must be recognized that all families do not fit into the traditional mold, nor do all families share common cultural and socioeconomic characteristics. These variations should be accepted and taken into consideration when planning for intervention.

Although Matkin's remarks were direted toward audiologists, the fact remains that SLPs share in the management of hearing-impaired students and may have more opportunities for intervention than their colleagues. Nevertheless, both groups of professionals must be cognizant of the needs of parents, as well as the needs of their hearing-impaired children.

Adolescence is a difficult period for most individuals; for the hearing-impaired youth, it poses even more problems. Atkins considered the impact of adolescence on the self-esteem of hearing-impaired teenagers (28). Like Matkin, she stresses the importance of a supportive family in the development of a confident hearing-impaired child. However, when the child approaches adolescence, much of the support and need for acceptance comes from peers, and these peers will have normal hearing. Even though hearing-impaired youth may want to connect with their peers, the fact remains that they are different at a time when it is important to be the same. Atkins reported on the success of a "rap" group of hearing-impaired youths conducted by an audiologist; this time for sharing served an important purpose for these adolescents. "Although their lives were full, their unique circumstances prohibited a shared perspective in the mainstream group; it made them feel lacking in some way" (28). As it did with parents of hearing-impaired children, the group counseling experience served a valuable purpose.

Deaf children face even greater challenges in terms of adjustment. Vernon and Andrews discussed parent counseling, as well as the deaf person's ability to benefit from counseling and psychotherapy (29). They acknowledged the need for strong support for parents at the time of the child's diagnosis and stressed that parents must be made aware of resource agencies and services. The counseling made available to parents "should be patterned, in general, after other self-help groups, but with professional direction" (29). With regard to psychotherapy, the authors discussed the problems encountered by deaf persons who use manual communication. "Helpful" therapy, they state, can be done by "a professional who is basically competent in using signs" (29). An interpreter could also be used as a last resort. Although the authors did not include SLPs in the following statement (nor did they allude to the profession as a part of service delivery), the implications are quite interesting. They said that "Ironically, hearing psychologists, psychiatrists, and social workers often have reacted to the sign language issue counterphobically" (29). In other words, they have "blamed" the deaf persons rather than acknowledging that they (the professionals) lack the necessary skills to communicate. They concluded that deaf individuals will never obtain appropriate counseling until "deaf therapists whose native language is ASL [American Sign Language] are trained and hearing professionals master ASL" (29).

Although parent counseling and direct counseling with the child are advocated, another important strategy with the student who stutters, is hearing impaired, or presents any other type of communicative disorder is play therapy. Rollin reviewed Axline's principles of play therapy (24). In addition to establishing rapport with the child in an atmosphere of acceptance and permissiveness, the SLP must remain alert to feelings expressed by the child. The child is permitted to direct the activities without interference from the SLP. Inherent in the play therapy process is the belief that the child will in time be able to solve his or her own problems. The only limitations within the sessions are those "that are necessary to anchor the therapy to the world of reality and to make the child aware of his responsibility in the relationship" (24).

There is little doubt that play therapy can provide an outlet for the child, as well as insights for the SLP. However, one must exercise restraint in making interpretations from what is observed. The author once watched as a child removed pliable dolls representing family members from a styrofoam container and then proceeded to "mow them down" systematically with a toy truck. After each doll's untimely demise, the child replaced it in its place in the styrofoam coffin. Did these actions reflect the child's hidden aggression toward his family? Perhaps so. However, it is quite conceivable that it was nothing more than a fun thing to do. Before coming to conclusions, additional observations and a second opinion should be sought.

On the other hand, one must not automatically disbelieve students' stories even when they seem outrageous. A colleague related an incident in which a preadolescent boy attending a private school for severely behaviorally disordered and emotionally disturbed youth shared some bizarre experiences during his language therapy sessions. The student's records indicated a rather chaotic home environment, which included a family history of mental illness and domestic violence. The SLP grew increasingly concerned when, for several sessions in succession, the student related fanciful, yet detailed accounts of his after-school activities; these included being in a kangaroo's pouch, playing with baby bears, and generally taking the role of Dr. Dolittle with a variety of exotic animals. Receiving a clear message that this "delusional" student might require additional professional services, the proper referrals were made. One school counselor/therapist, one social worker, and several meetings later, the "fantasies" were proved to be a reality. The young man did indeed spend much of his after-school time with a neighbor and his exotic animal collections. Hence, this word of caution with regard to interpretation of behaviors or stories is appropriate.

Throughout this discussion, it has become apparent that counseling with communicatively disordered students may take many forms. Children and adolescents may respond to direct counseling, as well as group sessions. Play therapy may also be effective with young students. In many cases, parent counseling should be included in the intervention process; that topic is considered next.

Parent Counseling

SLPs and parents have opportunities to interact in ways that are potentially beneficial to the child. Initially, the SLP may interview the parent. Additional opportunities for interaction occur during the IEP meeting and in conferences designed to obtain information from the parents or to suggest methods of managing the child at home. In most instances, the conferences take place in the school building although some SLPs prefer to visit parents at home. Group meetings may supplement individual conferences. After a general discussion of the problems of counseling parents of handicapped children, this section gives specific consideration to the counseling of parents of communicatively disordered students.

Counseling Parents of Exceptional Children

Stewart suggests that counseling parents of an exceptional child involves a helping relationship between those parents and a knowledgeable professional (30). This relationship should allow the professional to understand the parents' feelings, concerns, and problems. Further, "It is a learning process focusing upon the stimulation and encouragement of personal growth by which parents are assisted in acquiring, developing, and utilizing the skills and attitudes necessary for a satisfactory resolution to their problem or concern" (30). Finally, the counseling process should allow the parents to function fully as individuals, to be assets to their child, and to create a well-adjusted family unit. This appears to be a reasonable description of what counseling parents of exceptional children should be, and it is accepted as a working definition for this discussion.

Successful "helping" individuals appear to have certain attitudes and characteristics. According to Stewart, the counselor must be interested in people and must accept them as worthy persons. Empathy is an important quality. "As one counsels with parents, we must have (or develop) an ability to, so far as humanly possible, understand their meanings and feelings" (30). The counselor must possess sufficient security to be genuine and honest in the helping relationship and must be an attentive listener. Above all, counselors must be professional and ethical in their behavior. Not only must professionals handle confidential information discreetly, they must also recognize their limitations in the counseling role. Although these attitudes and characteristics are specified as necessary qualities for a counselor, they are also attributes of an effective SLP.

The counseling process, itself, involves several phases. Stewart suggests that although the steps may fuse, six phases may be identified. The initial interview, or Phase 1, affords the counselor and counselee the first opportunity to relate to each other. During this interview, the problem may be stated and explored and plans can be made for the future. Next, in Phase 2, the nature of the counseling process is defined. In Phase 3, the counselor seeks to understand the client's needs and to express this understanding to the client. Solutions to the problem are explored in Phase 4, and a plan of action is devised in Phase 5. Finally, the sessions are terminated by mutual agreement. Stewart indicates that not all counseling relationships will follow this sequence or include all steps but that it does represent the problem-solving process.

As noted earlier, several techniques are employed by trained counselors in conducting sessions. Traditionally, these have included the directive, nondirective, and eclectic approaches. Using the directive approach, the counselor is an active participant in guiding the counselee. It is assumed that the counselor, by virtue of his or her training and experience, is qualified to advise the client, whose background in certain areas may be deficient. The parents of a handicapped child, for example, may not understand the problems presented by that child as well as the professional. Therefore, a directive approach is employed by the counselor to obtain information and provide advice for child management.

There are those who feel that the directive technique places undue emphasis on the counselor's role in problem solving. In fact, it is sometimes referred to as the counselor-centered approach. Further, directive counseling may encourage the client to become dependent on the counselor. In using this counseling strategy, one should exercise care in giving personal advice to the client. According to Stewart, "A rule of thumb that can be followed is not to give advice unless it is in the form of tentative suggestions based upon solid expertise or in the form of possible alternatives that have been successfully tried out by other parents of exceptional children" (30).

Although the nondirective or client-centered technique is most efficiently employed by professional counselors, some of these strategies may be utilized in counseling the parents of a handicapped child. Basically, in this approach, the counselor views the client as possessing the ability to solve his or her own problems without the advice of the counselor. The professional's objective is to create a situation in which the client can identify and explore the problem objectively. In addition, the counselor must attempt to see the problem as the client views it and communicate this understanding to him or her. In order to achieve these goals, the counselor must listen attentively and reflect and clarify the client's attitudes and feelings.

As opposed to the directive technique, nondirective counseling tends to discourage client dependency since clients make their own decisions. Unfortunately, the fact that it is time consuming precludes extensive utilization of this strategy in the school setting.

The eclectic approach includes utilization of appropriate techniques from a variety of counseling strategies. The eclectic counselor believes that "a single orientation is limiting and that procedures, techniques, and concepts from many sources should be utilized to best serve the needs of the person seeking help" (30). Although this approach appears to be the most reasonable, there is some question whether a single counselor can become expert in all counseling strategies and capable of applying them effectively.

In summary, the traditional counseling techniques differ in terms of counselor involvement and in terms of the presenting problems to which they may be applied. Directive counseling revolves around the counselor and is appropriately applied in the educational, behavioral management, and vocational areas. In the nondirective approach, the role of the counselor is less prominent, and emphasis is placed on the problem-solving abilities of the client. This technique is employed when the presenting problems are in the personal or social areas. Finally, the eclectic counselor selects strategies from directive, nondirective, and other approaches according to the needs of their clients. According to Stewart, the effective application of the method, rather than the method itself, is the critical factor.

One additional counseling technique is the behavioral or action strategy. This method recognized that observation of behavior is the only certain way to determine whether change has occurred. Behavioral counseling "is a process involving a learning situation in which the counselee learns more appropriate behaviors" (30). Of concern to the counselor are the maladaptive behaviors, the supportive environmental contingencies, and the reinforcing stimuli that might be applied to alter the maladaptive behavior. These factors are explored in three phases. First, the client–counselor relationship is established. During the second phase, the counselor and client determine the approach to be taken and decide which techniques would be effective. In the third and final stage, the action planned in the second is taken and analyzed.

Behavioral counseling, because it has observable and measurable effects, is advantageous to both client and counselor. Conversely, one disadvantage is that the effective utilization of behavioral counseling depends upon the counselor's understanding of behavior theory; according to Stewart, many counselors are not sufficiently conversant with this theory and its application to employ it efficiently.

Stewart has also addressed specific issues related to the counseling process, including group counseling. When properly executed, group counseling allows the members to interact with others who have similar concerns and counseling goals. Counselors function in a group setting in much the same way they function in individual sessions. It is important that they create a situation in which group members feel secure and free to express themselves. Of equal importance is that all participants listen carefully and with understanding. The group might contain five to ten members, because, according to Stewart, it should be small enough to allow for personal interaction and large enough for group interaction. Group counseling with parents of exceptional children can be both efficient and effective when conducted by a properly trained professional.

Stewart also comments on the function of silence and nonverbal communication in the counseling process. Silence is sometimes feared by the inexperienced counselor, who feels that every moment should be filled with oral communication. "The counselor should realize that a great deal of communication takes place without sound and no rule exists that says all silence should be replaced with sound" (30). There are many reasons for silence, and the counselor should analyze and respect silent periods.

Similarly, the counselor should be alert to the nonverbal messages communicated by the counselee. One study involving a two-person conversation, for example, revealed that 65 percent of the social meaning was communicated nonverbally. Counselors should not only learn from the nonverbal communication of the client; they should also be aware of the nonverbal messages they themselves are relaying to the client. Such communications should not contradict the meaning they intend to convey and, in fact, do convey in speech.

Finally, Stewart discusses the referral process. Professionals who counsel parents but who are not trained counselors must not attempt to handle situations beyond their level of competence. "Learning when and how to make referrals and determining what purpose will be served is almost as important as learning to counsel" (30). It is imperative that clients be included in the decision to refer and that they be responsible for making appointments for the new service.

Counseling Parents of Communicatively Disordered Children

SLPs, guided by several members of their profession, have recognized the need to improve their counseling skills. Webster was an early leader in this area (31). In a 1966 article, she discussed counseling with parents of communicatively disordered children and defined the role of the SLP as a counselor (31). Initially, assumptions regarding the parents are made. For example, it is assumed that because of the child's communicative disorder, the parents and their child are not communicating effectively with each other. It is further assumed that this lack of communication interferes with interpersonal relationships and that this, in turn, further complicates communication.

The relationship between the child's problem and the parents' behavior must be explored. Although it cannot be assumed that the parents caused the problem, anxiety on the part of both the child and parents may be evident as they communicate. Guilt is sometimes a factor; parents may wonder if they have contributed to their child's problem. It is with emotions such as these — and frequently with a lack of information about communicative disorders — that parents may enter the counseling situation.

The SLP must realize that the parents are probably dealing with the problem as well as they can under the circumstances. Although SLPs can provide guidelines for managing a child, it is imperative that they not attempt to direct the child-rearing process. That is the parent's responsibility and privilege.

Lastly, it is assumed that the parents have the potential for growth and are motivated by the wish to do what is best for the child; to understand other people, including the child; to learn to communicate with their child on a more positive level; and to find fulfillment for themselves and their child. Concerning the last motivation, Webster emphasizes that parents must have an identity of their own. To deal with them strictly as parents, rather than as worthy human beings, would impede the counseling effort.

Webster cites three ways in which parents can benefit from counseling. First, counseling provides an opportunity for parents to discuss their feelings. Open discussion of fears and other emotions, motivations, and goals is encouraged in the counseling situation, and such discussion should lead to more open communication between parents and their children. Second, the parents are given information regarding their children's communicative disorders. Not only are they provided with facts, the SLP must also assist the parents in applying the information to their unique situations. Third and last, the SLP should afford the parents opportunities to experiment with effective ways of improving communication. Webster cautioned, however, that "the professional person's role is that of introduction and experimentation with tools; he cannot make others accept his ideas" (31). The "tools" Webster alludes to include a number of behavioral prescriptions for parents. For example, (1) the parents should try to understand what the child is feeling and to communicate this understanding to him or her; (2) the parents should learn to accept what the child is feeling even when the child's behavior is inappropriate; (3) the parents should provide opportunities for communication with the child when the latter will have their undivided attention, and these occasions should provide satisfaction and success for the child; and (4) the parents should attempt to communicate with the child at the child's level.

The role and attitudes of the counselor require consideration. According to Webster, the most important attitude is respect for the client. The counselor should also create a situation in which the client feels free to communicate; then the counselor should listen actively. The professional should also assist the parents in clarifying their feelings and ideas. An effective counselor must be knowledgeable about communicative disorders. Information provided to the parents must be accurate and must be presented in a relevant manner. The counselor must also be discreet in answering parents' questions. Some questions require direct answers; others, such as "what should I do if my child's friends tease him about his stuttering?" may often be referred to the parent for consideration and resolution. Patience is another quality of a good counselor. Counselors should realize that any modification of attitude or behavior occurs slowly. Finally, Webster warned that the counselor must keep counseling sessions parent centered rather than problem centered. Positive aspects of daily living should be discussed as well as specific problems. The counselor should "be able to laugh with them [the parents] even as he is able to view their suffering with compassion" (31).

Group counseling, according to Webster, is similar to individual conferences. Both require respect for the clients and open, attentive communication. In a group, however, the counselor must interact with more than one person at a time. An effective counselor will create a situation in which group members are supportive of each other; in effect, each may become a counselor. Group interaction may result in conflict between parents, however, and the counselor must be both alert to this possibility and prepared to resolve it. The effective group setting is one in which parents are permitted to disagree with each other but in which these conflicts do not interfere with the goal of counseling.

Since group interaction is necessary before the parents can learn from each other, the SLP must encourage an atmosphere that permits open discussion. This will not occur if the professional chooses to lecture to the parents or if the SLP is the dominant group member. As questions are asked, some should be answered directly, and others should be opened for group discussion. The counselor should be aware that some members will not participate as readily as others. Their wishes to remain silent should be respected although they may be encouraged to interact with the group. As Webster says, "It may be helpful to the clinician to remember that problem-solving can also begin in silence" (31).

Concluding her article, Webster addressed a question sometimes asked by SLPs: "Can't the speech pathologist or audiologist do damage to parents by attempting to counsel with them?" (31). If counseling is improperly done, the answer to that question is yes. The SLP who is too authoritative, who provides inaccurate information, or who focuses on the child's problem while excluding the parents' feelings may harm the parents. Conversely, the warm, accepting professional who listens and responds to the parents while providing them with sound information will be an effective counselor.

In a follow-up article, Webster elaborated on group counseling with particular regard for group discussion and role playing (32). Discussion constitutes the major portion of the group counseling process. Discussions should take place in a room containing comfortable furniture, arranged to allow all participants to see each other. The parents are encouraged to generate topics for discussion, but the SLP serves as the discussion leader. During the discussions, the parents are helped to recognize the common problems they are experiencing and are encouraged to solve these problems together. At the same time, the SLP is responsible for sharing information about communicative disorders with the less knowledgeable parents. The professional should also explain and demonstrate the tools (enumerated in Webster's earlier article) for improving child–parent communication.

Another technique to be utilized in group meetings with parents is role playing. The goals of role playing are to assist parents in understanding behavior and to permit them to experiment with different approaches to various situations. According to Webster, role playing consists of three phases. During the warm-up period, the SLP helps group members define the situation, assigns roles, and assists the members in creating their roles. In the second phase, the situation is acted out. And in the third phase, group members discuss what has happened.

Although role playing incorporates discussion in its first and third phases, it also requires actual bodily movement. This permits a demonstration of emotional behavior that may then be discussed. Because of this emotional component, role playing must be used cautiously. Further, this procedure lends itself to manipulation of the parents by the SLP, something to be avoided. Webster suggests that SLPs should have participated in role playing previously so that they will have an understanding of the process and of its benefits and dangers. In the professional situation, however, they should direct, not participate in the role-playing experience.

Emerick addressed the issue of the parent interview, concentrating on information exchange rather than the counseling aspect of interaction between SLP and parents (33). According to Emerick, an interview "is a purposeful exchange of meanings between two persons, a directed conversation that proceeds in an orderly fashion to obtain data, to convey certain information and to provide release and support" (33). The two participants in the interview should bring information to the meeting that will assist in understanding and helping the child.

Emerick identified several problems in the interviewing process. One of these difficulties resides in the fears of the SLP. Young professionals sometimes worry that parents will not recognize them as professionals because of their youth. This is usually an unfounded fear. SLPs are also fearful that the parents will become defensive during the interview or ask unanswerable questions. Again, these situations do not occur frequently. When the SLP experiences fear regarding an interview, the interview may be perceived as a threat or challenge; obviously, the latter reaction is preferable.

When the SLP perceives the parents as enemies, additional interviewing difficulties arise. Parents must be recognized as unique human beings rather than obstacles to therapeutic success. As Emerick points out, too often parents are blamed for the SLP's lack of success with a child. "It is very easy to explain away our failures by criticizing the parents of our cases, especially when we sit in the relative safety of the broom closet [therapy room] each week on coordination day" (33). Acceptance of parents as participants in the therapeutic process will alleviate this problem.

Finally, Emerick identified specific factors that interfere with communication during the interview. For example, (1) the parents may not remember critical information about the child, (2) emotional barriers may interfere with open communication, (3) the parents may conceal information, (4) the SLP may deal ineffectively with parents from social classes different from his or her own, (5) language differences may cause a breakdown in communication, (6) the parents may be suspicious of the SLP because he or she is associated with the school, or (7) the purpose of the interview may be unfocused. SLPs should be aware of these potential interferences and avoid them whenever possible.

According to Emerick, there are three objectives of a diagnostic interview. The first is to obtain information. In preparing the parent for this task, the SLP must define his or her role, as well as the role of the parents. The site of the interview is important for setting the tone of the session. It is Emerick's contention that the school setting is preferable to a home visit. Although many SLPs choose to open the interview with an assurance of confidentiality, Emerick suggests that the professional's manner alone should communicate such ethical behavior.

In seeking information, Emerick suggests that an interview guide be followed. Some SLPs utilize a questionnaire format, wherein the professional reads a question and the parent responds verbally. Emerick views such questionnaires as a barrier to effective interviewing or as a crutch for the inexperienced interviewer. The interviewing style (directive, nondirective, and so on) should be appropriate to the nature of the information sought. To obtain factual material, a directive approach may be required, whereas when emotionally charged information is discussed, a nondirective approach may be preferable.

Emerick feels that inexperienced interviewers are likely to make many strategic errors, and he singles out eleven of these as the most glaring. Table 6-1 describes these errors briefly.

The second objective of a diagnostic interview is to provide information

TABLE 6-1 Common Errors in Diagnostic Interviewing

The speech-language pathologist may

- Ask questions that can be answered yes or no
  This type of questioning tends to preclude discussions: an open-ended style is preferable.
- Bias an answer by the phrasing of a question
  The common example of this sort of questioning is the old line, When did you stop beating your wife?
- Talk too much
  Inexperienced interviewers are sometimes threatened by silence. By filling up pauses with conversation, they may miss opportunities to obtain valuable information.
- Dwell on etiology and physical symptoms, failing to respond to the parent's feelings and attitudes
  Some speech-language pathologists are so concerned with the pathology that they tend to ignore the emotional implications of the problem.
- Provide specific information too early in the interview
  Even though a parent may be laboring under a misconception, it is sometimes best to delay correcting such errors.
- Ask questions indirectly
  Sensitive questions should be asked directly. If, for example, the speech-language pathologist must know about the child's relationship with his or her siblings, the question should be phrased that way.
- Respond negatively to the parent's statements
  The interviewer must not impose his or her values on the parent's behavior or attitudes.
- Be incapable of delicately leading the interviewee who has wandered from the topic back to the discussion
  The interviewer should not attempt to do this by seeking new information but rather by returning to the answer the interviewee was giving when he or she began discussing tangential material.
- Accept superficial answers to questions
  There are numerous probes the interviewer can use to get beneath surface responses, and the speech-language pathologist should be familiar with these techniques.
- Attempt to obtain all information in one interview
  In some cases, the interviewee may reveal too much during the initial interview and then feel hostile or embarrassed for having done so.
- Fail to take notes
  A record of the interview is imperative. Note, however, that the intervieee should always be told that note are being taken or that the interview is being tape-recorded. Such record taking rarely interferes with the interview.

Source: Emerick, 1969.

to the parent. As Emerick points out, if professionals do not furnish accurate, nonemotional information regarding the child's communicative disorder, the parents will probably seek answers from persons unqualified to provide such information. Although the language used by the SLP must be nontechnical, it is important not to talk down to the parents. In imparting information to parents, Emerick suggests that the SLP should (1) refrain from lecturing to parents; (2) use appropriate language, and rephrase important points; (3) provide parents with something concrete to do; and (4) be direct, but pleasant, when discussing sensitive information.

The third and final objective of an interview is to provide release and support for the parents. One hopes that opportunities for the parents to ventilate will occur rather naturally throughout the interview. The SLP should empathize with the parents when the latter discuss their feelings and problems. When emotional scenes occur—and they will—the SLP has several options. He or she may leave the room, allowing the parents to regain their composure in privacy, or attempt to change the subject. Both of these approaches, according to Emerick, may be construed as rejection by the interviewee. Perhaps the most humane way to deal with this type of situation is for the SLP to communicate to the parents his or her understanding and acceptance of the parents' feelings. It should be understood that not all parents require an extensive interview. Frequently, information sharing is the sole purpose of the meeting. In other instances, however, parents may need support and opportunities to vent their feelings.

Finally, Emerick suggests ways in which SLPs may improve their interviewing skills. First, the professional or student in training should do research in the area of interviewing and should explore the problems confronting parents of both normal and handicapped children. It is also suggested that role-playing experience in interviewing can be beneficial. Finally, Emerick recommends that the SLP tape-record some actual interviews with parents and analyze these conferences with a supervisor or colleague.

Flynn also discussed interviewing techniques and identified several relevant facets of the interviewing procedures (34). With regard to the interview environment, Flynn notes that in addition to the privacy required for such a meeting, it is important that the area be clutter free. The client will have more confidence in the professional whose office is neat and whose records are carefully filed away. Chairs in the room should be placed at 90-degree angles so that eye contact is possible; this arrangement also allows for looking straight ahead when the client is attempting to think.

At the outset of the interview, Flynn suggested that the identity of the interviewee be verified so as to be certain that the correct person is present. She goes on to say that it is important that the SLP avoid excessive casual conversation. According to Flynn, this might indicate to the counselee that the problem is either too serious or not serious enough to discuss. The time frame for the interview should also be established at the beginning of the session.

In discussing interview behaviors, Flynn comments on the function of silence. Like the other authors cited here, Flynn acknowledges that silence is a useful interviewing technique. She cautions, however, that too much silence may be discomforting to the client and may make the interviewer appear to be a cold person. Finally, Flynn notes the significance of closing the interview with a summary of the session. This allows for the correction of any misconceptions and identification of gaps in information obtained during the interview.

Webster and Cole discussed the SLP's role as a leader of parent discussion groups (35). Essentially the SLP's function in this situation is to promote discussion by encouraging group members to talk; at the same time, the effective group leader is one who can remove himself or herself from the leadership role. Regarding skills that the leader should have, the authors suggest that the professional should become adept at perceiving and identifying similarities among the group members. As the counselees recognize these similarities, group interaction is facilitated.

Topic selection was also addressed by Webster and Cole, who suggested that several options are available. The SLP may select the topic, announce it, and have the parents discuss it. Another option is for the SLP to suggest a topic, subject to parental approval. If the majority of the parents agree, the topic is discussed. As discussion takes place, additional topics will be suggested by parents. There are occasions, however, when the SLP will identify a need to share specific information with the parents. When this occurs, it is the SLP's ethical responsibility to schedule this as a discussion topic.

With regard to the provision of equal opportunities for parents to participate in group discussion, Webster and Cole again caution that not all group members will participate orally; some participation will be in silence. When grossly unequal participation occurs, the SLP may want to tape-record meetings and analyze the participation of various members. This may assist in anticipating and correcting any inequities that may exist. Turn-taking may also be required when parents are competing for the opportunity to talk.

Douglass, while acknowledging that "no research indicates parent counseling will have a significant impact on the amelioration of a child's speech or language impairment," nevertheless advocates it as a "means of helping parents parent" (36). Her counseling format has four goals; first, she attempts to create a situation that will be comfortable for the parents. Assuming that both parents will be present, she seats them together on a couch. "This allows them to move closer or farther apart, avoiding the feeling of being separated from one another" (36). Douglass believes that this physical togetherness is important for the parents. The second goal is to obtain information about the child; to this end, she employs an open-ended format rather than a formal interview questionnaire. Next, she shares information with the parents regarding her philosophy of the etiology and intervention strategies for the child's specific communicative disorder. Finally, Douglass supports the "parents' belief in themselves" (36). If these goals are met, it is felt that parents have had an opportunity to problem-solve and to renew their self-confidence as parents. Douglass concludes with these important statements: "Most parents love their children and know what is best for them. Listen to them" (36). Back to the now familiar admonition to SLPs to listen.

Active listening was also stressed in a NSSLHA publication (37). Schum discussed the fact that the effective SLP counselor is able to recognize and react to the obvious; however, these responses should be carefully timed. "In counseling, *when* something is applied is as important as *what* is applied" (37). In other words, the SLP must be alert to what the child is attempting to communicate ("the obvious") but must not expect that student to be able to accept his or her feelings until the student is ready ("timing"). Schum suggests that counseling during speech-language intervention "underscores the concept of treating the *whole person*" (37). And it is with this holistic concept that this section on the SLP as a counselor began. "Our clients are not merely impaired ears or mouths. Our clients are people, each with a unique story" (37). School SLPs must be prepared to respond to each child's unique story and unique situation in a caring and competent manner as an SLP and a counselor.

Even as SLPs accept the challenge to counsel, certain precautions should be recognized. First boundaries must be established (38). The SLP is sometimes uncertain where counseling responsibilities stop and when a referral is indicated; is there a clear-cut boundary? What topics may be discussed and which are off-limits? Stone and Olswang suggest that limitations be set with regard to content or focus and style or the dynamics of the interaction (38). They stress that attitudes and questions that relate to the communicative disorder are within the content boundary; any topics not related to the communicative disorder are outside that boundary. SLPs must decide whether tangential issues are within or outside the focus boundary. "When a client frequently wants to discuss material that challenges or falls outside the boundaries, then the clinician has a good indicator that referral is needed" (38).

Regarding the interaction or dynamics between the SLP and client, the "style" may be considered acceptable if it is mutually supportive and respectful. According to the authors, the client must be active and feel empowered. When this respect is not apparent or if the client demonstrates extreme emotional or behavioral fluctuations, referral may be indicated. Another signal that the dynamics are not appropriate occurs if the client exhibits a dependency that reduces his or her self-confidence. SLPs may also become too involved with a particular client or feel uncomfortable with the situation. "Understanding that persistent uncomfortable feelings are an important clinical signal rather than a sign of clinician incompetence can make clinicians more open to their own feelings and reactions" (38). The SLP must be aware, however, of his or her own limitations as a counselor. Establishing boundaries and recognizing when these boundaries are being tested should assist the SLP as he or she pursues the challenge of counseling.

Throughout this author's career as a school SLP, supervisor, and university administrator, this challenge has presented itself frequently. School-aged children with family problems and school problems found the SLP a logical listener; college students presented similar complaints. Faculty members are not immune to numerous feelings of dissatisfaction and what better place to explore these feelings than the chair's office. In these roles, one shares in anger, failure, frustration, dependencies, death, and death wishes; on the flip side, one sometimes sees the anger turn to acceptance, the failure to success, the dependency to control, and the thoughts of suicide to thoughts of coping. It would appear that the SLP has no choice but to counsel; the only question is, how well. The question is considered next.

Evaluating the Effectiveness of Parent Counseling

Eisenstadt looked at parental counseling from the parents' point of view (39). Parents whose children had been involved in extensive therapeutic programs were interviewed in order to ascertain their level of satisfaction with regard to parent–client–clinician relationships. Although most comments were favorable, several problem areas were identified. Some of these difficulties were the result of faulty communication between the parents and the SLP; these problems might have been avoided if parental counseling had been more efficient.

Eisenstadt found, for example, that parents were unable to prepare their children for the initial diagnostic session because they, the parents, had no concept of what procedures would be followed. Prediagnostic preparation is particularly important when the evaluation will take place in a hospital setting. The consensus was that some indication of the nature of the testing procedures would have reduced the anxiety levels of both child and parent as they entered the diagnostic session.

Similar problems were identified when the SLP interpreted the results of the evaluation to the parents. Apparently some SLPs presented their findings to parents in the presence of the child. In these cases, the parents indicated that the first interpretation should be short; detailed results could be discussed at a later time.

The language used by the SLP also confused some of the parents. Although professionals are conversant with the jargon, they should remember that this terminology is new and unfamiliar to many of the parents. Vague directions were also given to the parents. They were instructed to work with their child at home but were sometimes not given specific directions on how much time to spend in such supportive work.

Another criticism offered by parents was that they were not kept informed of progress. And even though the parents realized that a specific prognosis was impossible, they wanted some idea of the time frame for habilitation–rehabilitation so that they could make necessary arrangements. Parents also indicated that they were unprepared to deal with emotional problems in the home that resulted from the program. Apparently, some nonhandicapped siblings resented the time parents spent in supportive work with the communicatively disordered child. Several parents, while talking with each other, found that many of them were faced with similar problems and suggested that group sessions led by the SLP would be helpful. Finally, the parents said that they were not always given specific information regarding the termination of therapy. It is important that the parents know what behavior is normal, in terms of fluctuating maintenance and of future needs for professional assistance.

In view of these comments from parents, it seems that counseling should not be limited to the time that the child is actually being seen for evaluation and therapy but should precede the child's initial interview. The exit interview also appears to be important.

Webster also considered ways in which SLPs could measure the success of their parent counseling efforts (40). Although an open-ended type of questioning can be employed to obtain the responses of parents to counseling, Webster suggests that specific questions be studied. These included the following:

- What SLP behaviors do parents identify as helpful to them?
- Do parents prefer group or individual counseling sessions?
- Should counseling sessions be intensive or are less frequent meetings more helpful?
- Do parents carry out supportive therapy in the home, and what is their response to such requests?
- What information regarding communicative disorders do parents find helpful?

Hoopes and Dasovich attempted to determine the views of public school SLPs on parent counseling (41). Specifically, they sought to explore the logistics of counseling procedures in the school setting. A total of seventy-six public school SLPs responded anonymously to a seventeen-item questionnaire. In considering the amount of time allocated for parent conferences, the investigators found differences between SLPs working in county schools and those employed in the city. City professionals spent less time in parent counseling (zero to one-half hour per week) than did county SLPs (fifteen minutes to one hour per week). Further, 27 percent of the city SLPs were not involved in any parent counseling. (Note that this study predated the passage of PL 94-142.) The difference between the groups might have resulted from the amount of parental cooperation given to the professionals in the two settings. County parents seemed to be more involved in the therapeutic process than did parents residing in the city. When asked if sufficient time were allowed for parent counseling, 40 percent of the professionals responded affirmatively. The majority of the city SLPs indicated that they would counsel with parents if time for such meetings were available. Many county SLPs, although they had time allocated for parent conferences, felt that more time was needed.

The survey revealed that conferences were held before, during, and after school hours or according to parent availability. In the city, parent availability seemed to be the determining factor; county SLPs were able to hold conferences during school hours.

The respondents were asked to list three factors that determined whether parent counseling was necessary. The severity of the communicative disorder presented by the child was considered to be the most important factor, with the need to provide or obtain information ranked second and third. The importance of parent counseling was also explored. Of the county SLPs, 59 percent ranked such conferences as "important," whereas 74 percent of those employed in the city felt parent counseling was "useful."

In summary, the logistics of parent counseling in the school setting must be considered. Hoopes and Dasovich's survey suggested that differences exist between SLPs working in city and county systems and that these differences influence the number and nature of counseling sessions. Regardless of the frequency of parental contacts, however, the majority of the respondents agreed that such conferences were important and useful.

Parent counseling, therefore, is a topic receiving increasing attention from SLPs. At one point, the question of whether the SLP should counsel at all was raised. However, because the EHA/IDEA mandates that parents be included in program planning for the child and that they be informed of the results of evaluative procedures, counseling is no longer an option. In looking at the qualifications of an effective counselor, one finds that they are similar to those of the effective SLP. This is a profession devoted to communication, and it is reasonable to assume that the SLP can use this communicative skill as a counselor.

The SLP as a Supervisor

SLPs have served in supervisory capacities almost since the beginning of the profession. A reference to the SLP's responsibilities as a supervisor appeared in the *Journal of Speech and Hearing Disorders* as early as 1937 (42). Although several conferences have been held to define the role and training of the supervisor, and articles regarding those subjects have appeared in professional journals, there are issues that still require resolution. Although some functions of a supervisor in various settings and at different levels of training may be essentially the same, for the purposes of this discussion, a distinction is made between the role of the supervisor of student interns in the schools; the SLP as a supervisor of paraprofessionals; and the function of the supervisor of school speech, language, and hearing programs.

Supervision of School Internship

In order to qualify for certification to work in the school setting in most states, the student must undertake student teaching or a school internship. The amount of time spent in student teaching, the academic credit hours or clock hours required, and the way in which student interns are supervised are among the factors that vary among the training institutions and states. Rees and Smith surveyed university supervisors, master clinicians (supervising school SLPs), and former students in California in an effort to ascertain whether practices in effect at that time were poor, satisfactory, or good (43). Although many factors were investigated, only the opinions regarding supervision are presented here.

A questionnaire devised by the researchers was sent to 25 university supervisors, 214 master clinicians, and 293 graduates of California training programs. Of the twenty-two university supervisors responding, 23 percent felt that the supervision provided by them was poor. Nine university supervisors (41 percent) felt that it was satisfactory, and eight (36 percent) judged their supervision as good. The majority of the master clinicians did not concur with the opinions of university supervisors regarding the adequacy of the latter's supervision. Of the 106 responding master clinicians, 49 percent felt that university supervision of students placed in the schools was poor. It was regarded as satisfactory by thirty-eight clinicians, whereas only sixteen rated university supervision as good. Of the 152 students returning the questionnaire, 32 percent (forty-eight students) felt that supervision by university personnel was poor, 23 percent (thirty-five students) judged it to be satisfactory, and 45 percent (sixty-nine students) rated it as good. Some discrepancies were apparent in this category, but general dissatisfaction with university supervision was expressed.

More positive feedback came in response to the question of the master clinician supervision of student interns. All the university supervisors rated such supervision in either the satisfactory or good categories; nineteen of the twenty-three supervisors judged it to be the latter. Of the 100 master clinician responses, only 7 percent felt that their supervision was poor. Supervision was considered satisfactory by 24 percent, and 69 percent judged it to be good. Of the 149 former students who responded to this question, only seventeen students (11 percent) regarded master clinician supervision as poor. The remaining students considered supervision by the school SLPs to be satisfactory (21 percent) or good (68 percent). Based on these results, the investigators did not view this as a problem area.

A major function of the supervisor is the evaluation of the individuals for whom he or she is responsible. Rees and Smith, in looking at this area of responsibility, found some inconsistencies. Although the majority of university supervisors (59 percent) felt that their evaluative procedures were good, only 32 percent of the master clinicians and 46 percent of the former students agreed. College supervisors' evaluative practices were judged poor by 9 percent of the university personnel, 33 percent of the master clinicians, and 30 percent of the graduates. The remaining respondents considered such procedures adequate.

Greater concurrence was found when the master clinicians' evaluative practices were rated. These practices were considered good by 87 percent of the university supervisors, 58 percent of the master clinicians, and 60 percent of the former students. None of the university personnel was dissatisfied with master clinician evaluative practices, and just 13 percent of the school SLPs and 16 percent of the former students judged these practices to be poor. Although this did not seem to be a particularly troublesome area, the investigators felt that revision of master clinician evaluation procedures might be considered.

The written evaluation criteria provided by the university were also analyzed. The majority of all three groups felt that the criteria were satisfactory or good, and only 6 percent of the university supervisors, 24 percent of the master clinicians, and 13 percent of the former students regarded them as poor. Again, enough dissatisfaction was expressed to warrant revision of the written evaluation criteria provided by the university.

Some districts in California provide master clinicians with written criteria for the evaluation of student SLPs. When such criteria were employed, the majority of the supervisors, master clinicians, and former students found them to be satisfactory or good. Of the 138 responses, 17 percent of the supervisors, 16 percent of the master clinicians, and 24 percent of the students regarded them as poor. These results suggested that revision of district criteria might be necessary.

With regard to supervision of student SLPs in the schools, then, Rees and Smith identified several problems. Areas requiring improvements were supervision by university personnel and evaluation procedures employed by both universities and individual school districts. The supervisory practices of master clinicians were well regarded by all three groups.

In a follow-up article, Rees and Smith reported on the results of the second part of their questionnaire (44). In this report, elements affecting the quality of the programs were discussed. One of the factors explored was the package of the recommended qualifications for university supervisors and master clinicians. It was agreed that the supervisor should carry university teaching assignments, hold ASHA certification, and have had experience in the public schools. The academic degree required for a university supervisor and the necessity of prior full-time clinical experiences were issues that required additional study. The qualifications of master clinicians were also explored. The respondents recommended that master clinicians have at least three years of experience, but they did not reach a consensus regarding the academic degree required or the necessity for the CCC-SP.

Supervisory practices were also investigated by Rees and Smith. It was recommended that the university supervisor confer with both the student and the master clinician whenever the supervisor visited the school. Further study was required to determine the number of visits the university supervisor should make to observe each student SLP. The respondents seemed to think that between three and six visits would be appropriate.

Regarding evaluation procedures, it was recommended that independent written evaluations of students be completed by the master clinician and the university supervisor. These evaluations should allow for both objective data and narrative judgments and should be presented orally to the student. Weekly oral evaluations of the student by the master clinician should transpire, and students should also be given the opportunity to evaluate themselves. Finally, it was recommended that students evaluate the school program in writing. No consensus was reached regarding the need for a cooperatively prepared written evaluation of the student by the master clinician and the university supervisor.

Similarly, the number of required oral evaluations of the student by the university supervisor and master clinician together was not determined.

Based on the investigation of Rees and Smith, the California Conference on Standards for Supervised Experience for Speech and Hearing Specialists in Public Schools was held (45). During the three-day conference, former students, master clinicians, and university supervisors discussed various components of the public school practicum program. A set of guidelines emerged from these discussions, and these guidelines were incorporated into the training program at California State University at Los Angeles. In addition to the creation of a directed-teaching program, the functions of university supervisors and the evaluative process were considered.

The university supervisor should visit the school on a "regular" basis to observe the student SLP. The university supervisor and the master clinician should discuss these observations; the university supervisor, student, and master clinician should also confer. When problems arise, additional supervisory visits and conferences can be scheduled. Concurrent with the student teaching experience, student SLPs were enrolled in a seminar taught by the university supervisor. Student contact and continuity in the directed-teaching program were considered to be facilitated by attendance at the seminar.

Formal evaluations of the student by the SLPs' master clinicians were conducted midway and at the end of the directed-teaching experience. The university supervisor prepared a written evaluation at the end of the assignment. Since grading was on a credit–fail basis, these written evaluations were critical. Finally, students were required to assess the directed-teaching experience, and their evaluations were utilized to analyze and make necessary programmatic modifications.

Baldes, Goings, Herbold, Jeffrey, Wheeler, and Freilinger addressed the evaluation of student SLPs and concurred that frequent evaluative sessions should be held (46). They also devised an instrument for evaluating students that assesses the student's capabilities in identification, diagnosis, scheduling, and therapeutic management. Additionally, the student's ability to maintain appropriate relationships with other professionals and with the client and his or her family is evaluated. Baldes et al. also recommended certain experiences, including opportunities to identify, evaluate, and schedule children, as well as to plan and deliver services to them. The students should also participate in record keeping, consultation, and public relations and have some administrative experiences.

Anderson developed a model of supervision that has applicability in the school setting (47). Recognizing that supervisors are frequently dominant in the supervisory process, this approach tends to decrease the dominance and focus on the process (48). In the initial stage, the supervisor provides feedback to the student; beginning student SLPs require this type of evaluative feedback, but it is important to prepare the student to move quickly to the transitional stage. At this point, the exchange, analysis, and decision-making responsibilities are moving away from the supervisor and toward the student SLP. The target stage is self-supervision; "at this stage, supervisees are responsible for their professional growth" (48). The amount of time required to move along the continuum from the feedback to the self-supervision stage depends upon the student's abilities, as well as the supervisor's willingness to relinquish dominance; some supervisors never seem to abandon their instructional role.

This model is appropriate for the SLP supervisor in the school although the emphasis may differ from a university setting. Assuming that students complete their initial work in a university clinic, it is probable that they will be struggling with content issues. That is, their concerns may lie in determining what should be done with a 6-year-old with an articulatory disorder. When the student reaches the school setting, procedural issues take precedence. The student should know what to do but may be uncertain as to how to execute intervention in a small pull-out group or if a collaborative model is employed. Nevertheless the supervisor and supervisee in both settings should focus on moving from a situation in which the supervisor is dominant to one in which the student serves as his or her own supervisor.

This sampling of the literature provides some idea of what supervisors involved in school practica are required to do. Ideally the university supervisor and the responsible public school SLP should develop the goals and objectives of the school internship program cooperatively. The time frame for the experience is governed by individual state requirements and university academic calendars. Although most supervision by cooperating SLPs is quite intensive, less frequent observations are made by university personnel. Evaluations, both oral and written, should be sufficiently comprehensive to keep students informed of their progress; similarly, student evaluation of the school internship experience should allow school and university professionals to analyze the program and make necessary adjustments.

Although the foregoing information should be of interest to the reader, one specific question remains unexplored. How does one supervise the student in training? Supervision, according to *Webster's Dictionary,* is "the direction and critical evaluation of instruction, especially in the public school." Direction of the student teaching experience should have been established prior to or at the beginning of the program. Both the student and the supervisor should be aware of the experiences the student is to have and of the means by which appropriate opportunities will be made available. The direction of the experience, therefore, should not be difficult. Evaluating the student's performance, on the other hand, may present problems.

The competent, confident school SLP recognizes that there are several ways of handling service delivery. Although one professional may feel more comfortable with programmed therapy, another may achieve positive results with traditional approaches. SLPs are also becoming more involved in providing services in other settings. For this reason, school SLPs must not attempt to create carbon copies of themselves and must not evaluate students in terms of their ability to fit into a specific mold. Acceptance of individual therapeutic styles, then, is a prerequisite for supervisors.

An instinct for when to be directive and when to allow students to make discoveries on their own is another attribute of a good supervisor. When student experimentation is not deleterious to the children in therapy, it should be permitted. Nothing is more disheartening or confidence-shattering than for the supervisor to take over a session for which the student is responsible. Demonstration therapy is perfectly acceptable, but repossession of a session reduces the children's respect for the student SLP, as well as the student's confidence in himself or herself.

A similar statement can be made with respect to critical analysis of the student's performance. Too often the supervisor recites a litany of the student's errors and shortcomings with little attention to his or her strengths. With experienced students, it is felt that self-evaluation serves a better purpose than supervisory assessment. Students should be given the opportunity to reflect on their own performances and to analyze them with the help of the supervisor. The ability to evaluate oneself is, after all, one of the ultimate objectives of training.

The supervising school SLP must also be alert to the student's readiness to assume responsibilities. Students must be introduced to new situations and duties in a systematic and gradual manner. Some school SLPs appear to hold a "sink or swim" attitude; others seem reluctant to relinquish any responsibility. The effective supervisor is sensitive to the student's readiness and delegates appropriate responsibilities in a carefully planned sequence.

Obviously, these observations do not begin to answer the question, "How does one supervise the student in training?" Supervision is an art, just as counseling parents or executing therapy are. Acceptance of and respect for the student along with a commitment to training students for public school work are important. In the author's experience with many supervising SLPs, however, the traits discussed above seem to separate the effective supervisors from those with lesser abilities.

Supervision of Supportive Personnel

In recent years, the utilization of paraprofessionals in a variety of disciplines has increased. The medical, social, and educational fields have recognized that employing supportive personnel can improve the quality of service delivery, as well as the quantity of such services. SLPs have been dealing with the issue of paraprofessionals, and many are experimenting with the utilization of both paid and volunteer supportive personnel. Although many questions remain to be answered, it is apparent that parents, students at the preprofessional level of training in speech-pathology, and high school graduates have been and are being used to provide specific services to speech- and language-impaired children and adolescents. The following discussion concerns the role of the SLP with supportive personnel.

Parents as Supportive Personnel

It is a recognized fact that the success of services delivered to children in schools and clinics depends to some degree on the involvement of parents. Neither the traditional service delivery schedule nor intensive cycle scheduling allows sufficient time for the monitoring necessary to modify speech and language patterns efficiently. Even more intensive programs, such as those available in self-contained or resource rooms, fail to provide the before and after school, weekend, and vacation stimulation and instruction that may be necessary. For years, SLPs have attempted to involve parents in the therapeutic process. These attempts were often sporadic and unorganized. Even today, the main communication between parents and SLP may take place during the required IEP conferences and in notes attached to the child's speech book. It is, therefore, encouraging that SLPs are defining the role of the parent in the habilitative process and implementing programs in which the parents can participate more vigorously.

Parental Involvement with Multiply Handicapped Children   Reports of the utilization of parents, specifically the mother, came as early as 1948. Lillywhite addressed the issue of the habilitation of severely handicapped children, including those with cerebral palsy, aphasia, and delayed speech (49). Although his specific concern was with supplementing work done in a university speech clinic, the confidence that Lillywhite placed in mothers to implement language-training programs is revealing. The original participant was the self-trained mother of a brain-injured child. Having been told that there was no hope for her son and that he should be institutionalized, this mother, a speech major in college, successfully undertook his habilitation. Later employed by the college, the mother then trained other mothers to deal with their aphasic children. Although success was reported in most instances, one failure was identified. The unsuccessful mother was hearing impaired and apparently suffered from severe guilt regarding her son. Lillywhite suggests that other factors may contraindicate the effective training of mothers; these include poor health, indifference in the program, outside employment, or inadequate intelligence. In general, the experiences reported by Lillywhite indicate that mothers can be used effectively. He suggests that appropriate reading material be assigned to supplement training sessions. Although time is required to train and supervise mothers, Lillywhite suggests that the time is well invested.

Parental Involvement with Articulatory Disorders   The issue of training time was also addressed by Fedula, England, and Ganoung as they considered the utilization of parents as supportive personnel with children with articulatory disorders (50).

Most school personnel do not have the luxury of time allocated to work with parents; instead, the greater portion of each day is spent in direct contact with children presenting communicative disorders. In order to alleviate that problem, the possibility that parental observation of therapy might serve as a training procedure was explored.

Participants in the study were ninety-two children with functional articulatory disorders and their parents. All the children had normal hearing and were of low, average, or above-average intelligence. Random assignment of the ninety-two children was to Group I, Group II-A, or Group II-B; the distribution of intelligence within each group was similar. Group I parents were asked not to observe therapy sessions but to work with their children 5 minutes per day if assignments were sent home. The SLP maintained contact with the parents via telephone or written communication. Group II-A contained twenty-three children; their parents observed therapy once per month (one out of every four sessions). Group II-B parents attended each weekly session and later participated in therapy sessions.

Posttesting after one semester of therapy revealed that children in Group II made almost twice as much improvement as the children assigned to Group I. No significant differences were found between Groups II-A and II-B. Subjective reports from teachers and principals indicated that the attitudes of the parents involved in Group II improved also. Fedula and co-workers acknowledged some problems in the logistics of the program but were optimistic regarding its effectiveness in the school setting.

Parental Involvement in Behavior Management   Carpenter and Augustine instructed the mothers of four children with communicative disorders in behavior management techniques (51). After a two-day workshop, the mothers were given lesson plans to be carried out with their children at home. Thereafter, the mothers maintained contact with the SLP by mail and telephone. Three of the four children made positive gains during the next few months; although the fourth mother reported progress, an assessment of the child failed to confirm such improvement. The authors concluded that a similar approach might be effective when daily therapy is needed.

Parental Involvement with Language Disorders   Bush and Bonachea initiated the Parents' Advice on Language (PAL) program (52). Assuming that the language-disordered child needs frequent stimulation in a variety of environments, parents were enlisted as supportive personnel. Initially, language specialists made home visits to parents of first- and second-grade children with deficiencies in receptive or expressive language. Later, the parents were invited to participate in a home language program.

Those parents who chose to join in the program attended weekly meetings to discuss their experiences and problems. Semi-instructional programs were presented at these meetings, and on occasion, there were guest speakers. Parents also exchanged ideas and prepared materials for language stimulation in the home. Specific instructions for home projects and experiences were also presented to the parents, and they were instructed in the use of corrective feedback. Weekly data charts were kept by parents to record the results of the parent–child projects.

The success of the PAL program led to its expansion to other grade levels and schools within the district. In addition to home projects, the PAL II program included more frequent field trips and neighborhood activities. The authors attributed the success of the PAL programs to several factors. Among them was the attitude of the SLP toward the parents; the latter were treated with respect, and their advice was given careful consideration in the program. Additionally, the fact that home projects were inexpensive and based on ordinary family and home activities seemed to contribute to the parents' enthusiasm for the program.

This sampling of research involving parents as supportive personnel suggests that they can play significant roles in the modification of their children's communicative problems. Those programs that provide specific instructions appear to lend themselves particularly well to execution by parents.

Other Supportive Personnel

Preprofessional Students   The utilization of preprofessional students in training as supportive personnel has received consideration. In some cases, a paucity of trained professionals prompts school districts to opt for utilization of uncertified persons. This need may be complimented by a university's need to provide training facilities for its students. Such was the case in Mississippi when student speech and hearing "teams" were deployed to the public schools (53). In this program, four undergraduates and one graduate student constituted a team. The students were assigned to centrally located public schools where they worked with communicatively disordered children. "Mild" problems were handled by undergraduates, whereas children with more complex communicative disorders were the responsibility of the graduate student. A staff member from the university provided one-third-time supervision. Wingo, in analyzing the "team" program, emphasized its positive aspects. He stated that university students were exposed to a variety of children presenting diverse communicative disorders; such exposure was impossible in the university setting alone. Further, school children received services that had not been provided previously. Finally, it should be added that these services were provided at no apparent cost to the schools.

In Iowa, a program designed to provide introductory clinical training to preprofessional speech-language pathology students was instituted (54). Eighteen students, having completed coursework in the basic communication areas and a course in articulatory disorders, were assigned to work with ten children with isolated articulatory errors. All the experimental children had been taught to produce the target phoneme in isolation by the supervising SLP. Following a two-part orientation session during which the communication aides were introduced to the school setting and had their roles defined, they began the three-month program. Each of the ten children was seen twice weekly for thirty-minute sessions; in some cases, a single aide serviced the same child on both days, whereas in others, the child had two different aides. Early in the program, session plans were devised by the school SLP. Later, the aides wrote their own plans. Supervision and consultation were provided by the school SLP.

Positive results accrued from the program. As was true in Mississippi, the researchers mentioned access to the school setting as being beneficial to the preprofessional students. At the same time, the public school children received services that might not have been available to them otherwise.

Nonprofessionals   In a frequently cited article, Alpiner, Ogden, and Wiggins described the utilization of speech aides in a pilot study conducted in Denver, Colorado (55). The investigators selected ten who met four minimum requirements: Each was at least 18 years of age, had a high school diploma, wanted to work with children, and had access to transportation. A three-week training program preceded the entrance of the speech aides into the school setting. Instructed by university and school personnel, the aides were introduced to such topics as the organization of public schools, the SLP's role in the school, the speech and hearing mechanism, and the nature of communicative disorders. Orientation was also provided to the fourteen public school SLPs who agreed to supervise the speech aides.

At the conclusion of the project, questionnaires were completed by the aides and the supervising SLPs. The results of the survey showed that the majority of the speech aides' time was spent in assisting with articulation therapy (51 percent) and that considerable time was spent in clerical activities (29 percent). Other responsibilities listed in descending order of frequency were assisting in language therapy (14 percent), in hearing therapy (4 percent), and in rate and rhythm therapy (1 percent). The aides did not participate in voice therapy. Of the fourteen supervising SLPs, eleven expressed interest in continuing to work with aides. Only two of the professionals did not want assistants and indicated that aides should not be imposed on the schools by the state. Eleven of the SLPs felt that the individual professional should have the right to determine whether an aide would be useful.

In addition to the four minimum requirements mentioned, it was suggested that aides should have clerical experience, two years of college, or university training in speech-language pathology. Although half the supervising SLPs felt that the three-week training session was adequate, several recommended that greater familiarity with equipment and experience with specific therapeutic techniques would be helpful. Generally, the attitudes of both the aides and the SLPs toward the project were positive. It was suggested, however, that guidelines be formulated regarding supportive personnel so that the professional status of school SLPs could be maintained.

It appears, therefore, that supportive personnel have been somewhat successful in providing speech-language services to children under the supervision of a qualified SLP. The questions that arise regarding supportive personnel include what entrance skills they should have, how they should be trained, and what they should be allowed to do. Those issues are considered next.

Issues Surrounding Supportive Personnel

Qualifications

In the previous discussion, it was apparent that different entry skills were required for supportive personnel. Lillywhite felt that parents needed good health, interest in the intervention program, and adequate intelligence in order to function adequately in supportive roles (49). The preprofessional students used in the Iowa study had completed coursework in the basic areas and a course in articulatory disorders (54). Alpiner et al. identified four requirements for supportive personnel: Candidates must be 18 years of age or older, possess a high school diploma, desire to work with children, and have access to transportation (55). Thus far, no mention is made of the candidate's ability to communicate effectively.

ASHA identifies three minimum entry qualifications (56). First, the candidate must hold a high school diploma or its equivalent. In addition, the individual should possess "communication skills adequate for the tasks assigned" (56). Finally, qualified applicants must be able to relate to the children and youths with whom they will work. California guidelines elaborate somewhat on ASHA's minimal requirements (57). These guidelines specify that the candidate be able to use "the primary language of the child"; applicants should also have "literate language and speech skills" (57).

Illinois has developed an *Inservice Training Manual for Special Education Program Assistants* (58). In the manual, criteria for the selection include assessment of the candidate's understanding of children; emotional, cognitive, and social development; physical status; and educational and employment background. On the application form, the candidate is required to explain why he or she is interested in becoming an assistant and what special qualifications could be brought to the position.

Remembering that minimal qualifications are specified in most guidelines, it might be well to speculate on these and additional skills that would be desirable in a supportive person. With regard to the need for a high school diploma, the relevance of this might be questioned; what exactly does a diploma prove about its possessor? Perhaps Illinois criteria for cognitive development (including the abilities to express ideas, think logically, be an accurate observer and reporter) reveal more about the applicant's abilities. Certainly, the candidate must be able to relate to clients and communicate in a common language. Finally, the applicant must have an honorable desire to work with children.

Are there other skills that would be desirable? The ability to perform clerical chores would be helpful. The itinerant SLP would also prefer an assistant who had access to transportation. Personal experience suggests that supportive personnel who have knowledge of children with disabilities are more successful than those who do not; this could not be considered a bona fide criterion, however. Organizational skills and attention to details (including time restraints) would also be important. Undoubtedly, the list of desirable traits and skills is endless. Nevertheless, minimal qualifications for applicants should be considered just that — minimal. Once the candidates have been selected, how should they be trained? That question is considered next.

Training

It should be obvious that the training of supportive personnel depends upon their entry skills, the tasks they are expected to perform, and the type of setting to which they will be assigned. Assuming that the supportive person meets the highest standards established for employment, consideration will be given to the last two points, moving from general to specific.

Paraprofessionals assigned to a self-contained classroom may receive training that is quite different from that received by those assisting SLPs who provide individual and small group intervention. In a classroom setting, it is important that paraprofessionals recognize their roles as partners with the teacher in the educational process.

Paraprofessionals: Training for the Classroom is a program that informs paraprofessionals about this and other responsibilities (59). The program stresses that the paraprofessional's role is strictly defined; supportive personnel are also informed that rules of confidentiality apply to them, as well as to teachers. This and other information regarding the paraprofessional's role in the educational process are delineated in the first training session.

Session two of the program is devoted to assisting the paraprofessional to understand children and their needs at various age levels. Included are physical, emotional, social, and cognitive characteristics of students from 5 to 13 years; the needs of some exceptional children are also addressed. Sessions three and four are devoted to instructing the paraprofessional in assisting both the children and classroom teacher. *The Leader's Guide* for the program comes with transparencies, a videotape, and reproducible ditto masters. Although not specifically designed for speech-language paraprofessionals, parts of the program could be utilized in the training of these individuals.

The inservice training procedures for special education paraprofessionals developed by the state of Illinois are also comprehensive. Not only do these guidelines outline the responsibilities of paraprofessionals and their effective utilization, but also twenty-two training modules are presented. The modules include general information regarding growth, development, and learning as well as procedural information. Behavior management and record keeping are also addressed. Training Module 15 is devoted to communication skills. Developmental milestones with regard to speech and language development are presented, and communicative disorders associated with various disabilities are outlined. Descriptions and pictorial representations of various communication aids are included. Paraprofessionals are also exposed to case study components and learn to recognize when material is missing. The training program employs audiovisual aids throughout, and recommended readings are specified. Three years were devoted to the preparation of the training manual, and the results should be very useful in the preparation of paraprofessionals.

The specific preparation of supportive personnel who assist SLPs may include all the aspects of training previously discussed plus additional areas. ASHA recommends that the communication assistant receive training in the normal aspects of speech and language, the various disorders of communication, behavior management techniques, auditory discrimination, administration, the utilization of equipment, and ethical concerns (56). Shinn-Strieker cites the need for training to include emphasis on interpersonal relations as well; she also recommends that aids be taught to communicate on the child's level in any form that is meaningful (60). It seems necessary to include task training if the paraprofessional is to be expected to execute specific programs.

Although the training procedures described thus far have included structured programs, additional structure is found in the model programs outlined by Shinn-Strieker (60). These training programs for communication assistants are offered through colleges. Students completing the training may earn associate's degrees and state certification, with specializations in either "speech therapy" or deaf education or both. Located in Rome, Georgia, one such program prepares students for roles in classrooms for speech-impaired or deaf children. A Seattle junior college also offers a ninety-hour program leading to an associates degree; included is coursework in sign language, therapy techniques, and mental health. In Oregon, Clackamus Community College offers instruction "that trains the paraprofessional to analyze the child's home environment and to develop a prescriptive plan for speech therapy" (60).

It is apparent, then, that a variety of approaches are employed to train supportive personnel to function effectively in the school setting. Once the person is trained, the next question is what should they be allowed to do. That is the next concern.

Responsibilities

Regardless of the setting (classroom, resource room, or therapy room), paraprofessionals may be expected to fulfill certain responsibilities. They may perform clerical tasks, prepare materials, assist with behavior management, and provide help to children with specific problems. Data collection, including tracking behaviors, may also be done by the supportive person. The Illinois guide classifies the responsibilities and duties of special education assistants as follows: monitoring, educational, and clerical (58). Special education assistants may also be involved in activities in the gym and library and may be required to assist with transportation of students.

Suggesting that the duties of the paraprofessional have lacked clarity, Frank, Keith, and Steil sought to determine which responsibilities teachers thought to be most important (61). Further, they attempted to learn if teachers considered the paraprofessionals skillful in completing those important tasks. Questionnaires that included statements regarding the relative importance of the clerical, instructional, and health-related responsibilities of the paraprofessional were completed by 254 teacher/paraprofessional teams. Teacher responses indicated that they felt that clerical and supervisory duties were most important and expressed satisfaction with their paraprofessionals' execution of these responsibilities; for the most part, the paraprofessionals concurred. The researchers suggested that individuals responsible for training supportive personnel make certain that these skills are addressed in the training program.

With regard to the duties assigned to communication assistants, ASHA recommends that a properly trained and supervised aid may be involved in screenings, evaluations, and intervention, as well as clerical tasks (56). The assistant may not interpret data, make clinical decisions, transmit information to other professionals, make referrals, or prepare reports. Further, the assistant must be supervised appropriately by a certified SLP who has had at least one year of experience. It is stressed that the SLP is totally accountable for the assistant's activities.

California guidelines indicate that paraprofessionals may "provide direct instruction in English or in the primary language of the students" (57). In states like California, where bilingual populations exist, this provision could be most helpful to the monolingual SLP. This type of intervention is also stressed in a report prepared by the ASHA Committee on Supportive Personnel (62). The report suggests that it is totally appropriate to employ assistants as interpreters when the SLP is not competent in a second language; similarly, an assistant may be used when the language used by the client is not used locally. The issue of bilingualism is one that will only become greater, and communication assistants may be very useful in meeting the needs of bilingual students.

Discussion

The foregoing discussions reflect some of the issues surrounding the utilization of supportive personnel. A review of the literature suggests almost complete agreement regarding the effectiveness of such persons, whether they be mothers, students in training, or high school graduates. Unfortunately for the objective reader, reports of the unsuccessful utilization of paraprofessionals may not have appeared in the professional journals.

With regard to whether supportive personnel should be utilized, the answer seems to be a qualified affirmative. The reservations are related to the task, training, and personal qualifications of the individual paraprofessional, as well as the attitudes and preparation of the supervising SLP. Regarding the tasks assigned to supportive personnel, they have been useful in performing clerical duties, as well as in intervention. Individuals implementing such intervention may receive either task-oriented training or task-oriented training supplemented by formal coursework. The training, entry qualifications, and titles of these persons have varied. One way of resolving these differences may be to follow the lead taken by other professions and create tiers of supportive personnel (63). For purposes of this discussion, only two levels are considered: the task-oriented tier (Level I) and the task-oriented tier that includes formal classroom preparation (Level II).

The personal entry qualifications for Level I and Level II would be similar. Candidates should have hearing within normal limits and adequate written and oral communication skills. They should be sensitive to the needs of communicatively disordered individuals and capable of dealing with persons presenting such problems in an objective manner. Further, applicants should be able to relate to the supervising SLP and other professional workers and be willing to accept constructive criticism. The final selection of candidates should be made by the supervising SLP based on the perceived needs of the clients and the abilities of the paraprofessional.

Most agencies or individuals establishing educational qualifications for paraprofessionals have cited a high school diploma as requisite. There is considerable evidence that possessing a high school diploma does not necessarily indicate any specific level of achievement and, therefore, may not serve as a discriminating qualification. Evidence of appropriate oral, written, and mathematic skills might be a better educational criterion. Additional competency requirements would vary depending on the specific job description. Level II personnel, for example, who were to work with language-disordered, mentally retarded children would profit from coursework in language development, language disorders, and characteristics of the retarded population. Competence in the use of specific language programs might also be required. The development of appropriate curricula would be the joint responsibility of the various agencies and a university department of speech-language pathology and audiology; a team instructional approach might be employed. If such specializations were available at Level II, educational background consistent with these specializations would be desirable.

The training of Level I and Level II personnel would differ also. Both tiers of personnel would be given an orientation to the specific job setting and instruction in the responsibilities peculiar to that environment. Level I persons would receive appropriate task-oriented training, particularly in the area of articulation therapy. Supportive personnel at the second level would also receive instruction in the implementation of therapeutic programs, but a broader spectrum of intervention tools would be included. The training of all supportive personnel should be the responsibility of the supervising SLP or employing agency.

With regard to the actual responsibilities of supportive personnel, flexibility is important. Research suggests that clerical duties, maintenance of materials and equipment, and execution of articulation therapy are tasks commonly assigned to paraprofessionals. Level II personnel might also be able to compile case history information, serve as monitors and reporters of communicative behavior outside the therapy setting, and participate in the implementation of language programs. If specialization with the Level II category were available, limited expansion into other areas of communicative disorders might be possible. Again, the duties of the supportive personnel would be determined by the supervising SLP, who would assume all ethical, moral, and legal responsibilities to the clients for any work done by the paraprofessional.

A final consideration concerns the qualifications of the supervising SLP. Minimally, that person should have a master's degree, be certified, and have several years of experience. Included in his or her training should be some background in supervisory techniques. The supervising SLP should also have an understanding of the role of the paraprofessional, respect that role, and be supportive of the concept. SLPs who feel threatened by supportive personnel will probably be inefficient in the utilization of such persons. Finally, the supervising SLP must be capable of assigning tasks commensurate with the abilities of paraprofessionals and monitoring their work objectively.

The advantages of using supportive personnel have been discussed throughout this section. One advantage is that the certified SLP is able to concentrate on providing quality services to children with complex problems, whereas the supportive person assumes responsibility of routine articulation therapy and housekeeping chores. Possible disadvantages include the professional time expended in orientation and supervision of the paraprofessional. There is also an inherent risk that the supportive person might assume more responsibility than he or she is capable of handling; prevention of this eventuality, however, is the responsibility of the supervising SLP. Finally, some SLPs have expressed the fear that school districts might employ supportive personnel rather than professionals. It has been shown that trained paraprofessionals can execute articulation programs and even language habilitation as efficiently as certified persons. Little evidence exists, however, that supportive personnel can deal effectively with individuals who stutter, have vocal disorders, or display multiple communicative disorders. Perhaps a redefinition of the role of the professional SLP is necessary; in such a definition, the responsibilities of the paraprofessional should be included since it appears that they are a part of the present and will be a part of the future.

Supervision of School Speech, Language, and Hearing Programs

Interest in the supervision of professionals employed in the schools has increased in the past decade. The state of Indiana pioneered in the study of supervision in the school setting (64). State and local supervisors as well as university personnel involved in supervision convened at Indiana University to discuss the supervision of school speech, language, and hearing programs. The following material is extracted from notes from that conference (as reported in Anderson, 1970).

During a panel discussion, the training of supervisors of school speech, language, and hearing programs was discussed. The total function of a supervisor may be broken down into those activities that are supervisory and those that require administrative skills. Supervisors, according to participant Peters, should be competent SLPs; further, some of the supervisor's clinical experience should be in the school setting. Training, however, is necessary to transform a skilled clinician into a competent supervisor. Peters suggests that this training should occur at the post-master's level after the SLP has had some experience. Such training should include exposure to theories and methods involved in the supervisory process. Supervisory experience in a practicum setting should supplement the coursework. A second area to be considered in training the supervisor is that of human interaction. Peters feels that many problems encountered by supervisors relate to their inability to relate to supervisees, "Whether we use sensitivity groups, encounter groups, therapy groups, individual counseling or whatever, it is important that we have a way to develop the ability of supervisors to understand themselves and others and to learn to interact effectively with others" (64). A third area of training deals with clinical research skills; according to Peters, there should be less emphasis in this area.

Regarding administrative functions, supervisors should understand and be competent in such areas as budget preparation and program management. Peters suggests that this competence might result from participation in courses dealing with organizational theory, business management, and educational administration.

Although Peters' remarks were conceptual in nature, Wood described the training procedures utilized at the University of Texas for the preparation of supervisors. Advanced graduate students with at least 200 clinical clock hours may participate in a graduate course in supervision while supervising a team of student SLPs. The student supervisors are supervised by a staff member. The thrusts of all coursework and supervisor experiences are in three areas: administration, instruction, and clinical supervision. In the administrative area, students discuss such topics as personnel management, relations with the public, and working conditions. Listening skills, behavioral observation and description, and methods of offering criticism are among the topics considered in the area of instruction. The final area of training is the application of supervisory or administrative skills in a practicum setting. Although Peters' concept of a training process for supervisors and the in-place program described by Wood are similar, the time at which students or professionals would receive such training differs. Wood points out, however, that some professional employment as a SLP should precede advancement to a supervisory position.

Prior to the Indiana conference, a survey was conducted to ascertain the status of supervision in school programs for communicatively disordered children (65). Questionnaires were mailed to 527 individuals thought to be supervisors of speech, language, and hearing programs. A total of 211 questionnaires were returned by 118 part-time and 93 full-time supervisors.

The respondents, who were variously titled "supervisor," "coordinator," or "director," typically were individuals with master's degrees although some had bachelor's degrees, and a small percentage held doctorates. Among the respondents, 27 percent of the full-time and 22 percent of the part-time supervisors reported that they had had coursework in supervision; only twenty individuals had had a specific course in the supervision of speech and hearing programs. The overwhelming majority of the respondents had had public school experience ranging from one to twenty-six years.

Respondents were asked not only to provide descriptive information about themselves but to identify the three biggest problems they had encountered as supervisors. Full-time supervisors varied in their responses; the professional inadequacies of the school SLPs and the need for additional personnel headed the list. Part-time supervisors identified insufficient time to execute their responsibilities as the most significant problem.

When asked whether special training for supervisory positions was necessary, 92 percent of the full-time and 81 percent of the part-time supervisors answered affirmatively. According to the respondents, the training should include information related to supervisory techniques, methods of evaluation, counseling and interviewing strategies, and inservice training. Business management material should be included, as should content information in speech-language pathology and audiology. Additionally, supervisors should obtain training in school administration.

Finally, the respondents were asked to estimate the amount of time consumed each week by various activities. Observation of school SLPs, staff meetings, program development activities, and diagnostic sessions occupied a large percentage of both the full-time and part-time supervisors' week. Other activities, including inservice training and correspondence, required considerable attention.

The results of this survey revealed that the preparation of supervisors is inconsistent and that supervisors of school speech, language, and hearing programs encounter a diversity of problems. It is apparent that the training of such professionals should be more specialized and should include information on program management as well as supervisory techniques.

Anderson identified four responsibilities that the profession must assume with regard to the supervision of school programs for the communicatively disordered (66). First, it is necessary to persuade school administrators of the need for supervisors. Next, the role of such supervisors must be defined; components of the supervisory process and the competencies of supervisors must also be identified. Finally, the profession should establish training programs for supervisors.

According to Anderson, the need for program supervisors becomes apparent if three factors are considered. Initially, when staff reductions occur, appropriate utilization of the remaining professionals is imperative. A competent supervisor can direct and coordinate this effort. Additionally, accountability trends in the schools demand that supervisors with administrative and supervisory skills be employed to manage program development and evaluation services. Finally, the mandate of education for all handicapped children requires that a more comprehensive continuum of services be provided to these students. This type of programming requires administrative skills that can be found only in a competent supervisor.

Regarding the role of the school supervisor, little specificity is evident. As indicated by others, both administrative and supervisory skills are necessary; in addition, the supervisor should be able to serve in a leadership capacity. Generally, however, all activities of the supervisor should be directed toward ensuring that competent services are delivered to communicatively disordered children.

The competencies of effective supervisors must be identified. According to Anderson, "The profession as a whole should begin to identify those competencies needed by all supervisors of the clinical process and those competencies needed in specific job environments" (66). Definition of these competencies will assist training programs in devising curricula to prepare supervisors for school speech, language, and hearing programs.

In discussing the training of supervisors, Anderson suggests that the profession should not be reactionary to state certification boards. Instead, university programs should develop a body of coursework that will include information on supervision, business management, advanced material in speech-language pathology, educational administration, and research techniques. Practicum experiences should also be provided. According to Anderson, the profession faces a challenge with regard to the issue of supervision. "It remains to be seen whether we will accept that challenge" (66).

ASHA responded to the need to establish guidelines for school programs with the publication of *Standards and Guidelines for Comprehensive Language, Speech, and Hearing Programs in the Schools* (67). Included in the manual were recommendations for program supervisors and five specific guidelines.

First, it was recommended that a supervisor be provided for each school speech, language, and hearing program. A part-time supervisor may serve when the total staff consists of fewer than ten SLPs. A staff containing ten to twenty-nine members should have a full-time supervisor, and one additional supervisor should be provided for every fifteen staff members over twenty-nine. Additionally, programs with more than twenty to thirty staff members should have a full-time administrator as well as a full-time supervisor.

It was recommended that the frequency and nature of supervision should depend on the qualifications and capabilities of the staff members being supervised. Specifically, the manual provides that (1) master's-level professionals in their initial year of employment should be supervised at least 15 percent of the time they are involved in service delivery, and (2) bachelor's-level staff in their first year must be directly supervised 20 percent of their service delivery time; thereafter, 15 percent of the student contact time must be observed.

Program management guidelines were also provided. The manual recommends that the supervisor should

- Develop program goals and objectives
- Develop data collection systems
- Participate in recruitment, employment, and dismissal of professional and subprofessional staff
- Deploy staff members according to their abilities and program needs
- Determine guidelines for case identification, selection, scheduling, and disposition
- Secure functional and appropriate physical facilities for staff members and the program

- Participate in increasing public awareness of services provided by the program
- Prepare budgets and request materials and equipment for the staff
- Coordinate school practicum experiences for university students in training
- Observe and assess staff and paraprofessionals

The supervisor should also play a consultative role by serving as a resource person to the staff and paraprofessionals, as well as in parent counseling. The improvement of direct services is one of the supervisor's responsibilities in this area, as is participation in educational curricular development. Finally, the supervisor must participate in program development and assessment. In this role, the supervisor may initiate inservice training programs, work with parents, create innovative service delivery strategies, and develop grant proposals.

The duties of the supervisor according to the ASHA guidelines, therefore, are extremely diverse. Certainly training is required to execute these numerous responsibilities with competence, and more than efficiency as SLP is required for the role of supervisor.

The American Speech and Hearing Association Committee on Supervision in Speech Pathology and Audiology has identified and defined nine issues that are related to supervision and that are of concern to members of the profession (68). The first of these issues is the need for data validating the effectiveness of supervision. According to the committee report, "We have no data to indicate that supervision makes a difference in the effectiveness of clinicians at any level of training or in the employment setting" (68). Furthermore, in the area of supervision, limited research is being conducted that might provide the necessary information. Research that has been done lacks a publication outlet. This need is critical since many other issues involved in supervision are related to the lack of validating information.

A second need, one that has been discussed previously, is for definition of the supervisor's role. The committee reported that too frequently supervisors begin to function in that role without preparation for it or a specific definition of their responsibilities. Guidelines in this area are imperative.

Although there appears to be a need for additional supervisors, the committee found this need difficult to support with hard data. Regarding supervision in the schools, it is estimated that there is one supervisor to every thirty-eight SLPs rather than the one-to-ten ratio recommended in the ASHA guidelines. Dublinske estimated that to meet those recommendations, over 1,900 supervisors should be employed (68). Finally, there is evidence that even when supervisors are employed, they may not be qualified to oversee staff activities. Again, information in this area is incomplete, but limited evidence suggests that additional supervisors are needed.

Other needs identified by the committee were the need for improvement in the quality of supervisors and the need for standards. For an individual to supervise in the schools, it is recommended that he or she have a CCC-SP, have had at least three years of experience in the schools, and be certified in the state of employment. Other competencies or characteristics required for effective supervision remain unclear.

The need for training of supervisors was identified by the committee. The results of some studies indicated that many supervisors have received little or no training before assuming supervisory positions. Similarly, it was determined that many university training programs do not offer appropriate coursework in this area. Supervisors responding to various surveys also indicated a need for training. It may easily be concluded, therefore, that additional training opportunities for supervisors must be provided.

Shapiro and Moses underscored this need and suggested that "most supervisors enter their positions without training in the supervisory process and, as a result, report feeling unprepared and anxious about participating and being observed in supervision" (69). In many cases, the supervisor of SLPs sometimes comes from another discipline. The current author experienced this type of situation. Her supervisor was a fine gentleman whose background was in mental retardation. Although he appeared to be committed to speech-language intervention programs, he had little knowledge of our services and was of no assistance. Because there were eight SLPs in the district who met on a regular basis, the staff did not experience the feelings of isolation that characterize some unsupervised SLPs. Nevertheless, a competent supervisor would have been a welcome addition.

Attempts are being made to prepare SLPs to assume supervisory roles. California State University at Chico has developed one supervisory preparation program (48). The nine-hour program is sequenced over a three-semester period and includes an introduction, a practicum, and an advanced seminar. According to Brasseur, "The content of each component has been strongly influenced by Anderson's philosophy and methodology" (48). The introductory course included an overview on components of the supervisory process, with time devoted to issues, research, competencies, and supervisory techniques. During the practicum experience, the twenty-five participants were able to apply the information they had learned. In the final seminar, the SLPs continued their study of the literature on supervision and developed dissemination strategies. Feedback from the twenty-five voluntary participants was quite positive, and additional follow-up was "planned to determine the extent to which skills and competencies have been maintained and new ones acquired" (48).

Discussion

It is apparent that supervision at all levels is receiving attention, and it may be assumed that the result will be improved competence among those who supervise. It may be important to determine how the consumers view supervisory effectiveness. Shapiro and Anderson, acknowledging that little evidence exists on the efficacy of supervision, investigated whether students in training "do anything differently after making commitments in a conference with a supervisor" (70). They believed this to be one measure of supervisory effectiveness. Thirty-two university supervisors and sixty-four students engaged in clinical practicum served as subjects; both beginning and experienced student clinicians were involved. Commitments were made by the supervisees; the majority of the commitments were related to clinical procedures or to the clinical process. Unwritten commitments were made under condition A, and written commitments were made under condition B. It was found that beginning clinicians completed more commitments under condition B than did experienced students. The reverse was true under condition A. In short, beginning students appeared to need the structure of a written contract, whereas advanced students responded better to less structure. The authors suggested that supervisors must be sensitive, therefore, to the students' levels of experience. The fact that the students' behavior changed as a result of a commitment made between the supervisor and the student suggests that supervision may be effective. "The need still exists to identify other effectiveness components in the supervisory process" (70).

Student perceptions of the supervisory process and the games played by supervisors were explored by Hagler and Casey (71). The authors asked students to describe supervisor-initiated games that they had experienced; these descriptions were categorized into those played by supervisors to "reduce responsibilities, to maintain an image, and to meet unfilled needs" (71). In the first category were strategies employed by supervisors to minimize their responsibilities; these were often used when an observer was present. Using this technique, the supervisor implies that the student is responsible for the client's care; this is especially useful when the third party is dissatisfied with the intervention. What the observer is not expected to know is that the ultimate responsibility for the client rests with the supervisor. Another game employed by supervisors wishing to reduce their responsibilities is initiated when he or she is unfamiliar with a given topic. If that topic relates to a specific disorder, the supervisor may suggest that the student should have learned about that in class. If not, the student should research it. "The student's willingness to do these things removes any need for the supervisor to research the matter" (71).

Supervisors engage in some games in order to preserve their images. This might occur when a student has an insight about a client that the supervisor had not had; the supervisor might say "I wondered when you would figure that out" (71). It is also possible for a supervisor to incorporate a student's original idea into his or her modus operandi and then claim credit for it. Finally, the supervisor may indulge in games to meet some unfilled needs. This may be seen when a supervisor takes over a session, leaving the student feeling incompetent and embarrassed.

Why do supervisors engage in games with supervisees? It may be that they, themselves, lack education in the supervisory role and are insecure. However, supervisors should have the maturity and insight to recognize when they are initiating or participating in gamesmanship. Clearly, something is wrong with the relationship when either party feels the need to engage in games. As supervisors learn more about the supervisory process, games should cease to exist; on the other hand, there are those who feel that people are inclined to play games whenever they interact. "The optimistic would reply that we have not yet learned enough or that which we know has not yet been taught to those who might put it into practice" (71).

Summary

Historically, SLPs have been responsible for identifying students with communicative disorders, assessing these students, and planning and executing competent intervention. Professionals have also interacted with teachers and parents in an attempt to obtain information about the child's functioning in other settings and to provide direction in the hope that carryover will be monitored. Elements of administration, assessment, direct and indirect intervention, consultation, and counseling are involved in the execution of these responsibilities; methods of assessing the SLP's effectiveness in these roles were considered initially in this chapter. Next, the status of the school SLP was considered. How do these professionals view themselves, and how are they regarded by colleagues? Consideration was also given to two specific responsibilities of the SLP: counseling and supervision. Problems and issues related to those roles were discussed. One obvious role of the contemporary SLP was conspicuous by its absence; that is the responsibility of the SLP in collaboration and consultation. That issue is considered in the next chapter.

Endnotes

1. R. J. Van Hattum, "Services of the Speech Clinician in Schools," *Asha* 18(1976): pp. 59–63.

2. M. Black, *Speech Correction in the Schools* (Englewood Cliffs, NJ: Prentice-Hall, 1964).

3. R. J. Van Hattum, *Clinical Speech in the Schools* (Springfield, IL: Charles C. Thomas, 1969).

4. *Program Guidelines for Language, Speech, and Hearing Specialists Providing Designated Instruction and Services,* California State Department of Education (1989).

5. M. H. Powers, "What Makes an Effective Public School Speech Therapist," *Journal of Speech and Hearing Disorders* 21(1956): pp. 441–467.

6. *North Carolina Public School Guidelines for Speech-Language Programs,* North Carolina Department of Public Instruction (1985).

7. R. J. Van Hattum, "The Defensive Speech Clinicians in the Schools," *Journal of Speech and Hearing Disorders* 31(1966): pp. 235–240.

8. J. B. Weaver, "An Investigation of Attitudes of Speech Clinicians in the Public Schools," *Asha* 10(1968): pp. 319–322.

9. T. Albritton, "The School Clinician and ASHA in the Seventies," *Language, Speech, and Hearing Services in Schools* 2(1970): pp. 3–6.

10. J. C. Bown, "The Expanding Responsibilities of the Speech and Hearing Clinician in the Schools," *Journal of Speech and Hearing Disorders,* 36(1971): pp. 538–542.

11. V. T. Falck, "Communication Skills—Translating Theory into Practice," *Exceptional Children* 10(1978): pp. 74–77.

12. S. Dublinske, "New Opportunities for Speech-Language Pathologist and Audiologists," *Asha* 21(1979): pp. 998–1002.

13. "A Class Act," *Asha* 28(1986): pp. 18–21.

14. "Serving School Children," *Asha* 31(1989): p. 37.

15. "Improving with Age," *Asha* 31(1989): pp. 39–40.

16. "Managing a Bilingual Program," *Asha* 31(1989): pp. 40–41.

17. "Conquering Carryover," *Asha* 31(1989): p. 42.

18. S. Dublinske, "Speech-Language Pathology and the Regular Education Initiative," *Asha* 31(1989): pp. 47–49.

19. L. B. Kohler, "Working in the Public Schools and Loving It," *Asha* 31(1989): pp. 44–60.

20. D. W. Sue, *Counseling the Culturally Different* (New York: John Wiley & Sons, 1981).

21. A. D. Wolvin and C. G. Coakley, *Listening,* 2nd ed. (Dubuque, IA: Wm. C. Brown, 1985).

22. J. G. Clark, "Counseling in Communicative Disorders: A Responsibility to Be Met," *Hearsay, Journal of the Ohio Speech and Hearing Association,* Spring/Summer (1990): pp. 4–7, 14.

23. D. Luterman, *Counseling the Communicatively Disordered and Their Families* (Boston: Little, Brown, 1984).

24. W. J. Rollin *The Psychology of Communication Disorders in Individuals and Their Families* (Englewood Cliffs, NJ: Prentice-Hall, 1987).

25. American Speech and Hearing Association Subcommittee on Housing of the Committee on Speech and Hearing Services in the Schools, "ASHA Recommendations for Housing of Speech Services in the Schools," *Asha* 11(1969): pp. 181–182.

26. L. E. Travis, *Handbook of Speech Pathology and Audiology* (New York: Appleton-Century-Crofts, 1971).

27. N. D. Matkin, "Key Considerations in Counseling Parents of Hearing-Impaired Children," *Seminars in Speech and Language* 9(1988): pp. 209–222.

28. D. V. Atkins, "Issues Faced by Adolescent Hearing-Impaired Clients and Their Parents: Implications for Audiologists and Speech-Language Pathologists," *Hearsay, Journal of the Ohio Speech and Hearing Association,* Spring/Summer (1990): pp. 15–21.

29. M. Vernon and J. F. Andrews, *The Psychology of Deafness* (New York: Longman, 1990).

30. J. C. Stewart, *Counseling Parents of Exceptional Children* (Columbus, OH: Charles E. Merrill, 1978).

31. E. J. Webster, "Parent Counseling by Speech Pathologists and Audiologists," *Journal of Speech and Hearing Disorders* 31(1966): pp. 331–340.

32. E. J. Webster, "Procedures for Group Parent Counseling in Speech Pathology and Audiology," *Journal of Speech and Hearing Disorders* 33(1968): pp. 127–131.

33. L. Emerick, *The Parent Interview* (Danville, IL: The Interstate Printers, 1969).

34. P. T. Flynn, "Effective Clinical Interviewing," *Language, Speech, and Hearing Services in Schools* 9(1978): pp. 265–271.

35. E. J. Webster and B. M. Cole, "Effective Leadership of Parent Discussion Groups," *Language, Speech, and Hearing Services in Schools* 10(1979): pp. 72–80.

36. L. W. Douglass, "Counseling Parents of Speech-Language Impaired Children," *Seminars in Speech and Language* 9(1988): pp. 223–235.

37. R. L. Schum, *Counseling in Speech and Hearing Practice,* Clinical Series No. 9 (1986).

38. J. R. Stone and L. B. Olswang, "The Hidden Challenge in Counseling," *Asha* 31(1989): pp. 27–31.

39. A. A. Eisenstadt, "Weakness in Clinical Procedures—A Parental Evaluation," *Asha* 14(1972): pp. 7–9.

40. E. J. Webster, "Questions Regarding Parental Responses to Parent Counseling," *Language, Speech, and Hearing Services in Schools* 3(1972): pp. 47–50.

41. M. Hoopes and M. O. Dasovich, "Parent Counseling: A Survey of Use by the Public School Speech Clinician," *Journal of the Missouri Speech and Hearing Association* 5(1972): pp. 9–13.

42. American Speech and Hearing Association Committee on Supervision in Speech Pathology and Audiology, "Current Status of Supervision of Speech-Language Pathology and Audiology," *Asha* 20(1978): pp. 478–486.

43. M. Rees and G. Smith, "Supervised School Experience for Student Clinicians," *Asha* 9(1967): pp. 251–256.

44. M. Rees and G. Smith, "Some Recommendations for Supervised School Experience for Student Clinicians," *Asha* 10(1968): pp. 93–103.

45. L. M. Monnin and K. M. Peters, "Problem Solving Supervised Experiences in the Schools," *Language, Speech, and Hearing Services in Schools* 8(1977): pp. 99–106.

46. R. A. Baldes, R. Goings, D. D. Herbold, R. Jeffrey, G. Wheeler, and J. J. Freilinger, "Supervision of Student Speech Clinicians," *Language, Speech, and Hearing Services in Schools* 8(1977): pp. 76–84.

47. J. Anderson, *The Supervisory Process in Speech-Language Pathology and Audiology* (Boston: College-Hill Press, 1988).

48. J. Brasseur, "The Supervisory Process: A Continuum Perspective," *Language, Speech, and Hearing Services in Schools* 20(1989): pp. 274–295.

49. H. Lillywhite, "Make Mother a Clinician," *Journal of Speech and Hearing Disorders* 13(1948): pp. 61–66.

50. J. B. Fedula, G. England, and L. Ganoung, "Utilization of Parents in a Speech Correction Program," *Exceptional Children* 28(1972): pp. 407–412.

51. R. L. Carpenter and L. E. Augustine, "A Pilot Training Program for Parent-Clinicians," *Journal of Speech and Hearing Disorders* 38(1973): pp. 48–57.

52. C. Bush and M. Bonachea, "Parental Involvement in Language Development: The PAL Program," *Language, Speech, and Hearing Services in Schools* 4(1973): pp. 82–85.

53. J. W. Wingo, "Student Speech and Hearing 'Teams' in the Public School," *Asha* 12(1970): pp. 605–606.

54. P. K. Hall and C. L. Knutson, "The Use of Preprofessional Students as Communication Aides in the Schools," *Language, Speech, and Hearing Services in Schools* 9(1978): pp. 162–168.

55. J. G. Alpiner, J. A. Ogden, and J. E. Wiggins, "The Utilization of Supportive Personnel in Speech Correction in the Public Schools: A Pilot Project, *Asha* 12(1970): pp. 599–604.

56. "Draft Addendum to the Guidelines for the Employment and Utilization of Supportive Personnel," *Asha* 29(1987): pp. 45–48.

57. *Program Guidelines for Language, Speech and Hearing Specialists Providing Designated Instruction and Services,* California State Department of Education (1989).

58. *Inservice Training Manual for Special Education Program Assistants,* Illinois State Board of Education, Department of Special Education (1986).

59. C. S. Houk and R. G. McKenzie, *Paraprofessionals: Training for the Classroom,* American Guidance Service (1988).

60. T. K. Shinn-Strieker, "Trained Communication Assistants in the Public

Schools," *Language, Speech, and Hearing Services in Schools* 15(1984): pp. 70–75.

61. A. R. Frank, T. Z. Keith, and D. A. Steil, "Training Needs of Special Education Paraprofessionals," *Exceptional Children* 55(1988): pp. 253–258.

62. "Utilization and Employment of Speech-Language Pathology Supportive Personnel with Underserved Populations," *Asha* 30(1988): pp. 55–56.

63. K. L. Moll, "Issues Facing Us—Supportive Personnel," *Asha* 16(1974): pp. 357–358.

64. J. L. Anderson (ed.), *Conference on Supervision of Speech and Hearing Programs in the Schools* (Bloomington, IN: Indiana University Press, 1970).

65. J. L. Anderson, "Status of Supervision in Speech, Hearing, and Language in the Schools," *Language, Speech, and Hearing Services in the Schools* 3(1972): pp. 12–22.

66. J. L. Anderson, "Supervision of School Speech, Hearing and Language Programs—An Emerging Role," *Asha* 16(1974): pp. 7–10.

67. American Speech and Hearing Association, *Standards and Guidelines for Comprehensive Language, Speech and Hearing Programs in the Schools,* Washington, DC, 1973–1974.

68. American Speech and Hearing Association Committee on Supervision in Speech Pathology and Audiology, "Current Status of Supervision of Speech-Language Pathology and Audiology," *Asha* 20(1978): pp. 478–486.

69. D. A. Shapiro and N. Moses, "Creative Problem Solving in Public School Supervision," *Language, Speech, and Hearing Services in Schools* 20(1989): pp. 320–332.

70. D. A. Shapiro and J. L. Anderson, "One Measure of Supervisory Effectiveness in Speech-Language Pathology and Audiology," *Journal of Speech and Hearing Disorders* 54(1989): pp. 549–557.

71. P. Hagler and P. L. Casey, "Games Supervisors Play in Clinical Supervision," *Asha* 32(1990): pp. 53–56.

7

Consultation and Collaboration

Speech-language pathology in the schools is like a kaleidoscope. There is an everchanging pattern of challenges to be met (1).

Introduction

A perusal of the literature in consultation and collaboration reveals that these terms have been used and misused rather consistently. Denotatively, the verb *consult* means "1. to seek advice or information from: ask guidance from: refer to for information" (2). A person who serves as a consultant is "1. one who consults someone or something. 2. One who gives professional or expert advice" (2). Finally, consultation is "1. the act of consulting: conference. 2. a meeting for deliberation, discussion, or decision" (2). When speaking of consultation, therefore, one is referring to an exchange of information between an expert and one with less expertise. The employment of the term is appropriate when one consults with a physician on medical matters; a distinct disparity of expertise exists. However, if consultation takes place between an SLP and a teacher, both have expertise but in different areas; the same situation occurs when an SLP consults with any other professional. It might be more accurate, therefore, to say that consultation is the sharing of information between professionals with different areas of expertise, with the intent of assisting the child.

In some contexts, consultation has an additional meaning; it infers that the consultant (SLP) provides information to the teacher, who then provides services to the student. The SLP in such cases is not involved directly in service delivery. In other contexts, though the terminology remains the same, the consultant and the teacher may both be involved in direct intervention. The reader will become aware of these inconsistencies as this discussion continues.

The other term that may cause confusion is the verb *collaborate,* which is defined as follows: "1. to work with one another. 2. to cooperate willingly, with an enemy of one's country" (2). Although the author and others have experienced situations in which the second definition may apply, it is better to think of the process in terms of the first meaning. The noun *collaboration* is defined as "1. the act or process of collaborating 2. the product resulting from collaboration" (2). With regard to speech-language service delivery, collaboration involves the SLP working with other professionals in order to help the child. In the literature, the participation of the collaborators in that service delivery is sometimes unclear.

If this explanation of consultation and collaboration was not sufficiently confusing, it should be added that some authors also speak of "collaborative consultation." Although all these terms will be employed throughout this chapter, it is only to be consistent with the terminology employed by individual researchers and authors. It appears that more equity exists among participants when the term *collaboration* is employed. Nevertheless, the chapter is titled "Consultation and Collaboration," and both terms will be used in the discussions.

Before considering the role of consultation/collaboration in the educational setting and its specific application by SLPs, it is important for the reader to recognize that consultation/collaboration is not a new concept but one modified to be consistent with recent trends in education. For example, one type of consultation/collaboration that has been used by SLPs throughout the years is that designed to improve or enhance speech or language. Usually, such intervention was provided when assessment and observation suggested that the majority of children in a given classroom would benefit from instruction. The teacher and SLP would then formulate a program to be executed by one, or preferably, both professionals. An illustration of such collaborative work comes from the author's experience. All the students in a first grade serviced by the author came from depressed environments and required language stimulation to acquire age-appropriate linguistic competence. The program, collaboratively designed by the teacher and author, was projected for a semester. During that time, the author (SLP) worked in the classroom for an hour each Friday; the teacher remained in the classroom and observed the presentation and interaction. The SLP also provided session plans and materials for the teacher to employ throughout the week to reinforce the concepts presented on Fridays; approximately thirty minutes each day were devoted to the language stimulation program. Being inexperienced and naive, neither the teacher nor the author thought to do posttesting to objectify what were perceived to be positive results. This illustration should confirm that collaboration is not new to the profession; however, the focus of this delivery system has expanded beyond just language and speech enrichment. The reasons behind this expansion are considered next.

Historical and Contemporary Perspectives

Much of the historical information regarding consultation comes from the area of special education. Friend, recognizing that interest in consultation in special education had grown rapidly, identified a need to explore the history of its utilization and examine consultation from contemporary perspectives (3). Historically, consultation was employed primarily in the fields of counseling and school psychology. Beginning in the mid-1970s, provision of services to students with special learning needs through the consultation model emerged as a viable delivery option. Fearing that this option might be employed indiscriminately, Friend warned,

> *In the midst of this almost frenetic activity, it is too easy to lose sight of the fact that consultation is a discipline with a history, that it is only one of many forces affecting schools, and that decisions made now about the practice of consultation will affect the character of services in the future (3).*

To this end, Friend proposed to reexamine consultation as it had been used in various human service agencies, to explore forces influencing school consultations, and to hypothesize about the future of consultation in the school.

As noted previously, school psychologists were among the first to use the consultation model in the educational setting; this delivery system option was implemented when the demand for services exceeded the number of professionals available to provide them. The reported success of consultation by psychologists and counselors led other special educators to explore this service delivery option. Coupled with this positive factor was the mounting dissatisfaction of many special educators with the segregation of students into special education classrooms. As the reader is now aware, a concept that evolved from that dilemma was that of the least restrictive educational environment (LRE). One of the LRE outcomes was the development of resource rooms. Instead of being segregated from peers for the better part of the day, students who required special services were to be placed in resource rooms for only an hour daily. Theoretically, these children were in the regular classroom during the rest of the day. Even with this type of programming, however, the fear continued to exist among educators that more students might be identified as needing services than could be served in existing programs. There was also concern that another delivery system, one that was even less restrictive than the resource room, was needed; that system was consultation.

"By the 1980s a research base suggesting that consultation could be an efficacious model for educating handicapped students had emerged" (3). Additional impetus came from the continuing belief of many that segregating students for any amount of time during the day might have detrimental effects. All these factors led to experimentation with the consultation model, and this experimentation continues in the 1990s; among those involved are SLPs and occupational and physical therapists. According to Friend, contemporary SLPs who formerly provided services on an individual basis are recognizing "the importance of overall communication for school success and the relevance of language acquisition as an essential domain in which speech pathologists may provide assistance" (3). In addition, SLPs have acknowledged that "the most ecologically valid setting in which to offer language remediation is the general education classroom" (3). To meet these needs, SLPs are turning to consultation. The ways in which SLPs are providing consultative services are considered in some detail later in this chapter.

Occupational and physical therapists are also exploring consultation as a service delivery model for children who present mild or moderate disabilities. Using this model, "The teacher or consultee is viewed as having the expertise to assist the student, but not the ability to make subtle therapeutic judgements, the latter remaining the responsibility of the therapists" (3). Questions remain unanswered regarding the legality and ethics of consultative service delivery by occupational and physical therapists, but it is apparent that it is an important and developing concept.

Although the LRE has been important in the consultation movement, Friend identified two other factors that may influence the utilization of consultation: the educational reform movement and the Regular Education Initiative (REI). "The latter seems to enhance the likelihood that consultation will continue to be a significant school service approach, and the former suggests that it is doomed" (3). The reform movement may impact negatively because it emphasizes achievement and educational accomplishment without consideration of the unique needs of individual learners. If it is to be assumed that problem learners can succeed in the regular classroom as long as adaptions are made (through consultation and other strategies), then any reform that generalizes rather than individualizes instruction will disadvantage these students. For this reason, Friend considers the educational reform movement to be potentially deleterious to the utilization of consultation.

The REI, on the other hand, encourages consultative intervention. Jenkins et al. discussed the REI and its implications for special education (4). According to some educators, the system now employed to instruct children with learning problems is flawed. One problem is the fragmentation of categorical programs: "This fragmentation not only impairs the programs' effectiveness, but also causes children to fall through the cracks created between the separate programs" (4). Additionally, some feel that regular classroom teachers and administrators have lost control of the instruction of children with learning problems; instead, special educators control the programming of these children with little consideration of coordination. As noted earlier, segregation of students from their peers is problematic and may affect their self-esteem. Finally, the placement of a child in special education has the potential for creating problems between parents and school officials.

In order to overcome these perceived problems, it has been suggested that principals be given control with respect to managing and coordinating categorical services. In addition, instructional time should be increased. A support system should also be generated for teachers; team teaching and inservice training should be included. Finally, new approaches should be devised "such as curriculum-based assessment, cooperative learning, and personalized curricula" (4). These suggestions and others have been referred to as the REI.

Reaction to the REI has been positive in that some consensus has been reached that current strategies for educating children with learning problems are flawed. On the other hand, not all would agree that the REI is the solution. Further, the REI is a concept rather than a well-defined plan. Jenkins et al. state that, "beyond a call for partnership (which is not spelled out) and less restrictive, more mainstreamed, education for at-risk students with disabilities, the REI is largely without definition" (4). If one agrees that teachers and special educators do share responsibility for a given child (partnership) and that the child should remain in the least restrictive environment (the classroom), then the consultation model is consistent with the REI. However, additional focus on the role of consultants in this model is necessary.

It is apparent, then, that historical and contemporary issues have motivated special educators to consider consultation and collaboration as service delivery options. Early experience with this system was gained primarily by school psychologists and counselors who employed consultation to accommodate inflated caseloads. Additional impetus was generated by the LRE and the REI. Those involved with the various consultation and collaboration models have identified strategies designed to maximize success and minimize failure; those strategies are considered next.

Implementation Strategies

General Guidelines

Successful implementation of the consultation or collaboration model in the school setting may depend on four factors (3). Initially, the concept of consultation must be clarified; it is important to define the specific intent of a consultation or a consultation model. "Second, consultation should be explicitly placed in the continuum of services available to students" (3). As the reader is aware, SLPs have already included consultation as a service delivery option. Next, discussion of consultation as a decision-making model should be initiated. Finally, if professionals are to engage in consultation, they should receive preprofessional and inservice training particularly related to transdisciplinary efforts. "If professionals are attempting to create service delivery approaches that rely on professional cooperation, the model for that cooperation should be rooted in training" (3).

Although these factors are undoubtedly important to the future of consultation in the school setting, Phillips and McCullough identified other issues that require resolution (5). One factor that may complicate successful collaborative consultation (the terminology sometimes employed by the authors) between regular and special education professionals involves attitudinal differences, differences that may result from insufficient knowledge about the demands of each other's role. Further, although special education personnel may not be experts in the consultation process, they "have been introduced to basic principles and terminology, if not exhaustive consultation theory and process" (5). Teachers are not likely to have similar exposure. Finally, in many cases, the consultation effort sometimes is unstructured due to practical barriers, including time constraints. "Consultation which develops informally, without structure and predictability, generally proves ineffective and shortsighted" (5).

Because these and other barriers exist, it is felt that a collaborative ethic must evolve. Involved in this ethic would be the belief that professionals are jointly responsible and jointly accountable for the students. They must further believe that sharing expertise and resources is advantageous and that the resolution of problems is worthy of the professionals' time and energy. Finally, there must be a "belief that correlates of collaboration are important and desirable"; these correlates include group morals and cohesiveness, as well as increased knowledge (5). Assuming that these ethics are accepted, it is possible to develop and implement a consultation program.

Initially, it is important to seek the support of administrators; this support and understanding is critical at both the building level (in the form of the principal) and at the district level. Additionally, staff at all levels should be involved in determining which consultation formats will be employed and in developing plans for implementation; this involvement affords the participants a sense of ownership. The feasibility of the consultation formats must be demonstrated to the classroom teachers and accepted by them; the teacher "may not implement, or may not do so with integrity, interventions they perceive as incompatible with classroom ecology" (5).

As noted previously, teachers, as well as other professionals, may not have the preservice education to prepare them for collaborative consultation. Therefore, the need for staff development exists. In achieving this end, three factors must be considered; these include program establishment, maintenance, and enhancement. According to Phillips and McCullough, "three critical features of staff development facilitate program establishment: (a) specificity, (b) expectancy and motivation, and (c) interdisciplinary training" (5). Specificity is required so that program participants have clear and concise concepts of what is targeted and what strategies are to be employed. Next, the participants must receive training in the skills they are expected to demonstrate; the participants are more likely to support the program if they feel confident in their abilities to execute target behaviors. Although the potential consultants are not expected to become knowledgeable about the areas of expertise of their colleagues, they are expected to become knowledgeable about the art and science of the consultation process. This constitutes the interdisciplinary training function of program establishment.

Program maintenance, the second phase of staff development, requires that collaborative consultation training be conducted over a long period rather than during a day-long inservice. Effective programs involve training over time, "organized around demonstrably efficient instructional and support strategies (for example, observation, practice, experimentation, feedback, coaching) that promote skill acquisition and maintenance" (5). In order for program enhancement to occur, refinements and adaptations should be ongoing. This phase of staff development should occur after the consultants have acquired the necessary consultation skills and have had sufficient time to solidify these skills. With a systematic approach, such as that advocated by Phillips and McCullough, collaborative consultation may be successfully implemented.

One of the pitfalls of collaborative consultation that may occur is the resistance of classroom teachers. Phillips and McCullough attempt to reduce this potential resistance by including teachers in all phases of program planning and implementation. Polsgrove and McNeil also explore resistance problems that may occur and the means by which they may be surmounted (6). They acknowledge that while consultees who request services are eager participants in the process, others may resist involvement in both the planning and implementation of a proposed plan of intervention. According to the authors, the resistance may be related to the consultee or the system. As indicated previously, successful programs require administrative support; administrators who are neutral or oppositional may undermine consultative efforts. In some cases, their lack of support may "serve as a hidden source of resistance" (6). For example, the administrator may verbally endorse the plan but then not allocate time for the provision of services.

Another resistance to consultation may be related to funding. Children placed in special education classes or those receiving special education classes or special education services through pull-out intervention present reimbursement sources to the district. "Under a traditional approach, a system receives funds based on the number of children tested and placed in special education classes" (6). When the consultation model is successfully implemented, a reduction of children receiving special education services occurs with a corresponding reduction in financial support. According to the authors, reduced accountability may accompany the consultant model of service delivery, and this type of indirect intervention may be less convincing to school boards. For these reasons, administrators may not be totally supportive of the consultant model.

Resistance may also occur at the building level when teachers who had formerly been encouraged to refer students for special services are now asked to participate in planning and executing classroom intervention. Here the resistance is to the system rather than to the many interpersonal or intrapersonal factors associated with the model. Other variables related to the model itself that may result in teacher resistance are its novelty and uncertainty. Teachers may prefer more structure than the consultant model may afford. These factors, when coupled with administrative lack of support, may make successful implementation quite difficult.

Intrapersonal variables may increase teacher resistance. "They may be threatened at having to admit they must rely on outside help to deal with a problem" (6). Teachers may also feel uncomfortable when the consultant observes in the classroom or with the prospect of managing a child collaboratively within the classroom environment. Teachers who were relieved when a "problem child" left the classroom for services may resent having to deal with that child in the room. "Finally, a consultee may experience anger, resentment, or anxiety at having to bear the major responsibility for implementing an intervention plan and for its possible failure" (6).

Interpersonal stresses must be considered as well. The terms *consultant* and *consultee,* as used by Polsgrove and McNeil, may contribute to a lack of parity in the consultant process. The expert (consultant) appears to control the power, whereas the teacher (consultee) bears the burden of implementing the plan; this in itself may create problems. In addition, in the case of the SLP, a disparity in education between the consultant and consultee may exist. Teachers may assume a defensive posture when this gap exists. Teachers may also feel overwhelmed by the additional responsibility of implementing programs for individual children while attempting to respond to the needs of twenty-five other students. The consultee may question what the consultant does to earn his or her keep if the former is providing actual intervention. Finally, interpersonal problems that arise in the course of normal interaction among and between persons may interfere with the consultation process.

Successful consultation or collaboration is dependent on a number of factors. Participants must be aware of their roles and responsibilities and should receive sufficient training to execute these responsibilities. It is essential that all professionals accept the concept of the consultation/collaboration model and work to recognize and remove any barriers that may preclude successful service delivery to the students.

Thus far, for the purposes of establishing historical and contemporary perspectives and of providing general implementation guidelines, consultation and collaboration have been considered as a general entity. In the next two sections, each is discussed, insofar as possible, as distinct service delivery models.

The Consultation Model

In the introduction to this chapter, questions were raised regarding the use and misuse of the terms *consultation* and *collaboration*. In some cases, it was noted, the terms are used in combination (collaborative consultation) or interchangeably. However, individual authors sometimes define their terminology concisely and present materials specific to those definitions. In this section, ideas from those who use "consultation" or describe a consultation model are presented.

"Consultation is a three-person chain of service in which a consultant interacts with a caregiver (consultee) to benefit an individual (client) for whom the caregiver is responsible" (7). For example, the SLP, serving as the expert consultant, devises a plan that is implemented by the classroom teacher (consultee/caregiver); in so doing, the behaviors of both the student and the teacher are modified. According to Frassinelli et al. "consultation provides input to the teacher in an effort to facilitate the functioning of both the teacher and the child" (7). It may also allow the SLP to serve more clients in a classroom setting and "achieve preventive effects" (7).

One impact of consultation upon direct service caseload is relatively obvious. If SLPs work with teachers whose classrooms have a high representation of children with communicative disorders, the direct service caseload will be reduced. In districts in which the need exists for additional SLPs if service delivery is to be direct, the utilization of consultation would be beneficial. One must remember, however, that the child's needs, not the availability of services, should be the determining factor in selecting the consultation model.

Another advantage of this model is that intervention is provided in a more naturalistic environment. SLPs have always recognized that the provision of services twice or three times weekly in a speech room was unnatural and did not contribute to carryover into other environments. Classroom intervention, on the other hand, may occur periodically during the day in connection with academic pursuits; in this environment, it is more likely to be meaningful and to generalize. Further, the classroom teacher having received guidance from the SLP may be inclined to employ appropriate strategies to enhance the learning of all the students. The teacher may become more astute at identifying problems and in planning and implementing programs. This may serve to prevent problems before they become problems.

Frassinelli et al. suggest that SLPs preparing to employ the consultant model must be aware of three principles. First, they must believe that the consultation model will benefit their clients. In addition, SLPs must commit themselves to a collaborative, not an authoritarian, posture; they must believe that the teacher and SLP form a partnership. Finally, SLPs must recognize the necessity for careful data collection and analysis in order to evaluate the efficacy of the delivery system.

Several consultation formats are available to the SLP considering this as a service delivery option, and Frassinelli et al. identify three variations (7). Type I involves ongoing direct contact. Both direct intervention, either individual or small group, and collaborative consultation are involved. In effect, work done by the teacher in the classroom augments direct intervention by the SLP. For example, carryover of a newly acquired phoneme may be monitored and reinforced by the classroom teacher; again, both direct and indirect services are provided.

Type II consultation involves one-time or periodic contact between the SLP and the child; consultation occurs after a diagnostic session. The SLP assesses the student and then confers with the teacher to design a program to be implemented by the classroom teacher. Such consultation may be appropriate for a young child who is dysfluent in the classroom. The SLP identifies factors that may contribute to fluency and, together with the teacher, designs classroom strategies that will promote and reinforce fluency.

No direct contact is involved in Type III collaborative consultation. In such cases, the teacher accumulates data on a child or a group of students and presents the information to the SLP. Based on the SLP's analysis and recommendation, the teacher makes appropriate adjustments.

In order for any type of consultation to be effective, numerous factors must be considered. Although some of these factors have already been discussed, Frassinelli et al. identify four that they feel to be significant. First, some sort of a contract should be negotiated between the SLP and the classroom teacher. This oral or written contract should outline the roles and responsibilities of both participants. Also included should be logistical items including consultation meeting times and frequency, specific responsibilities for data collection, commitment to problem solving, and "the teacher's option to accept or reject any recommendations" (7).

Another factor, emphasized frequently in this text, is the importance of active listening by the SLP. Teachers must be aware that the SLP understands the formers' concerns and feelings. Through classroom observation and listening to teachers, the SLP should gain a better understanding of the teachers' perspectives. Only through active listening can the SLP achieve this understanding.

Earlier, it was noted that successful consultation requires specificity and focus. The child's problem must be described concisely so that both the teacher and SLP have a complete picture of its scope. "As specifics of the problem are discussed and data collected, solutions become clear" (7).

Truly collaborative consultation requires that the SLP avoid assuming the role of expert, nor should the SLP attempt to provide immediate solutions. In a partnership, both parties are expected to participate in problem solving. Moreover, "immediate solutions, based on insufficient data, are often inappropriate or have already been tried" (7). Therefore, the teacher and SLP should attempt to solve problems and plan intervention strategies cooperatively. This type of programming is more likely to be effective since the teacher's frame of reference is considered.

Even when these and other factors are addressed prior to implementing a consultation model, additional concerns and questions may arise. For example, will teachers (and for that matter, SLPs) be willing to sacrifice unassigned time for consultations? Most will if they understand the benefits of the consultation system. Will the teachers be willing and able to accept the additional challenge and responsibilities associated with this model? Frassenelli et al. suggest that once teachers understand the advantages of collaborative work, both for themselves and their students, they participate willingly. In this regard, the specificity of expectations mentioned previously may be a convincing factor. Some teachers may challenge the notion of consultation since they may perceive that they are assuming the responsibilities of the SLP. Most teachers expect their students to receive direct services and must be convinced that collaborative consultation may serve their children better. To convince these individuals, it is well to select suitable teachers and students for the initial collaborative efforts. Nothing is more convincing than success.

With regard to children who might benefit from the consultation model,

Frassenelli et al. identified students in special education classrooms as particularly good candidates. A fair number of these children will require speech-language services, and it may be less disruptive and more productive to provide intervention in the classroom via the classroom teacher. Language learning-disabled children may also profit from classroom intervention, as may preschool, kindergarten, and first-grade students. In effect, children with all types of communicative disorders may benefit from collaborative consultation if planning, implementation, and tracking are appropriate. With these as general guidelines, specific strategies for implementation of the consultant model are considered next.

In a previous discussion, trends in education were identified; included were educational reform and the REI. These modifications of the educational system were partially due to the recognition that not all students appeared to benefit from the system as it was. Additionally, it was found that educators were "re-discovering the role language proficiency plays in the educational process" (8). Unfortunately, these same educators may feel incompetent in addressing the issue and students, as a result, may be disadvantaged. According to Damico, the solution to the language issues may be the effective deployment of the SLP as a language consultant who can assist school personnel in addressing language concerns in special and regular education. To be effective, this consultative model must be carefully structured and implemented.

The consultative model must be designed to meet the needs of school personnel without burdening the SLP. Without prior consideration of this factor, a long-term commitment is not possible. According to Damico, decisions should be made regarding the amount of time the SLP will devote to consultation, the style of the interactions, the manner in which group interactions will be handled, and strategies to be employed to manage interactions.

With regard to time commitment, it has been found that the SLP serves the students best if both direct and consultative service are available. However, the time allocated for consultation should be at least one hour per day, preferably on a variable schedule. It is important that specific times be set aside for consultation rather than on an as-needed basis; random and infrequent consultations tend to be ineffective. Equally important is that the time specified for consultation be profitably spent. The SLP should maintain records of the time spent in consultation and evaluate these records regularly with the building principal or a supervisor. In the event that a scheduled consultation is canceled, the SLP should substitute classroom observation or a similar activity consistent with the consultation model.

Collaborative interaction is the style most effective in the consultative process. Rather than the SLP directing the interactions, both the teacher and SLP should "create a plan of action for addressing the student's particular language needs based on what is practical to implement in the classroom" (8). The SLP, therefore, should serve as a facilitator. In addition, the student's perspectives must be considered. "Both the SLP and teacher need to view the student in the situational context and observe not only the interactions of the student, but also the interactions of teachers, peers, and others in relation to the student" (8). Using this model, the student is not just the target of services; rather, his or her language needs are perceived in terms of both intrinsic and extrinsic factors. It may be that the student's language skills are not generally inferior; rather, it may be that the educational approach is inappropriate considering the child's abilities. Through collaborative observation and interaction, the SLP and teacher may be able to identify negative factors and modify the language approach.

Teachers and SLPs should not function alone in the consultative process. Parents, school support staff, and the student should be encouraged to participate through group interactions. One method of disseminating information about consultation to large numbers of interested parties may be through an inservice. Small informal meetings specific to subject areas, grade levels, or types of teachers should follow. When specific problems are to be addressed, an IEP meeting might be an appropriate forum. In general, although group meetings may be effective in sharing general information, "one-to-one interactions are recommended as the 'workhorse' of consultations" (8).

Finally, decisions must be made regarding the interactional strategies to be employed. Damico suggests that there are ten such strategies. One involves information giving; the SLP shares information with the teacher, and the latter may then use it to solve a problem. If the need is for more extensive information, then instruction is required. This strategy involves an intense learning experience that allows both participants to explore intervention principles and their theoretical framework. When intervention techniques are to be employed by the teacher, the SLP may choose to model the strategy. "The consultant may provide information and then actually model the approach with the teacher, providing opportunities for the teacher to imitate the technique with immediate feedback" (8). Demonstration is another useful strategy. Although it is similar to modeling, "demonstration attempts to achieve a deeper understanding of the clinical or classroom interventions by providing information on the underlying rationale and by actually working with a student over a period of time" (8). Although it is a time-consuming strategy, demonstration has the advantage of encouraging greater growth on the teacher's part.

Thus far, the strategies that have been described focus on behavioral changes; cognitive restructuring, on the other hand, is designed to modify teacher attitudes. Attitudinal adjustment will eventually lead to modifications in teacher behavior although this may be a long and complex process. In some cases, the SLP is called upon to mediate problems. In this consultative role, the SLP studies the problem, envisions possible solutions, and then attempts to mediate a resolution among the concerned parties. The SLP consultant may also serve as an intervention coordinator. This need may arise when several professionals are involved in intervention and when the SLP's expertise may place that professional in a leadership role.

Once any of the strategies outlined above has been implemented, the SLP may incorporate additional techniques. One of these, reinforcement, involves positive feedback to the teacher for appropriate behaviors (old, new, or modified) and no feedback when inappropriate behaviors are observed. Confrontation may also be incorporated. "It is viewed as an opportunity to demonstrate a positive, non-territorial approach to problem-solving, operating on the idea that people cooperate rather than compete" (8). In employing this strategy, an individual devises, presents, and defends a specific approach. Objections to the plan from others are to be viewed from a clinical, rather than a personal, perspective. It is felt that this strategy leads to sound decision making based on selection of the most effective plan without regard to the individual responsible for the plan; it is regarded as a team effort.

It may be seen, then, that the SLP as a consultant must prepare himself or herself to assume this role. It requires a time commitment, as well as a determination of style. Group interactions may be useful, and the SLP must be alert to opportunities for conducting these meetings. Finally, at least ten interactional strategies may be utilized during consultation. The selection of specific strategies "depends on the aim of the interaction, degree of rapport, type of intervention used, and [the] consultant's own effectiveness" (8).

As discussed previously, the effective consultation model must first be accepted in theory and must then be executed efficiently. Supervisors, administrators, and peers must be convinced that the consultation model is necessary and workable. To this end, the influence of language on educational performance and social interactions would be stressed. Once the need for language-based consultation is established, the SLP must demonstrate that he or she is the most capable person to serve as consultant. Credibility is established by virtue of the SLP's education and experience, as well as a consequence of "making the need for the consultative model known" (8). In addition, the SLP must present a concise written plan for consultation and must be prepared to delay implementation or move toward this goal in small increments once it has been accepted.

The actual implementation of the consultation model should begin with a dissemination of information focusing on the need for this alternative method of service delivery and the specific proposal. Concerns of the teachers should be anticipated and addressed during these inservice presentations. The SLP should also outline specific procedures that will be employed. If all this groundwork has been properly laid, it may be assumed that the process will be accepted and understood, and implementation may begin. As the SLP operates within the consultative model, it is important for that person to maintain a team perspective, respect the individual interactive styles of the other team members, employ terminology that is concise and clear, utilize demonstrations when appropriate, be open to the insights of others, and listen actively.

The role of language in the total educational process is receiving increased attention, and the school SLP must respond to the need to be involved; one method is through language consultation. Damico was general in his approach to consultation in the school setting; Fujiki and Brinton specifically address ways in which the SLP can assist the teacher as the latter deals with language-disordered children in the classroom (9).* Their suggestions are considered next.

Application with Language-Disordered Students

One of the problems involved in combined service delivery to language-disordered children is that the two service providers (the teacher and the SLP) have infrequent opportunities to interact. Like others, Fujiki and Brinton suggest that inservice presentations may be time efficient; small group discussions may also be useful. The former may be used to explain the nature of language in terms of content, form, and use; the SLP may also include information regarding the influence of such processing skills as attention, memory, and retrieval. With this background, the teacher is better prepared to discuss the specifics of an individual child's language problem. As a result of these discussions, it is hoped that the teacher will understand the child's linguistic strengths and weaknesses and be able to interact with the child more effectively.

Fujiki and Brinton also provide concrete suggestions for teachers; some of the advice is general and applies to interactions with normal and language-disordered children. For example, teachers are urged to "create a climate of emotional acceptance in the classroom that emphasizes communication" (9). Specific techniques to be employed by teachers when talking to children include modeling, expatiation, and expansion. The authors also provide suggestions to teachers on handling unintelligible utterances. Activities that may facilitate language learning in the classroom setting are suggested; included activities are classification, labeling, sequencing, and sentence completion tasks. Verbal absurdities may also be used. The authors stress that although these activities are designed to assist children with language disorders, many of them will also be beneficial to children without such problems. They also suggest that a teacher knowledgeable about language, language disorders, and the effect of a language problem on a specific child will modify his or her behavior and "make a language-disordered child's classroom much more pleasant and rewarding" (9).

The California Model

The utilization of the consultation model has not been limited to language-disordered children but has been employed in a variety of settings with a variety of intents. California, for example, provides consultative services to personnel working with nonverbal and bilingual populations (10). They also identify and define the roles of the diagnostic consultant; the community-based language, speech, and hearing consultant; and the mentor teacher consultant. In all these roles, the SLP is "a resource person and adviser to teachers, parents, administrators, and other support personnel in the schools" (10). Positive results have

---

*It should be noted that the authors, though describing a Type I consultation model, do not employ the term *consultation* in their article.

been reported from California when the consultation model has been applied; one such report came from The Fountain Valley School District (11). According to the report, improvements in test results and the attitudes of the students have occurred; moreover, the SLP has become "just another teacher" (11). It is predicted that the program of consultation will lower the dropout rate in the district.

At the outset, it was suggested that different utilization of terminology makes separation of consultation and collaboration difficult. The preceding paragraph was included to illustrate this point. California guidelines suggest that the primary function of the consultant was as a resource person and an advisor. The model "is intended to answer questions, provide information, present demonstrations, and facilitate access to resources" (11). However, the "success story" from Fountain Valley, California, describes a program in which the SLP works with communicatively disordered children in their classrooms rather than pulling them out for individual intervention. What has been described as successful employment of the consultation model does not seem to be consistent with the state's definition of consultation. It is no wonder that confusion exists.

Without belaboring the point further, perhaps it is best to summarize. Most of what has been included in this section falls under the category of consultation in its strictest sense. According to the opening definition, consultation refers to an exchange of information between an expert in a specific area (the SLP) and one with less expertise in that area (the teacher). In most cases, the consultant provides guidance, answers questions, and may demonstrate intervention strategies. Also, in most cases, on-going intervention is provided by the classroom teacher. Collaboration also involves these processes but usually encompasses additional components. The topic of collaboration is considered next.

The Collaboration Model

Collaboration may be defined as follows:

> *Individuals with equal status voluntarily participate in shared decision making to work toward a common goal, requiring the meaningful identification of a mutual goal, clarification that each individual's contribution during collaboration is equally valued, active participation on the part of each person, and the sharing of resources and accountability (12).*

It can be seen that this definition removes the disparity between the teacher and SLP in terms of status and emphasizes shared responsibility in terms of goal setting, planning, implementation, and accountability. Marvin offers a similar description of what she terms "collaborative consultation" (13). She describes it "as an interactive process between two or more professionals who have mutual respect, educational philosophies, and communication goals for targeted students" (13). The SLP and teacher also have clearly defined roles and responsibilities in the implementation of the intervention plan. The process, according to Marvin, is triadic; that is, "the SLP interacts with a teacher, who then acts as a mediator for change in a targeted student" (13). Using this model, the SLP and teacher are interdependent, and both are responsible if the child succeeds or fails.

The principles and behaviors underlying consultation are appropriately applied to collaboration. The professionals must have mutual respect and recognize that they share ownership of goals, intervention, and outcomes. The positive personal and professional ethics that characterize the SLP in other roles are equally essential in the collaborative process. Emphasized, as always, is the importance of active listening by both participants in collaboration. The similarities between consultation and collaboration are quite apparent; the differences might best be illustrated by describing programs that employ the collaborative model.

The Pennsylvania Programs

Gerber presented descriptions of a variety of models of interdisciplinary collaboration employed in Pennsylvania (14). Although not all these programs were conducted in school settings, those involving preschool and school-aged children are included since adaption to the public schools would be possible.

The first model was developed at Temple University to meet the needs of preschool children enrolled in Headstart programs. Responding to the expressed desires of the teachers to learn more about language, the university devised a course covering language and the preschool child; sixty Headstart teachers attended four, three-hour sessions weekly for a month. Lectures, outside readings, and videotaped demonstrations were included. "Each of the four class sessions included presentation of some theoretical information on a selected topic, followed by discussion about the application of this theory to principles of intervention" (14).

According to questionnaires completed by the participants at the completion of the course, the majority (forty-two) found the information appropriate, and forty-four of the sixty teachers felt that they needed no further training to implement the information in their classrooms. Unfortunately, no formal follow-up assessment of the effect of training on actual classroom instruction was conducted. However, SLP observations that Headstart teachers were making more language referrals suggested that the training was effective, if only by virtue of making teachers more aware of language and language disorders.

Another collaborative model was designed to solve the problem of screening preschool children in Philadelphia (14). The first phase of the program involved training teachers to administer a language screening test. In the second phase, "the goal of training teachers to provide language stimulation in the classroom was added" (14). Three SLPs provided instruction to groups of teachers regarding common error patterns revealed by the screening test results.

Videotapes of intervention strategies were followed by discussions of how these strategies could be employed in the classroom. Next, the SLP conducted language stimulation demonstrations in the classroom. The SLP demonstrated the importance of "increased talking to the children, decreased directives to and demands of the children, providing answers before asking questions, and developing hierarchies of task difficulty" (14). Although the teachers were responsive to SLP demonstrations, there appeared to be some reluctance on the part of the teachers to implement these activities themselves. One positive result was the heightened awareness of teachers of the importance of language and how it relates to learning and child development. These findings were consistent with those of the Headstart program.

Although the next collaboration model employed graduate students rather than certified SLPs, Gerber suggests that the format could be adapted to the school setting (14). Temple University received a request for assistance in dealing with nonstandard-speaking students in parochial schools. "The original goals of the program were to train nonstandard-speaking students to be functionally bidialectal and to foster elaboration of the use of language and as an aid to learning and academic performance" (14). Several components comprised the program: research into the attitudes of the teachers with regard to language differences, coursework, analysis of the speech and language patterns of the students, consultation with teachers and specialists, demonstrations with follow-up discussions, and implementation of procedures by teachers. The program was implemented for one semester. At the end of this period, a naive judge evaluated the experimental and control classrooms. "Teachers were rated for the quality of the communicative climate they established and for the incidence of the techniques employed in the program for the development of oral communication skills" (14). The evaluator ratings of the experimental classes with regard to communicative climate were more than twice as high as those of the control classrooms. Observed in the experimental rooms were 135 instances of facilitative techniques; only 26 were noted in the control classes. Objective evaluation of the program was not done, but the majority of participants felt that both students and teachers had benefited.

It may be debated that some components of the collaborative process appeared to be absent in the programs just described. However, at the beginning of this chapter, it was noted that the language of the original author (as opposed to the current author) would be maintained. Gerber, in her presentations, refers to the implementation of the collaborative model, hence, the inclusion of these programs.

"Into the Classroom"

One of the proponents of collaboration as a service delivery model is Simon (15). Along with Myrold-Gunyuz, Simon has prepared two instructional videotapes along with a manual describing the role of the SLP in collaboration. Although the curious reader will want to consult the original works, it is appropriate that some attention be given to them in this discussion.

Simon and Myrold-Gunyuz, employing the term *collaborative communication programming* (CCP), describe this as a shift in philosophy from a medical to an educational model. This modification was made necessary by the recent emphasis on viewing communication in situational context; in this case, the situation is the educational setting. Further, the least restrictive environment mandate of the EHA/IDEA and the REI (discussed earlier in this chapter) has contributed to the need for a change in service delivery. Finally, the authors submit that cost effectiveness is an issue; relatively few students benefit from pull-out intervention, and gains resulting from this delivery option sometimes do not generalize to the regular or special education setting. In order for SLPs to function effectively within the school setting, they must be aware of the literature from the educational field and cognizant of the skills of the classroom teacher. Only then can the SLP participate effectively as a team player in the educational setting.

The CCP, itself, recognizes that school is a language-based context. The theoretical rationale for the CCP incorporates socialinguistic research and the holistic language approach; the literature from the study of pragmatics is also taken into consideration. For example, it has been determined that levels of demands shift at various points in the educational process. Students who have been able to cope with content and curricular demands at a lower grade level may find themselves unable to cope as they advance. It is possible, however, to identify students at risk for making the necessary transitions; the educational model of service delivery is appropriate for these children and youth.

Although previous discussions have focused on promoting the consultative or collaborative model for service delivery and on overcoming resistance from administration and teachers, Simon and Myrold-Gunyuz confront a problem that must be resolved before the SLP attempts to sell the concept. That problem involves selling the SLP on the model. How does the SLP shift mentally from a self-perception as a "white coat SLP" accustomed to a medical model to an "educator SLP"? According to the authors, the metamorphosis is easy if the SLP is willing to spend time in various classrooms and observe how classrooms work. The SLP must be especially alert to the techniques employed by students who are successful classroom participants. Once the SLP has changed his or her self-image, that image may be projected to others. Only then is it possible to promote the CCP confidently.

Simon and Myrold-Gunyuz identify three collaborative models. The Communication-Enhancement Model allows the SLP to guest-teach in classrooms on a scheduled basis. The SLP first observes the students and analyzes the instructional and interactional demands of the class or the age group. The SLP then designs "lessons to help clarify 'the basics' underlying instruction and curriculum content" (15). In scripted lessons contained in their instructional manual, the authors target such goals as identifying parts of written language (educational vocabulary), distinguishing among confusing words (including homophones, homographs, and words with multiple meanings), and coping with the language of science and math. This model is appropriately used with students in resource rooms and those who are poor readers.

The Formula Model provides "an ongoing structure for collaborative partners" (15). A communication- or curriculum-related program is selected; this decision is made collaboratively. Once a core program has been chosen, "the 'formula' for collaborative communication programming permits the insertion of 'micro objectives' into a predictable structure" (15). This formula is implemented in three-week intervals. After deciding upon a communication goal for the period, the SLP works with one half of the class on language; the teacher employs the supplemental curriculum with the other group of students. The groups are switched for the second week. During the third week, the materials are reviewed with the teacher and SLP sharing the leadership role. An introduction week precedes the initiation of the program. A scripted lesson is provided to introduce the module, and sample lesson plans for the Formula Model are provided; warm-up communication plans are also included.

The last model presented by the authors is the Curriculum-Based Model. As its name suggests, the leadership for this strategy must be provided by the teacher, with the SLP providing language lessons in support of the specific curriculum units. "The format, based on three four-week curriculum units, is probably the most versatile of the three models presented in *Into the Classroom*" (15). The time involved with this model varies from once weekly to as little as one session per month. Again, the SLP must observe in the classroom to determine which language skills should be emphasized in order to help the students grasp the material. The authors suggest, for example, that if the teacher is presenting a unit on humor, the SLP might instruct the students on the role of multiple-meaning words in puns. The SLP has "two basic jobs in the curriculum-based model: provision of (1) preparatory activities and (2) clarification activities" (15). The first responsibility requires that the SLP and teacher attempt to anticipate student problems with the language demands of a given unit. Secondly, the SLP should "address those difficulties and help the students understand the objectives within a curriculum unit" (15). Again, the authors present both scripted and general lesson plans to illustrate the implementation of the Curriculum-Based Model.

Although some descriptions of the utilization of collaboration have been general, Simon and Myrold-Gunyuz presented collaboration models that are very concrete and specific. In addition, they confront the issue of the SLP's perception of himself or herself as an educational collaborator. Many speak of the changing expectations of SLPs, but these authors suggest ways in which SLPs can assume these changing roles confidently.

Other Types of Classroom Intervention

Not all classroom intervention strategies have been placed exclusively in either the consultation or collaborative camp. SLPs, for example, may enter the classroom to work with a specific child on a particular communicative disorder; in effect, the SLP is providing individual intervention within the classroom setting. Presumably, the student is less stigmatized than if he or she were pulled out and received services in the speech room. Also, presumably, the probability of carryover of newly acquired skills in this naturalistic environment is improved.

Other types of classroom intervention have been described in the literature. Anderson and Nelson integrated language intervention and education in an alternative classroom for adolescents (16). Larson and McKinley also discussed a continuum of services for this population, including classroom intervention (17). SLP involvement in classroom language services for mentally retarded students has been reported (18). Miller discussed various approaches to language intervention in the classroom; in addition to the SLP's role in consultation and as teacher of a self-contained classroom, she described team teaching and one-on-one classroom intervention (19). The SLP's responsibilities in curriculum-based intervention and in incorporating language and reading have also been described (20, 21).

SLPs, by virtue of their expertise in language, have additional opportunities for classroom intervention in schools in which the whole language philosophy is employed. "Whole language is a term, originated by Ken Goodman, that is used to designate an educational philosophy regarding language and how it should be taught" (22). In essence, the theory evolved from research in the area of normal oral language development and from what is known about natural language learning (22). Those who support this movement contend that children encounter reading and writing problems in school because the instructional approach is incorrect. "Children are taught language that has been broken up into small, abstract pieces with the expectation that if they master the parts they will eventually master the whole" (23). Proponents of the whole language approach believe that the opposite strategy facilitates learning; that is, language should move from the whole to the abstract pieces.

All language areas—including listening, speaking, reading, and writing—are emphasized in the whole language learning environment. Instead of teaching the students, classroom teachers act as facilitators. "Adults make it possible for children to become literate by providing a language-rich environment that enables them to learn the 'rules' of reading and writing through active engagement with that environment" (23). In addition, the various skills are viewed as developing concurrently rather than sequentially. For example, children in whole language classrooms are encouraged to write from the time they enter school; this "writing" may be in the form of a picture, but it is, nevertheless, an attempt to communicate something. This early emphasis on writing is not observed in a traditional classroom.

The SLP in schools that emphasize the whole language concept must be prepared to provide services that are consistent with this approach (23). Assessment strategies "should focus on meaning and the communicative process" (23). These strategies should not include tests that examine isolated language skills but should focus on total language functioning. Unfortunately, many districts will require the administration of specific tests, and the SLP is obligated to meet these requirements. Nevertheless, the assessment of holistic skills, rather than fragmented abilities, should be the basis for intervention.

As would be expected, whole language intervention should be functional, based on strengths, and incorporate all aspects of language (23). As would also be expected, such intervention should take place in the classroom, with either the teacher or SLP providing the services. Among the responsibilities of the SLP in whole language environments are the following: First, the SLP should assist the teacher in developing effective literacy environments. An additional function is to help children with the oral language skills. The SLP may also be involved in assisting students with written language; it is this responsibility that may be least comfortable for the SLP. However, resources are available to assist the SLP in becoming a competent participant in the whole language environment.

Summary

Current trends suggest that the school SLP is moving out of the therapy room and into the classroom; does this infer that uncharted waters are ahead? It is doubtful. Responsible SLPs have always attempted to provide functional intervention; activities, materials, and procedures were selected to assist the child in his or her communicative interactions in specific environments. Perhaps less functional intervention took place in the school setting; it may be that what happened in the speech room had little relevance to what was occurring in the classroom. Sammy Snake and the Angry Kitty undoubtedly contributed to this disassociation. Nevertheless, most SLPs attempted to find ways to make pull-out intervention meaningful.

Evidence exists that, in some cases, SLPs may increase the impact of intervention by altering service delivery. Although school SLPs have historically interacted with other personnel regarding specific children or groups of children, consultation and collaboration models now add structure to these interactions. Further, SLPs have guidelines for presenting the concepts of consultation and collaboration to administrators and teachers and have a variety of models from which to choose. Consultation and collaboration should not be viewed as the only approaches to intervention with communicatively disordered students, nor should they be employed as a convenience. Rather, these various models should be analyzed and applied when they meet the needs of the children.

Similar judgment is required for other types of classroom intervention strategies. For example, although the SLP may predict that service delivery to an individual child might best take place in the classroom, that student might consider this individual attention in the presence of peers quite stigmatizing. The whole language approach discussed previously has inherent flaws as well (24). Although it is important that the SLP be familiar with the continuum of services available, it is equally important that the professional be able to evaluate these options with respect to the needs of his or her clients.

The choice to treat collaboration and consultation in a separate chapter was not based on the quantity of information available (although more is being generated daily) but on the recent emphasis placed on these service delivery models. The reader is once again advised to remain abreast of current research in these areas.

Endnotes

1. S. Maxwell, "Public School Caucus: A Professional Partnership," *Asha* 28(1986): p. 26.

2. *Random House Dictionary of the English Language,* 1966.

3. M. Friend, "Putting Consultation into Context: Historical and Contemporary Perspectives," *RASE* 9(1988): pp. 7–13.

4. J. R. Jenkins, C. G. Pious, and M. Jewell, "Special Education and the Regular Education Initiative: Basic Assumptions," *Exceptional Children* 56(1990): pp. 479–491.

5. V. Phillips and L. McCullough, "Consultation-Based Programming: Instituting the Collaborative Ethic in Schools," *Exceptional Children* 56(1990): pp. 291–304.

6. L. Polsgrove and M. McNeil, "The Consultation Process: Research and Practice," *RASE* 10(1989): pp. 6–13, 20.

7. L. Frassinelli, K. Superior, and J. Meyers, "A Consultation Model for Speech and Language Intervention," *Asha* 25(1983): pp. 25–30.

8. J. S. Damico, "Addressing Language Concerns in the School: The SLP as Consultant," *Journal of Childhood Communication Disorders* 11(1987): pp. 17–40.

9. M. Fujiki and B. Brinton, "Supplementing Language Therapy: Working with the Classroom Teacher," *Language, Speech, and Hearing Services in Schools* 15(1984): pp. 98–109.

10. *Program Guidelines for Language, Speech and Hearing Specialists Providing Designated Instruction and Services,* California State Department of Education (1989).

11. "Consultation Model: One School District's Success Story," *Language, Speech, and Hearing Services in Schools* 21(1990): p. 63.

12. *Department of Special Education Administrative Bulletin,* Illinois State Board of Education (1990).

13. C. A. Marvin, "Consultation Services: Changing Roles for SLPs," *Journal of Childhood Communication Disorders* 11(1987): pp. 1–15.

14. A. Gerber, "Collaboration between SLPs and Educators: A Continuing Education Process," *Journal of Childhood Communication Disorders* 11(1987): pp. 107–123.

15. C. S. Simon and P. Myrold-Gunyuz, *Into the Classroom: The SLP in the Collaborative Role* (Tucson: Communication Skill Builders, 1990).

16. G. M. Anderson and N. W. Nelson, "Integrating Language Intervention and Education in an Alternate Adolescent Language Classroom," *Seminars in Speech and Language* 9(1988): pp. 341–353.

17. V. L. Larson and N. L. McKinley, *Communication Assessment and Intervention Strategies for Adolescents* (Eau Claire, WI: Thinking Publications, 1987).

18. M. A. O'Brien and T. S. O'Leary, "Evolving to the Classroom Model: Speech-Language Service for the Mentally Retarded," *Seminars in Speech and Language* 9(1988): pp. 355–366.

19. L. Miller, "Classroom-Based Language Intervention," *Language, Speech, and Hearing Services in Schools* 20(1989): pp. 153–169.

20. N. W. Nelson, "Curriculum-Based Language Assessment and Intervention," *Language, Speech, and Hearing Services in Schools* 20(1989): 170–184.

21. J. A. Norris, "Providing Language Remediation in the Classroom: An Integrated Language-to-Reading Intervention Method," *Language, Speech, and Hearing Services in Schools* 20(1989): pp. 205–218.

22. J. A. Norris, "Clinical Forum," *Language, Speech, and Hearing Services in Schools* 21(1990): p. 205.

23. M. E. Schory, "Whole Language and the Speech-Language Pathologist," *Language, Speech, and Hearing Services in Schools* 21(1990): pp. 206–211.

24. C. Chaney, "Evaluating the Whole Language Approach to Language Arts: The Pros and Cons," *Language, Speech, and Hearing Services in Schools* 21(1990): pp. 244–249.

8

Contemporary Issues

Introduction

*Potpourri, n. 4. any mixture, esp. of unrelated objects, subjects, etc.**

Perhaps every author reaches a point in preparing a text when issues remain, but these issues do not have clear relationships to each other. Such is the case with this chapter. Each item is important and must be addressed. For example, some school districts are experiencing a modification in payment for service delivery. Instead of employing full-time SLPs, the districts are contracting and paying for services through third-party reimbursement. That topic is considered initially. Marketing of speech-language services in the school setting is considered next. Augmentative communication systems are necessary with certain clients and a summary of the types of systems available is presented in the following section. Contemporary school SLPs also must be prepared to deal with individuals from birth to 21 years, who represent populations somewhat foreign to yesterday's clientele. Therefore, the communicative problems and needs of some of these special populations are discussed. Finally, the utilization of computers in administration, assessment, and intervention is considered.

Third-Party Payment

With the passage of PL 94-142, the door was opened to allow educational agencies to take advantage of third-party reimbursement. Specifically, the EHA/IDEA in Sec. 1414 (as well as in other sections) states that the local or state agency must provide assurance that federal funding will be used "to sup-

*From *The Random House Dictionary of the English Language,* 1966.

plement and, to the extent practicable, increase the level of State and local funds expended for the education of children with disabilities" (1). The key word in this sentence is "supplement"; local and state agencies were not relieved of this responsibility, nor were they to disregard other funding sources. Part H of the EHA/IDEA (PL 99-457), Sec. 1481, was more specific regarding funding. It states: "Nothing in this subchapter shall be construed to permit the State to reduce medical or other assistance available or to alter eligibility under title V of the Social Security Act (relating to maternal and child health) or title XIX of the Social Security Act (relating to medicaid for infants and toddlers with disabilities) within the State" (1). It further states that PL 99-457 funding should not be used when other public or private funding is available unless services would be delayed; in such cases, reimbursement is expected. The language of the laws, then, appeared to demand that state and local agencies take advantage of all funding opportunities.

According to Dublinske, many third-party payors stopped payment (2). Medicaid refused to cover services prescribed in IEPs, and there were questions about private policy coverage of prescribed services. As a result, the Department of Education, in 1980, put forth a policy interpretation that allowed private insurance payment for services. "However, the use of private insurance must be voluntary on the part of the insured and all costs or financial losses that may incur as a result of filing a claim for private insurance payment must be paid by the state or local education agency" (2). Included in the potential losses were premium increases and payment of deductibles.

Another important interpretation came on June 29, 1988. On that date, the U.S. Supreme Court ruled on the *Bowen* v. *Massachusetts* case (3). The Supreme Court upheld an earlier ruling by the U.S. Court of Appeals for the First Circuit, which required reimbursement to the state by Medicaid for the provision of services to mentally retarded individuals housed in intermediate care facilities. The services had been provided by both educational and mental health personnel. "By implication, this ruling supports the view that services provided under a handicapped student's IEP are not automatically excluded from Medicaid reimbursement" (3). According to Dublinske, "The ruling indicated also that determination of whether it is educational versus health should rest on the nature of the service and not the state's method of providing or administering the service" (2).

On July 1, 1988, PL 110-360, the Medicare Catastrophic Coverage Act of 1988, was signed by President Reagan. This legislation "bars Medicaid from refusing to pay for medical services covered under a state's plan and included in a handicapped child's IEP" (3). This law became effective January 1, 1989, and nationalized the Supreme Court decisions in *Bowen* v. *Massachusetts*. Medicaid-elligible children with disabilities, therefore, were the responsibility of state Medicaid for related services (including speech-language intervention if covered in the individual state plan); educational services must be provided and funded by state education agencies (2).

In light of these various decisions and interpretations, it is apparent that a number of sources may be tapped to provide educational and related services for children with disabilities. And states are just beginning to explore these funding possibilities even though they have been available for some fifteen years. A proper clearing house for investigating the issues involved in third-party and Medicaid funding was ASHA and the legislative council; the council charged the Committee on Governmental Affairs (CGA) to review these issues and generate policy and procedural guidelines. The discussion that follows is derived from unpublished written reports of the CGA deliberation (furnished by ASHA President Elect Ann Carey, July, 1990).

On July 7 and 8, 1990, the CGA met in Rockville, Maryland, and developed guidelines in two topic areas: (1) child and family issues and guidelines and (2) professional issues and guidelines (4). With regard to child and family issues, the CGA stressed the importance of informing the parent of the implications of third-party billing. That is, parents should be informed that third-party billing is voluntary and failure to give consent will not adversely affect the provision of services to the child. Parents should also be advised that this may be a risk to the cap on their lifetime health insurance. As written consent is obtained from parents, they should also be apprised of the projected amount of the annual bill submitted to the insurance company.

The committee also recognized that parents would probably be uninformed about third-party billing and recommended that SLPs be prepared to provide appropriate information. This requires that SLPs remain current regarding each individual state's policies. Addressing uniform quality of services, the CGA advised that SLPs and audiologists should meet the federal and state minimal standards requirement.

Among the professional issues discussed by the committee were documentation requirements, the logistics of billing, appropriate fees and charges, and the qualifications of service providers. In general, the CGA recommended that SLPs become knowledgeable about the various state and federal laws, insurance regulations, and professional liability. They concluded that:

> *Eligibility of schools to receive third party reimbursement does not change the mission of school based services, that is, to provide appropriate special education and related services. Availability of funding should not be interpreted as an incentive to expand services to children who are not eligible for special education and related services and whose services are not otherwise covered by other education funds (4).*

Among the resolutions sent forward to the legislative council by the CGA were those that (1) affirmed the rights of children to services regardless of funding source, service location, or consent of the parent for third-party billing; (2) recommended that service providers hold Certificates of Clinical Competence; (3) mandated uniform treatment standards; and (4) charged ASHA to continue to advocate for the rights of children with disabilities and for appropriate funding from both education and health care agencies.

During their deliberations, the CGA had access to information regarding state activity in third-party billing and to comments from members of the Council of School Supervisors, Coordinators, and Administrators of Language, Speech, and Hearing Services in Schools (CSSCALSHS) who had had experience with third-party billing. Information from the ASHA State Policy Workshop (June 1990) indicated that ten states were billing Medicaid or private insurance companies on at least a trial basis; other information suggested that as many as nineteen states are implementing billing (memorandum to the CGA from ASHA National Office, April 4, 1990). Some respondents indicated no knowledge of third-party billing or suggested that the issue was under consideration. Among the negative issues identified were professional liability, caseload management, payment for different service delivery models, and documentation requirements; in all, twenty-five negative issues were raised. Included in the nine possible benefits identified were additional funding, the possibility of better salaries, and upgrading of professional standards. Clearly, the majority of respondents did not view third-party billing positively.

The twenty CSSCALSHS respondents who returned surveys regarding their experiences with third-party billing were not much more enthusiastic (5). The respondents were asked to make pro and con statements, to identify positive and negative experiences, and to add comments. Four pro and thirteen con opinions were elicited; two responses indicated that the respondents could think of few or no positive aspects. Additional comments questioned the efficiency with regard to existing personnel, unhealthy competition between work sites, and the high costs of billing. In this instance, also, SLPs did not demonstrate confidence in the third-party payment system.

At this point, it is apparent that issues regarding the third-party billing system require resolution. It is doubtful that most SLPs are sufficiently knowledgeable about the ramifications of third-party billing to provide accurate information to parents. For example, private insurance premiums may increase, or the parents may be required to pay deductibles. As unethical as it may seem, the possibility also exists that parents who do not consent to billing may find services withheld from their children. Confidentiality of information may be at risk when districts are required to release materials to insurers. The question also arises about uniformity of service provision; will that be compromised based on who provides that service and which delivery system is utilized? Will direct services be provided to students with third-party insurance support and the collaborative model employed for students without such support? These and other issues must be considered as third-party funding is explored.

Despite the somewhat negative reviews given to third-party funding, it is too early to dismiss it as a viable financial resource. It required fifteen years for the possibilities of third-party funding to get recognized; it may take at least that long to make it efficient. As with other evolving practices, students must remain current with state and federal guidelines.

Marketing

For years, SLPs have attempted to explain to parents, colleagues, and administrators their roles in and contributions to the total educational program. For the most part, these attempts may have fallen on deaf ears as teachers and others continued to perceive the SLP as someone who came into the building two or three times a week, took small groups of children to a small room somewhere in the building, and played games. This was not the image that SLPs wanted to project. One wonders if teachers still view SLPs in that light.

A graduate student in speech-language pathology conducted a miniresearch project as a part of the requirements in an education course (6). Twelve teachers, with an average of almost twelve years experience, responded to questions such as the title of the "speech person," how important the SLP's work was, how often the SLP was in the building, and what coordination should exist between the SLP and classroom teacher. Although one respondent reported that the SLP held that title, (SLP), "speech therapist" was reported most often. Two thought the "speech person" was called the "speech teacher," and one offered the title "special district speech technologist."

On a scale of one to ten (ten being most important), the respondents' average response was nine, indicating that they considered the SLP's work to be important. Eight respondents were aware of the days the SLP was in the building, three did not know, and one wrote "when they need spelling and writing skill lessons." Finally, the teachers expressed a willingness to cooperate with the SLP; it should be noted that only two indicated that it was a "good" idea, whereas the remainder stated that it was "fine" or "ok." Their responses were not overenthusiastic. Whether the results of this poll can be generalized is questionable. However, it suggests that the profession should improve its image in the school setting, but how? The answer may be marketing.

Individuals in private practice have been in the business of marketing for years, but this concept is still somewhat novel to school SLPs. Granted, most SLPs have participated in marketing but have not been so bold as to use that terminology. Each time the SLP does an inservice for teachers or talks to the parents' organization or wears a "May is Better Hearing and Speech Month" badge marketing is taking place. Johns suggests that SLPs go even further in "Marketing in the Schools: A Class Act." (7). Marketing is based on product, price, place, and promotion; all the basic elements are present in the school setting.

With regard to the four P's of marketing, the *product* that the SLP has is a service. If the SLP desires to pursue more service delivery in one area (the classroom, for example), it is imperative to research the need and the potential benefits. These benefits may be felt by the teachers as well as the child.

In the school setting, the *price* involves time rather than money. A child who is pulled out of the classroom for intervention loses instructional time that needs to be compensated for at another time during the day. Both the child and the teacher are affected. The SLP must convince the teachers that whatever delivery option is offered will provide sufficient benefits to offset the time commitment.

Place, in a school marketing setting, refers to the physical area of service delivery. Is speech-language intervention best conducted in the SLP's room or in the classroom? This decision should also be based on the needs of all concerned, including the SLP, child, teacher, and administrator.

Promotion, according to Johns, is "what makes marketing fun" (7). In the case of the school SLP, promotion amounts to letting others know what the SLP does and can do. Inservice presentations may accomplish this, but the SLP should look for other forums as well. Johns refers to materials available from ASHA that could be employed by the school SLP in marketing.

Unlike teachers whose functions in the school setting are well understood, SLPs have always faced an uphill battle in acquainting others with their roles. Perhaps through active marketing techniques with emphasis on the four P's, SLPs will succeed in selling themselves and the services they are prepared to deliver.

Augmentative Communication

"My biggest handicap isn't having cerebral palsy. It is people's ignorance about the nonspeaking person" (8). This statement, made by a 36-year-old man, reflects the state of the art in terms of communication for the speechless when the speaker was in school. He did not have access to the augmentative devices available today. In this section, procedures for assisting the speechless are considered.

ASHA addressed the need to develop a position statement in 1980 (9). Included in the statement were clarification of terminology, historical information, specification of the SLP's roles with the nonspeaking population, and ethical considerations.

With regard to the group under consideration, the statement referred to them as "nonspeaking" even though some of the population may produce some speech. In essence, nonspeaking persons have insufficient communication to meet their needs. "Augmentative communication system" referred to the "total functional system of an individual which includes: 1) a communicative technique (or means to transmit an idea); 2) a symbol set or system (or means to represent an idea); and 3) Communication/Interaction Behavior (as necessary to have an idea received and understood)" (9). In the position statement, "unaided" indicated that no physical aids are required; thus, signs and gestures are employed. "Aided" referred to the utilization of devices or objects such as communication boards.

Historically, nonspeaking persons were either placed in programs designed to elicit speech as a means of communication or not treated when the acquisition of speech appeared to be an unreachable goal. Some enterprising SLPs developed communication boards or taught manual signs to their clients with disabilities. Today, a wide array of devices is available for implementation with severely involved persons, and the SLP should be cognizant of such devices and prepared to utilize them appropriately in intervention. Therefore, the SLP should be able to determine if a specific client requires an augmentative system and select such a system when the need exists. Not only must the nonspeaking person be taught to employ the system, but the SLP must also teach the client to "utilize the augmentative technique and symbol system in such a manner as to be able to achieve communicative competence as defined by the message-receiving community" (9). This included the training of individuals with whom the client interacts, as well as the client. Finally, the SLP must be involved with follow-up.

Clearly, SLPs must receive adequate preservice or inservice training in order to carry out their professional responsibilities in an ethical manner. They must be properly trained by those with credentials and experience to provide such instruction. When the SLP lacks this training, referral must be made to someone who is competent in the area of augmentative systems. Finally, SLPs involved with dispensing products must abide by the code of ethics with regard to clients requiring augmentative devices.

Since the position statement in the early 1980s, numerous publications have focused on communication for nonspeaking persons. A National Student Speech Language Hearing Association (NSSLHA) publication was devoted to alternative forms of communication (10). Included in the pamphlet was valuable information on assessment of severely impaired clients and strategies for intervention. Case histories illustrated the implementation of augmentative communication systems with actual clients. A special issue of *Language, Speech, and Hearing Services in Schools* contained a variety of articles on nonvocal communication (11). The utilization of augmentative systems with autistic, mentally and physically handicapped, and other nonspeaking children was highlighted. Musselwhite and St. Louis outlined both vocal and nonvocal communication programs for the severely handicapped (12). The appendix, including an annotated bibliography, a review of various programs, and assessment strategies, was no doubt a welcome publication for SLPs.

A comprehensive text on communication for nonspeaking individuals was authored by Silverman (13). He classified the augmentative strategies into three categories: gestural, gestural-assisted, and neuro-assisted. "The defining characteristic of a gestural strategy is that it requires no instrumentation, only patterned muscle gestures, or movements" (13). Two types of gestures are those that stand for concepts and those that represent linguistic units. American Sign Language, American Indian Hand Talk, and pantomime are considered gestural communication strategies. Since most people employ gestures normally, such techniques "are taught to severely communicatively impaired persons to enhance their abilities to transmit messages gesturally" (13).

Gestural-assisted techniques are defined by the presence of a "readout device" (or display) that is activated directly or indirectly by muscle gestures or movements. These are considered aided strategies. Gestural-assisted strategies may be categorized as follows: First, a "symbol set is a group of sensory (visual, auditory, or tactile) images, or signs, that suggest, or stand for, something else by reason of relationship (association) or convention" (13). Visual symbol sets include photographs and printed words; synthesized speech is an example of an auditory symbol set ,and Braille represents a tactile set.

A second type of gestural-assisted strategy includes those that are nonelectronic. Communication boards may be the most familiar examples of nonelectronic gestural-assisted strategies; however, strategies that include the manipulation of symbols to communicate are included. Drawn or written symbols that may be sequenced by the client in order to communicate are also exemplified as nonelectronic gestural-assisted strategies.

Electronic gestural-assisted devices comprise the third type of communication strategies. All these devices have three components: "switching mechanisms, control electronics, and displays" (13). The switching component allows the client to interface with the device; the switches may be activated by pressure (push switches), by changing the position of the switch in space "by a patterned movement (or gesture) of a body part," or by moving a body part within the field of the switch (proximity switches) (13). Other types of switches include pneumatic and sound-and-light-controlled devices.

Electronic gestural-assisted devices always have some sort of a display component. The display may appear on a television or computer screen, may be printed out on a typewriter or computer printer, or may be heard as synthesized speech. Other types of displays are also available. The interface between the switching device and the display component is completed through control electronics. The reader is referred to Silverman for a more technical explanation of electronic gestural-assisted strategies.

For individuals who are too severely impaired to use gestural-assisted strategies or electronic gestural-assisted devices, neuro-assisted strategies might be considered. "These aids differ from gestural-assisted ones intended to perform the same function in only one way: they are activated, or controlled, by electrical signals generated by the body rather than by muscle gestures or movements" (13). Usually, muscle action potentials are employed to activate the communication aid; however, it may be that brain waves could achieve the same results. The utilization of neuro-assisted strategies should be considered only when the other two communication strategies would be impossible.

Silverman suggests that careful consideration be given to a specific client's needs prior to determining which augmentative strategy would be most appropriate. There are six areas that must be explored. First, the cause of the disorder must be established. It is also necessary to determine the client's current method of communicating and his or her communicative needs. Assessment is also needed in the areas of inner, receptive, and expressive language. Finally, it must be decided which strategies the client would be capable of employing and which would be the most efficient in meeting his or her needs.

Assessment procedures are also being applied in school settings. Michigan has provided its SLPs with evaluation guidelines for severely handicapped children when augmentative communication may be necessary (14). Using Piaget's stages of cognitive development, a summary sheet profiles a given child's abilities in the areas of cognition, receptive and expressive language, and social development. This summary is then employed to arrive at placement and program decisions. If it is determined that an augmentative strategy is appropriate, a flowchart is utilized to decide what methods or devices will be required. The need for team assessment, decision making, and intervention is emphasized throughout the Michigan documents.

Silverman, too, stresses the interdisciplinary aspects of intervention with the speechless (13). He suggests that the team may include members of these professions: "audiology, clinical psychology, education, engineering, medicine, nursing, occupational therapy, optometry, physical therapy, social work, speech-language pathology, and vocational counseling" (13). Silverman considers the SLP to be the individual who should assemble and coordinate the team's efforts with regard to augmentative communication. In addition to the normal intervention procedures of goal setting, treatment implementation, and on-going assessment, it is also necessary to motivate the potential user of an augmentative system to accept that strategy. Of equal importance, is that others in the client's environment understand the need for the augmentative strategy and accept it as an alternative to speech. If this latter step is omitted, the individual with augmented communication will have no one with whom to communicate.

Like Musselwhite and St. Louis, Silverman includes an extensive bibliography, as well as sources of materials for those who may want to develop and employ augmentative strategies. School SLPs will undoubtedly be increasingly involved with augmentative communication and will require more knowledge than this brief summary has provided. This point is illustrated next.

Blackstone estimated that between 2.5 and 6 percent of children found in the schools are unintelligible and legally in need of augmentative and alternative communication (AAC) (15). Recognizing that this is a low-incidence but high-cost population, she suggests that this group requires specialized attention, and in some cases, the SLP is not a specialist. Therefore, a need exists for preparing SLPs for AAC. In addition, frequently excessive attention is given to the acquisition of AAC materials and devices (due to lack of SLP preparation), without equal attention being given to the utilization of these materials and devices. "Equipment and materials do not solve communication problems" (15). In an effort to make SLPs better informed about AAC and its utilization in the school setting, Blackstone reviews AAC application in various service delivery models.

The center-based model has been used more extensively for AAC programs than other delivery systems. The severely communicatively disordered student attends a center where assessments are conducted and intervention programs are prescribed. A Florida program exemplifies a center-based model. The Communication Systems Evaluation Center provides AAC services to children in the state; a team approach is employed. Although the professionals at the center are highly skilled, Blackstone cites disadvantages in the delivery model. First, children sometimes do not perform well in settings that are not familiar to them, especially when the professionals are also unfamiliar. Next, individuals who accompany the child to the site may not be involved in the assessment except as observers; these may be the same people who will be responsible for implementing the prescribed programs. Finally, local school personnel may fail to implement these programs. Although attempts have been made to neutralize these limitations, they have not met with total success.

Another service delivery model is that which is community based. Because it is important for AAC to be utilized within the child's home and school setting, this appears to be a more appropriate model. Blackstone outlines three methods of staffing a community-based model. If the district has a large population, it may determine that staff and equipment can be maintained within the district; in some cases, full-time AAC staff are employed, and equipment libraries are available. In smaller districts, part-time personnel may be involved; these AAC experts may also fulfill other roles. When the district's need for AAC services is inconsistent, it may be most cost effective to utilize a consultant's services. When consultative services are employed, it is important that the consultant be strategically located geographically. This allows for consultant involvement with teachers and parents, as well as with the child; it is this involvement that is crucial to the success of AAC utilization.

A final approach combines the community-based and center-based models. The collaborative model "recognizes the strengths and constraints of school personnel, AAC center teams, vendors and manufacturers, and consultants" (15). In other words, the effective collaborative model employs qualified community personnel and taps the expertise of AAC center professionals while involving equipment vendors and expert consultants. According to Blackstone, the collaborative model, when well defined and implemented, is the delivery system most consistent with the intent of legislation and most likely to meet all the child's needs.

In summary, augmentative communication strategies are becoming increasingly important, and the contemporary SLP must be knowledgeable about the appropriate utilization of these techniques. Because of the complexities of assessment and the technical aspects of the devices themselves, a multidisciplinary approach is required. Moreover, the involvement of all members of the child's environment is critical to the successful implementation of any augmentative system. Severely impaired school-aged children may be candidates for augmentative communication strategies, and school SLPs must be prepared to participate in the management of this special population of the speechless.

Special Populations

Multicultural Concerns

Once upon a time, the majority of U.S. citizens were Caucasian; today, about one-quarter of the population is a minority (16). In some areas of the country, more than 50 percent of the population are minorities. "Thus, minorities are the majority and majorities are the minority" (16). Further, it is anticipated that the number of minorities will increase at a rather steady rate. As this society becomes more pluralistic, SLPs are called upon to broaden their horizons with regard to multicultural issues. Cole outlines "eight multicultural imperatives that will affect the delivery of speech-language pathology and audiology services to multicultural populations" (16).

First, it may be predicted that 33 percent of the children served by SLPs will be minority students. Next, more minority children may be considered at risk by virtue of being economically disadvantaged. Further, minority children may present communicative disabilities related to different etiologies; for example, lead poisoning and sickle cell anemia may affect black children more than other populations. It is also difficult to establish norms among the diverse populations being seen today. Another complication is that different cultures view health-related matters in diverse ways; these differences could influence the perception of the disorder and whether or not intervention is accepted. As the following discussion reveals, cultural differences, if not recognized and understood, may create conflict in the clinical setting. The SLP must also recognize that certain minorities prefer intervention by persons other than the SLP; as Cole explained, some lay practitioners are believed to have spiritual connections and "a 'higher' credential than the Certificates of Clinical Competence" (16). Finally, SLPs must recognize that Hispanic, Asian, and Indian children may have a variety of languages; for example, approximately 250 different languages are found among American Indians.

These, then, are the multicultural imperatives outlined by Cole. In the following discussion, cultural and linguistic differences presented by Asian, black, Hispanic, and Indian children are considered. This is followed by a presentation of special problems encountered by SLPs with regard to two populations who, by virtue of their ages, are somewhat unfamiliar: infants and toddlers and adolescents. Also considered are students who have been abused and neglected, those with head injuries, and youths identified as behaviorally disordered.

Asian Students

SLPs, throughout the years, have become more competent in differentiating disorders from differences with regard to black English, and those from states with a high representation of Hispanics are learning to make the same distinctions with references to children for whom Spanish is the first language. Now, with an influx of students with Asian language backgrounds, SLPs must become as conversant with differences presented by this group of limited English proficient (LEP) students as those who are native speakers of Spanish.

Chen discussed both cultural and linguistic considerations with regard to Asian populations (17). Certain cultural influences should be understood by SLPs. First, Asians have strong family orientation and high regard for education. They do not, however, advertise their educational accomplishments since humility is considered an important virtue. Asian parents, though wanting their children to experience success in the United States, also want the children to retain their native language and culture. "These dual expectations, common in traditional Asian families, often result in conflict and confusion" (17).

In addition to these cultural differences, the SLP must keep pragmatic variations in mind. Asian children are expected to be quiet—"to be seen and not heard" (17). During intervention and in the classroom, these children may seem to be passive. Because extended families are important in the culture, titles for family members are quite specific; an older sister has a different title than a younger one. Nonverbal communication also differs. For example, children avoid eye contact with their teacher. (How often do SLPs direct children to "Look at me?") Displays of affection among Asians do not occur in public. Laughing or giggling by an Asian child may reflect only embarrassment, not amusement. Unless these pragmatic differences are understood by educators, serious misunderstandings may occur.

With regard to the speech differences presented by LEP students, they vary according to the child's native language. For example, consonant clusters do not occur in Vietnamese or Chinese, and children learning English may have difficulty acquiring these blends. In addition, many Asian languages are monosyllabic as opposed to the polysyllabic characteristics of English. Final consonants may present problems to LEP children since some Asian languages have a limited number of consonants that appear in the final position of words; Japanese words all end in vowels. The phonology of Asian languages also differs from English; some vowel and consonant productions may be difficult for these LEP students.

Morphology and syntax will also present problems for Asian speakers learning English. They may omit plural markers and confuse the order of questions. Although semantics in this literal sense will be troublesome, idioms present an even greater challenge. With college students, it is the latter problem that concerns them most. Although appropriate materials for dealing with speakers of Asian languages are limited, Cheng directs the reader to tests appropriate for use with this population and resources for additional study.

Black Students

The legitimacy of black English was established in 1979, in what is commonly known as the Ann Arbor decision (18). The plaintiffs in the case were the parents of children enrolled in the Martin Luther King Junior Elementary School of Ann Arbor, Michigan. They contended "that their children's use of 'Black English,' 'Black dialect,' or 'Black vernacular English' created a barrier to their learning to read in particular" (18). The parents were not asking that instruction be delivered in black English; rather, they petitioned "the court to require the Ann Arbor School Board to adopt a policy whereby teachers would become more sensitive to the 'home language' when teaching standard English to Black children" (18). In essence, they were asking that any language barriers that impeded instruction be removed. It was found that the teachers were rejecting the home language of the minority students, whether consciously or unconsciously. The judge ruled that the school board of Ann Arbor had failed to guide the teachers properly and ordered that the board "develop a plan to help teachers at King School identify speakers of Black English and to use that knowledge in teaching such children how to read standard English" (18).

As a result of the decision, teachers at King school were required to attend a minimum of twenty hours of inservice training. Teachers learned to be cognizant of linguistic features, dialectal differences (including black English), and instructional methods that might encourage code switching. Follow-up seminars were also required of the teachers. Unfortunately, little is known about the outcome of the teacher education program. According to Bountress, "while the plan had been implemented, no information had been gathered and disseminated which indicated whether teacher attitudes had been altered or pupil performance had been improved" (18). Therefore, the Ann Arbor decision may not have had the impact it could have had.

Bountress, in reviewing the decision, acknowledged that the "courts cannot legislate teacher sensitivity nor can they develop more effective educational programs" (18). Rather, impetus for educating teachers and SLPs should originate at the university level, with courses emphasizing the history and characteristics of social dialects. SLPs should learn to differentiate between dialects and disorders. Teachers might learn the value of exposing dialect-speaking children to code-switching black role models; this might motivate these children to recognize the value of standard English in the marketplace. Finally, according to Bountress, SLPs should learn to capitalize on their expertise in both normal and disordered speech and language, as well as their knowledge of dialectal differences, in order to work with dialect-speaking children. Or should they?

In 1982, in response to the Ann Arbor decision, as well as other significant events involving civil rights, the legislative council of ASHA issued a position paper on social dialects (19). It was the position of ASHA "that no dialectal variety of English is a disorder or a pathological form of speech or language" (19). Because standard English is used by mainstream society, however, speakers of nonstandard English may see an advantage to learning the former. In cases in which intervention is elective, the SLP may intervene. Therefore, in the school setting, the SLP may provide services to speakers of nonstandard English if it is requested by the child or adolescent and if it does not interfere with service delivery to communicatively disordered individuals. It is necessary for the SLP offering services to be knowledgeable about social and dialectal differences, however.

Taylor provided guidelines that might assist the SLP in understanding both the verbal and nonverbal aspects of black communication (20). For example, eye contact is not necessary to demonstrate attentiveness. Turn-taking rules are not always observed; the most assertive individual may control the conversation. With regard to question asking, directiveness may be construed as intrusive or harassing. Many of these differences in communication behavior may be observed in a school setting, and the SLP must be aware of their social appropriateness.

Linguistic variations also occur in social dialects. North Carolina guidelines provide school SLPs with examples of syntactic and phonological variations that may be expected (21). Identified as syntactic characteristics are differences in possession, negation, subject-verb agreement, pronomial opposition, and the use of "is" and "be." Phonological differences include the /θ/, /ð/, /r/, and /l/ phonemes; cluster reduction and devoicing of certain phonemes may also occur. Semantic variations may be anticipated as well.

As with all dialectal differences, only the well-informed SLP will be able to anticipate these variations and discriminate differences from disorders. Further, the school SLP should be aware that "the majority of Black English speakers are Black. However, due to social factors, not all Black individuals are Black English speakers" (19).

Hispanic Students

SLPs in certain regions of the United States have become familiar with interacting with children whose native language is Spanish. In fact, assessment tools have been modified to accommodate these students for whom English is a second language. In this brief discussion, cultural and linguistic characteristics of Hispanic children are considered, as well as efforts designed to meet their needs.

"Hispanic" refers to individuals of Spanish descent and origin (22). "Hispanics are members of a single culture group in the sense that they share a fairly common history, beginning with the Spanish conquest" (22). Although they have a common language, Hispanics actually represent many diverse subcultures. Some generalizations about Hispanics in the United States are possible, however. First, compared to the general population, "Hispanics are a significantly undereducated group" (22). As such, they are also underemployed and underpaid. With regard to family structure, nuclear Hispanic families are found in urban regions, with extended families more common in rural settings. The degree to which Hispanics have been assimilated or acculturated into U.S. society can best be viewed on a continuum; however, the majority seem to fall somewhere in the middle. Most, according to Ruis, are bicultural.

Taylor identified both verbal and nonverbal differences exhibited by Hispanics that might result in miscommunication (20). First, Hispanics may use hissing noises in order to gain attention; this may be interpreted by others as impolite. Hispanics may also touch each other as they converse, a practice not generally followed by other cultural groups. Eye contact may be regarded by Hispanics as "a challenge to authority" (20), whereas gaze aversion may signify attention and respect. Most Americans maintain some spatial distance while engaging in conversation. Hispanics, on the other hand, are physically close during interactions. Finally, Hispanics preface important conversations with "lengthy greetings, pleasantries, and other talk unrelated to the point of business" (20). Knowledgeable SLPs will make every effort to identify and respect these differences in Hispanic children and adolescents.

The production of certain phonemes will be difficult for Hispanic children. Among the consonants, $/\theta/$, $/v/$, $/z/$, and $/r/$ may present problems (23, 24). Dentalization of $/t/$ may also occur. Hispanic children also tend to use pure vowels for dipthongs or substitute one vowel for another, such as $/i/$ for $/I/$. Hispanics speak each syllable within a word carefully, with vowels retaining their identity. "This quality is the one sure to carry over into the English of every speaker of Spanish" (24).

The SLP working with Hispanic children must be prepared to deal with cultural characteristics and distinctive phonology, as well as the obvious linguistic differences. The state of Texas has been involved in servicing bilingual students for many years and has developed a number of programs for such children and adolescents. Austin employs seven bilingual SLPs and, when a student requires bilingual services, the child is transported to the school closest to his home where he can receive these services (25). In Dallas, when a Spanish-speaking child is determined to require intervention from a bilingual SLP, several options are available (26). The monolingual and bilingual SLPs may trade portions of their caseloads; this is termed a "trade-out." Another option is to utilize a bilingual student in intervention. Consultation from a bilingual SLP may also be employed until the child's proficiency in English has improved. Finally, the student may be provided services in the classroom, with the SLP consulting with the child's teacher. In Fort Worth, a bilingual diagnostic SLP assesses Spanish-speaking children (both preschool and school-age), assists in developing intervention strategies, and serves as a translator (27). Given the fact that a single bilingual diagnostic SLP is available to serve all Spanish-speaking preschoolers, and school-age children from 100 elementary, middle, and high schools, this must be one busy person.

Although the number of Hispanic SLPs who are members of ASHA continues to increase yearly, a similarly growing need to service bilingual and Spanish-speaking children exists (28). School SLPs must be prepared to provide culturally and linguistically appropriate services to these children. Those whose professional coursework has not offered opportunities for preparation for this population must seek out information through regional and national conferences.

Indian Students

Historically, Indian children have been an underserved population. Recognizing that language experiences are prerequisite to successful entry into school and hypothesizing that some Indian children lacked these experiences, Canadian researchers undertook a four-week summer enrichment program initiated in 1968 (29). According to the researchers, good spoken language is not stressed by Indians, and they lack facility in reading. Further, Indian children display many characteristics of educationally disadvantaged children in that they lack self-confidence, do not come from educationally stimulating environments, are frequently undernourished, and display reduced language skills. A program was devised by the researchers to attack these deficiencies.

Following the four-week program, which emphasized language development, posttests revealed that the eight preschoolers involved had made significant improvement. The study indicated "that within the language areas assessed, a dramatic improvement in disadvantaged children's verbal patterns can be realized in a short period of time by actively involving the children in specific and well planned language experiences" (29). The authors further suggested that, without direct intervention, it is doubtful that the children's language would have improved.

Berman (30) has reported on her experiences with Sioux Indian children in North Dakota. There she found families struggling with economic problems (the estimated mean annual income in 1972 was $3,000), social problems (including substandard housing, a high incidence of alcoholism, juvenile crime, and child neglect), medical problems, and educational problems. The educational difficulties were reflected by the fact that approximately 50 percent of all children who entered high school did not graduate. This was related, in part, to the utilization of traditional curricular programming; special education was not incorporated until 1971.

In August of 1972, Berman established her speech-language program. Supported by federal grant funding, she was able to order all the equipment she needed. Her speech room was located in a dormitory (many students lived in the dormitories during the week) near the elementary and high schools. Screening and teacher referrals revealed that 79 of the 763 children and adolescents required speech-language services. During the next year, Berman's caseload was reduced to thirty-three students. Only four of these students presented isolated articulatory disorders; the remainder had disorders of language in isolation or in combination with articulation. Three additional children had cleft palates, one was cerebral palsied, and six were mentally retarded. Berman also conducted language stimulation classes in the two kindergartens.

Discussing problems that she encountered, Berman mentioned that there was a space shortage. Additionally, the children involved in therapy did not practice outside of therapy sessions, and parental cooperation was poor. Berman rectified this situation in 1973 when she trained five aides to provide additional assistance to the children; four student aides were later trained to work with students with interdental lisps.

In reviewing the situation on the Standing Rock Sioux Reservation, Berman emphasized points made by Mickelson and Galloway. The Indian children were generally shy and quiet; they also exhibited reduced vocabularies. Although problems were encountered, the author indicated that the children did profit from intervention. She recommended that SLPs working with Indian children should have a good understanding of language disorders.

Although additional provision of services to Indian children may have occurred prior to 1975, the enactment of the EHA/IDEA had particular implications for these students. This previously underserved population is entitled to free appropriate educational services, including speech and language programming. SLPs who work with Indian children have an obligation to familiarize themselves with the culture and environment of the reservation, as well as with the expectations of Indian children and their parents. The ways in which these children differ from the average — like the characteristics that distinguish any culturally different children — must be taken into account in assessment, intervention, and referral.

Discussion

It is acknowledged that culturally different children do not always reside in inner cities or on reservations, nor are they always black, Indian, Hispanic, or of Asian descent. They may come also from rural areas or from the suburbs. Regardless of people's origins or places of residence, their educational, social, and vocational success tends to be related to their ability to conform to a "standard" pattern of behavior. If a child is unable to employ "standard" language patterns, he may be impeded in attaining such success.

The responsibilities of the SLP in working with children displaying culturally different communication patterns have been defined by ASHA and the EHA/IDEA. If the child displays differences, rather than disorders, intervention is not warranted; the key is to discriminate between the two. If, on the other hand, the student wishes to achieve standard communication skills, the SLP may become involved. When disorders are present, appropriate goals must be established; the student and parents should be involved in setting these goals and objectives. Intervention strategies should be adapted to the needs and motivations of the students. Finally, the SLP dealing with communicatively disordered children must be aware of referral opportunities. To suggest that parents of such a student take their child to an otolaryngologist might produce negative results; to refer them to a free clinic for equivalent services would probably be more useful.

Infants and Toddlers

As noted frequently throughout this text, students in training gain clinical experience working primarily with preschool and school-age children. Less familiar are the problems presented by infants and toddlers and adolescents. ASHA has attempted to fill this void with regard to infants and toddlers with a series of assessment and intervention workshops (31). Participants in the workshops come away with a great deal of knowledge and every SLP's dream, a notebook full of hand-outs. The suggestions for intervention with infants and toddlers that follow come from that notebook.

Although intervention for this population may be delivered using a variety of service models, the concern here is on school-based services. Caufal prepared a report on such a delivery system in Nebraska (31). In 1979, that state mandated the provision of services to the zero to 2-years-of-age population; at that point, the intent was to provide services only to infants and toddlers presenting the most severe problems. The number of children served by the program increased from approximately 100 (1979) to 450 (1986). Of this number, 15 percent presented communicative disorders.

The delivery model of choice in the majority of cases was the home-based model. It was reported that mothers involved in this model had more positive attitudes, asked more questions, and followed through with the programs more completely than when other models (including the school based) were employed. This may have been the result of being in a familiar environment since location appeared to be an important variable. The Omaha Public Schools implemented an intervention program for children under 3 years. Following assessment of the infants and toddlers, the SLP provided consultative or direct services as a member of the intervention team. The services were either related (when the child had other handicapping conditions) or primary (when the most serious problem was in the area of communication). Even though school personnel provided the services, it was possible to implement the program using a home-based or combined model.

In considering the preparation of personnel to work with this population, it was noted that SLPs require "substantial training and experience" in several areas (31). These include infant vocalization, infant development and learning theories, collaboration with parents, and a variety of service delivery models. In addition, SLPs should have some exposure to genetics, augmentative communication systems, therapies delivered by other professionals, pharmacology, and counseling approaches.

Rossetti also discussed intervention with infants and toddlers in school settings (32). He suggests that the SLP, after becoming familiar with all the legal ramifications concerning service delivery to this population, "begin to educate those in decision-making positions" (32). The needs of these children and their potential problems should be stressed. Further, the SLP must inform others of the effect that early intervention might have in lessening developmental problems; this instruction might include audiovisual presentations. Parents should also be included as advocates for early intervention. These "parents of young children with known mental and physical disabilities are aware of the difficulty of meeting the needs of their children" (32); therefore, they would be most convincing in their advocacy of early intervention.

Some parents, however, require education about the needs of their at-risk children. Rossetti suggests that media presentations, as well as speaking opportunities, be employed by the SLP. The parents, themselves, should be given developmental checklists with which to compare their own child's development.

With regard to specific programs for infants and toddlers, Rossetti cites a Missouri project that targeted pregnant mothers and followed the family for three years. Experts in child development met with the families of 380 children twice each month until the infants were 5 months old; one meeting was held in the home and one at school. Thereafter, the teachers visited the homes once each month, while parent groups met every six weeks. When these children were tested at 3 years of age, their scores exceeded those of other 3-year-olds in both the mental and language areas. Rossetti considers the results of this study of early intervention to be most significant.

Adolescents

An age-group that has not received much attention in the past is that comprised of adolescents. A notable exception to this neglect is found in works by Larson and McKinley (33, 34). They explain that this population has not been served in the school setting for a number of reasons. First, SLPs have not been trained to work with these students; now that the law requires that service be provided to adolescents, that void should be filled. Additionally, educators have incorrectly assumed that early intervention is the most appropriate strategy; unfortunately, some speech and language problems may not be identified until "the student faces the more rigorous demands of junior and senior high school" (33). Moreover, SLPs have not been aware of normal adolescent development, assessment procedures based on that development, or strategies appropriately employed with adolescents. Finally, the techniques, materials, and delivery models familiar to most SLPs are not applicable to older students.

To remedy these deficiencies, McKinley and Larson outline a delivery system comprising four components. Initially, the SLP must disseminate information to school personnel regarding speech-language services; students must also be informed of availability of assistance. This marketing strategy should include information regarding "the interrelationship of communication with academic and social performance," "the expectations for cognition and oral communication," and "the developmental nature of language and communication skills" (33). Particular emphasis should be placed on the interactions among listening, reading, writing, and speaking.

The second component is the identification of adolescents who may require services. If the first component—information dissemination—has been successfully accomplished, this step will be more easily done. Referrals from teachers, as well as screenings, should be employed in identification.

Next come evaluations and, when indicated, program planning. Both formal tests and language-sampling techniques should be used to pinpoint problems. Specifically, SLPs will be concerned with disorders in the areas of cognition, comprehension and production of linguistic features, appropriateness of discourse, nonverbal communication, and survival language (34). With regard to planning for intervention, the youth should have input in establishing priorities and objectives. The student must also recognize that he or she shares the responsibility for his or her progress (or lack thereof). "If the adolescent does not want responsibility, denies the existence of a problem, or remains unmotivated to change, the authors recommend that the adolescent not be forced into intervention services, if indeed, force is even possible with this age group" (33).

Intervention is the final component of the delivery model. The authors suggest that three principles be applied in intervention regardless of the specific model selected. First, the SLP should determine the state of the adolescent's development. Is the youth in early, middle, or late adolescence? Next, the SLP should recognize that counseling will constitute as much as half of the intervention. Finally, pragmatics must receive attention. To facilitate effective intervention, McKinley and Larson suggest that SLPs work within existing time modules and employ group intervention. Language intervention that receives course credit also is appropriate.

As noted at the outset of this section, the dearth of information available to SLPs working with adolescents is beginning to be filled. Larson and McKinley deserve a great deal of credit for bringing the attention of SLPs to this neglected population. The reader is encouraged to refer to their text for additional information on working with adolescents.

Abused and Neglected Students

In recent years, the reported prevalence of child abuse and neglect has increased. There is little doubt that instances of abuse and neglect have existed in the past, but it was not always reported. The author recalls many children in her public school caseload who appeared to be neglected; that is, there were visible signs that caretakers were not taking care of the children's physical needs. Others appeared to be emotionally unsupported as well. Evidence of abuse was sometimes apparent; there were children who repeatedly came to school bearing unexplained cuts and bruises. One little girl who displayed signs of neglect, including a mouth full of decaying teeth, also had marks on her arms that bore a strong resemblance to cigarette burns. Although neglect and abuse were strongly suspected, the school staff had no satisfactory legal means of reporting the abuse. Today, school personnel are mandated reporters although not all reporters have had satisfactory responses from child-protection agencies. Nevertheless, in mentally reviewing the children who might have been abused or neglected, they consistently displayed language disorders, ranging from mild to severe. This recollection is consistent with what researchers are learning through controlled investigations. Fox, Long, and Langlois conducted one such study (35).

Initially, the researchers distinguished between "abuse" and "neglect"; the former refers to a willful action by the caretaker that harms the child either directly or indirectly. Neglect, on the other hand, is harm done to the child through inattentiveness although that inattentiveness may be deliberate. Although ambiguity in the use of these terms is apparent in the literature, the intent of the action should distinguish between them. "Abuse," therefore, is regarded by the researchers as intentional, whereas "neglect" is the result of caregiver inattentiveness.

In reviewing the literature on child abuse and neglect, the authors discussed studies that focused on the attributes of the abusive parents and those that concerned attributes of the abused child. Parents who abuse their children have been described as immature, poorly socialized, and emotionally unstable. Although most are categorized as low, socioeconomically, abusive parents are found in every socioeconomic group. Many abusive parents were also abused as children.

With regard to characteristics of abused children, boys outnumber girls;

the majority of abused children are between the ages of 1 and 5. Children may be at risk when they display medical or developmental disorders, making them difficult to manage; the mother–child relationship has been disrupted; the parents have unreasonable expectations for the child; and the child internalizes the "bad" perceptions of the parents and behaves in a manner consistent with this label. It should be noted that some of these factors might also contribute to language learning problems.

Specific research regarding speech and language problems among abused and neglected children has indicated that abused children have impaired expressive skills. One study found that abused children may talk but do not necessarily communicate or use mature linguistic structure. It was learned that neglected children appeared to be more depressed in the area of language than abused children.

Fox, Long, and Langlois isolated the linguistic skill of comprehension for this research. The *Peabody Picture Vocabulary Test* (PPVT-R), the *Token Test for Children* (TTC), and the *Miller-Yoder Language Comprehension Test* (MYLCT) were administered to twenty-eight children; the age range was 3 to 8. Ten of the children had been abused, with the other eighteen considered to have been generally or severely neglected. Ten nonabused children served as the control group.

On both the PPVT-R and the MYLCT, the control group's mean scores were highest; in descending order were the scores of the generally neglected children, the abused children, and the severely neglected group. TTC mean scores were highest for the generally neglected children, followed by the control, abused, and severely neglected children.

In reviewing the results of this study, it is apparent that severe neglect impacts more on language comprehension than abuse although abused children scored below the control group. General neglect did have consistent effects on the scores of children involved in this study. The authors conceded that generalizations may not be drawn based on this study. However, given the relationship of the factors thought to be involved in both child abuse and neglect and language disorders, further investigation is warranted.

Sparks, acknowledging that additional study is required, suggests that researchers contemplating such work keep five points in mind (36). First, matched (control) groups must be employed "to determine that a given speech or language problem is the result of maltreatment, rather than social class" (36). Next, studies should be longitudinal so that the long-term effects of abuse and neglect are measured. The interaction of multiple variables over time must be considered; prospective research should be conducted after these variables are defined. Sparks cites a study in which the subjects were selected prenatally, according to their mothers' potentials for abuse or neglect. That is, certain behavior displayed by the mothers led the researchers to predict that these mothers might eventually abuse their children. This is the type of research advocated by Sparks. Finally, researchers must apply statistical analysis procedures that account for the numerous variables across time.

School SLPs may not be involved in conducting the type of research advocated by Sparks, but they will undoubtedly work with children who have been neglected or abused. SLPs must be alert to evidence of physical, sexual, or emotional abuse and report these suspicions to the designated school official; such reporting is not an option, it is a mandate. SLPs working with children who are known to have been abused or neglected should note the patterns of language or speech disorders displayed by these children and share those observations with colleagues. Only through this exchange of information, as well as well-controlled research, will the total impact of mistreatment on speech and language be understood.

Head-Injured Students

Sometimes, as the result of abuse or accidental occurrences, school-aged children and adolescents present themselves as closed head injured (CHI) students, and the school SLP must be prepared to provide appropriate speech-language services to them. De Pompei and Blosser have attempted to orient SLPs to the types of problems associated with CHI and the means by which the SLP can assist the CHI child in reentering the school setting (37).

Individuals with CHI have experienced diffuse brain damage due to some sort of blow. As a result, they may experience physical, cognitive, behavioral, perceptual, and social problems, as well as disorders in communication. With regard to communication, "problems can occur in language, articulation, word-finding (anomie), reading, writing, computation, abstraction" (37). Blosser and De Pompei have developed a worksheet that medical and educational personnel may employ for charting the behaviors of the CHI child in these areas.

Once the CHI child is ready to reenter school, it is not uncommon for him or her to be returned to the same class he or she was in prior to the accident. Given the possible extent of his or her disabilities, success in that setting is unlikely. Even though teachers, administrators, and special education personnel are more familiar with a variety of disabling conditions than they were prior to the EHA, "educators are unfamiliar with the problems associated with head injury and strategies for teaching them" (37). CHI children differ from other students with disabilities in that many had had positive experiences in school prior to the accident; learning-disabled and multiply handicapped students have not experienced such success. The CHI student is also inconsistent in his or her performance and has difficulty with integration, association, and structure. In order to create an educational environment in which the CHI student may experience success, these distinctions and variables must be taken into consideration. Further, a team approach is required in order to implement an appropriate educational plan.

The SLP must participate actively as an educational planning team member. That person should be able to provide expertise in the areas of the neurophysiology involved in language, evaluation procedures, linguistic subtleties, pragmatic factors, and the impact of communication on learning. The SLP should also have knowledge of the functioning of the educational system.

The transition between the rehabilitation facility and educational setting is extremely important and requires cooperation between personnel in both settings. De Pompei and Blosser specify procedures to be followed by the SLP who represents the rehabilitation facility and contacts school personnel, as well as procedures to be followed by the school SLP when a CHI referral is received. Topics that must be considered during the student's IEP conference are also presented. Included are procedures that the school should follow with regard to grading, behavioral control, and coordination of the rehabilitation program. The authors also outline techniques that will assist the CHI student in the classroom. Generally, educators are encouraged to minimize ambiguity and distraction and maximize structure, clarity, and redundancy. The reader is encouraged to consult De Pompei and Blosser's contributions in the area of CHI for additional guidelines.

Like abused and neglected children, CHI students will be seen more frequently in the school setting. Individuals who might have died as the result of injuries they had sustained are now surviving, thanks to 911 numbers and expedient medical care. It is imperative that the school SLPs be prepared to meet the challenges presented by the CHI population.

Behaviorally Disordered Students

For many years, SLPs have dealt with children and adolescents who displayed concomitant disorders of behavior and communication. As noted in the Preface, the current author suspected that some relationships between the two deviant behaviors existed and used this question as the basis for her doctoral research. Tests of language, articulation, and hearing were administered to 119 male juvenile delinquents incarcerated in the Missouri Training School for Boys (38). Clinical judgments were made regarding voice and fluency. Only nineteen of the youths demonstrated communicative abilities that were within the normal range. Among the 84 percent with communicative disorders, the predominant disability was in the area of language. This type of disorder was found in 50 percent of the boys, and an additional forty-one presented disordered language and concomitant problems. Although this study was limited to a single state institution, the results did suggest that male adolescents with behavior problems as defined by law experienced more communicative disorders than would be expected in a similar group of nonincarcerated adolescents.

Prizant et al. also considered the relationship between communicative and behavioral and emotional disorders, not only in adolescents but also in children (39). The authors suggest that many have noted that children with communicative disorders sometimes display aberrant behavior but that frequently researchers have looked for a cause-effect relationship. Perhaps it is wisest to understand the various psychiatric disorders, as well as the communicative disorders that may coexist, rather than attempt to establish which caused which.

With regard to psychiatric disorders, they are classified according to a rather complex system identified as DSM III-R (39). Included in the DSM III-R are five axes. Axis I includes clinical syndromes, such as schizophrenia; Axis II includes developmental disorders, including mental retardation. Personality disorders are considered a part of Axis II, and physical disorders and conditions, including cerebral palsy, are classified under Axis III. The severity of psychosocial stressors is identified by Axis IV ratings, and Axis V is a global assessment of functioning on a scale of 1–90, where 1 is the most severe. Even this brief review of the various psychiatric classifications suggests that communicative disorders may be involved in many of the axes. For example, children and adolescents with cerebral palsy or who are developmentally disabled are prone to a variety of speech, language, and hearing impairments. According to Prizant et al., the fact that some psychiatric diagnoses have speech and language characteristics "specific to the overall diagnosis . . . poses a challenge to differential diagnosis between communicative disorders and psychiatric disorders" (39).

After reviewing the research on the relationship between communication disorders and behavioral disorders, the types of psychiatric disorders presented by communicatively disordered children and adolescents, and models of causality, Prizant et al. address the implications for SLPs. The first consideration is the area of assessment and differential diagnosis. Although it may be possible to differentiate some communicative disorders from psychiatric problems with ease, in many cases it is necessary to be "concerned with the degree of contribution of each on a child's daily functioning" (39). This requires a detailed case history and careful observation of the child or adolescent, not only by the SLP but by a variety of professionals. Obviously, a multidisciplinary approach is necessary. Through careful assessment, it may be possible to make an accurate diagnosis; a complicating factor, however, is that many of the assessment tools used by psychiatrists are language based. All the professionals must be made aware of the level of language functioning of the subject because "deviant language skills could lead to a misinterpretation of information a psychotherapist would obtain during remediation" (39).

Intervention with the child or adolescent identified as presenting concomitant communicative and behavioral disorders must also be multidisciplinary. The first responsibility of the SLP is to have an awareness of the potential that the speech-language-impaired children whom they see may be experiencing emotional or behavioral problems. Further, the SLP must be cognizant of appropriate referral sources. Through the intervention process, the SLP must be alert to positive or negative changes in the child's behavior, as well as his or her progress in intervention. "Tracking changes in both communication abilities and emotional and behavioral problems with the assistance of mental health professionals could provide important information about the effect of improvement in communication on the emotional or behavioral problems" (39). A final responsibility of the SLP is to inform other professionals about communicative disorders and their potential relationship with other aspects of behavior.

With regard to the SLP working in the school setting, Prizant et al. warn that children with coexisting disorders of communication and behavior are sometimes overlooked by the SLP. This is the result of early classification of the child as behaviorally or emotionally disordered. "Because of this tendency to separate issues of behavior from communication, it is not uncommon for a child's communicative needs to be overlooked if priority is on dealing with emotional or behavioral problems" (39). Once again, it is imperative that the SLP inform other professionals about the possible coexistence of such disabilities and participate in the multidisciplinary approach to intervention.

Anyone who has dealt with communicatively disordered children or those displaying emotional or behavioral disturbances would concur with the importance of determining what relationships exist. The author's early observations and the results of her research with juvenile delinquents bear this out. These findings were reinforced by more recent work with children and adolescents displaying behavioral disorders in attendance at a private school. The majority of these students displayed pragmatic disorders, with a large number presenting various combinations of related linguistic deficits. Although articulatory problems were evidenced by some students, very rarely were these the focus of intervention. One young man who stuttered attempted suicide without success; the role that stuttering played in his depression is unclear. Other students with communicative disorders directed their aggressive tendencies toward others, including the SLP, both verbally and physically. At the other end of the spectrum were those students who were withdrawn and noncommunicative. Because SLPs may anticipate seeing increasing numbers of behaviorally and emotionally disordered students in their caseloads, sensitivity to potential problems is required. In addition, SLPs should maintain professional currency on the subject through the literature and attendance at appropriate conferences.

The Utilization of Computers

Introduction

Software now exists for the SLP in the areas of assessment, intervention, and reporting, and professionals are responding to these new opportunities in a positive manner. That was not always the case, however. A 1986 survey of directors of special education revealed that only 37 percent of the SLPs in 250 school districts employed microcomputers (40). This compared to computer usage by 92 percent of learning-disabled teachers, 87 percent of the teachers working with mentally handicapped children, and 75 percent of those servicing emotionally disturbed youth. Another survey conducted that year yielded dissimilar results. Questionnaires were sent to 4,000 ASHA members; one of the questions asked concerned computer usage (41). Sixty-seven percent, or 2,628 persons, responded. Of those respondents employed in the school setting, approximately 25 percent indicated that they used computers occasionally (less than once each month), and an additional 10 percent used computers at least once each month. Approximately 15 percent reported frequent computer usage. In all, 49.5 percent of the school SLPs utilized the computer in some aspect of their professional functioning. Only those in residential health settings used computers with less frequency.

Houle attempted to determine if certain factors characterized school SLPs who used computers in their employment settings (42). Of a possible 600 respondents, 274 completed the fourteen-question computer usage survey. The majority were female (92.7 percent), Caucasian (92 percent) individuals between the ages of 30 and 39 years; over 90 percent of the respondents held the master's degree. As would be expected, those SLPs who were frequent users were employed by districts that funded software and hardware specific to their needs. They also "saw computers as desirable professional tools and viewed early computer training in a positive light" (42). Those individuals who did not consider themselves to be frequent users apparently have the ability to use computers, but "philosophical, psychological, or sociological factors may induce them to continue to resist computerization" (42).

This perceived underuse of technology in the school setting is not new; historically, school SLPs have employed equipment sparingly. According to Palin and Cohen, "the most pervasive and popular implementation of technology by speech-language pathologists has been in the area of augmentative communcation" (43). In other areas, however, SLPs have remained somewhat inactive with regard to technological advances despite the increasing quantity of software available for specific purposes. An ASHA computer conference attempted to determine why a gap exists between reported interest in computer application and the actual use of computers by SLPs. One factor appeared to be a "lack of quality application software" (43). Dissemination of information regarding software application may also be ineffective. In addition, SLPs may be uncertain about methods of employing this technology within specific work settings. Finally, both a fear of computers and lack of knowledge about computers may prevent school SLPs from entering the computer age. Schetz and Sheese propose that other factors may be operative (44). They suggest that "the work conditions of this population (in the school setting) discourage the application of computer technology" (44). They feel that travel, limited financial resources, and the large number of clients seen by the school SLP are not perceived as factors conducive to the utilization of computers. It may also be that information concerning computer applications is too general to be useful. In the next sections, some of these concerns are addressed.

The Basics

In order to approach computers fearlessly, one must have some general idea of basic terminology and functions. The following limited and simplified explanation is not intended to make the reader a computer expert; rather, it may serve to take some of the mystery out of the computer and create an interest in seeking additional information.

Although any owner's manual would provide similar information, the *Apple II GS Owner's Reference* offers the following definitions and explanations (45). The term *hardware* refers to the various components that make up the computer system. The term applies to the computer itself, the keyboard, the mouse, cords, external switches, and so forth. To understand the computer, other terms are important. A major component of the computer is the main circuit board. The circuit board contains numerous integrated circuits (commonly called chips). One of these circuits is called the central processing unit (CPU) or the microprocessor. The CPU is often referred to as the "brain" of the computer. Devices are also needed in order to communicate information and data into the computer system, to display the information that is in the system, to store the input, and to print the information and data. The information printed is referred to as hardcopy. The hardware that enables the user to do these functions are called peripheral devices. This term is used because these devices exist upon the periphery or outside the basic system. A few of these devices are the keyboard, the mouse, and the disk drive.

The computer cannot function alone. It needs directions and input to perform the necessary functions. This is done by means of the programs or software. Software can be separated into two separate types. System software are programs that are concerned with the integral processes that the computer needs to function. Application software are the programs concerned with allowing the computer to complete specific functions. These functions can include word processing, the generation of class lists or IEPs, test scoring, and other functions too numerous to mention.

The software of the computer is usually stored and saved on disks. A startup disk contains the information necessary for the computer to run. A data disk contains no information for the computer. It is merely a place where information is stored.

Firmware refers to the programs that are a part of the computer's permanent memory. The permanent computer memory is called ROM (read-only memory). This information is protected so that it cannot be altered or changed because it is necessary to the workings of the computer system. RAM (random-access memory) is the temporary memory that is lost when the computer is shut down. It is important to remember that information placed in the computer is in RAM and must be saved on a disk before the system is shut down. If not saved on a disk, the information can be lost forever. There is nothing more tragic than entering an important document and suddenly realizing it is erased. It is also a good practice to save data as you go along and keep backup copies of all system disks and important data disks.

Computer information is translated and stored in a special computer language. All the characters on the keyboard are understood by the computer as varied combinations of ones and zeros. This system of language is referred to as the binary system. In most computers, memory is stored in bits; the term *byte* refers to 8 bits. A byte can then be said to store one single character of the computer, such as one letter, one number, or one sign. Further, 1024 bytes equal a kilobyte, and 1024 kilobytes equal a megabyte. This term is important because it refers to the amount of computer memory available.

With this basic introduction to computer hardware, it is now necessary to move to the next step: software.

Software

Factors that seem to contribute to the underutilization of computers in the school setting are first locating appropriate software and then finding that the software is within financial reason. Many individuals are not aware of the various sources of software available and the costs. Also, they are uncertain as to how to select the best software for a specific task. There are numerous groups and organizations that review software and assist the professionals in making informed decisions.

Commercial Software

This term represents the expanding number of programs on the market. These programs are often expensive, and the quality ranges from inferior to superior. In the field of speech-language pathology, the amount of software available is growing rapidly. It is important to remember, however, that it is both illegal and unethical to copy protected software except for a backup purpose when allowed. Although commercial catalogs advertise specific programs, the reader should also be aware of such publications as *Apple Computer Resources in Special Education and Rehabilitation* (46). This resource guide categorizes computer application according to disability. Not only are general applications discussed (for example, for intervention or administration), but also specific software is described. Reviews of software also appear in *Asha*. Naive and even veteran users of software should consult reviews such as these before purchasing programs.

Public Domain Software

These programs are not copyrighted and are developed to be used as free access software (47). There is no fee or royalty on this software. In this category, there also exists a group of software that can be used free of charge, but it may not be altered in any way. These programs can be of great assistance to the SLP since the cost is very small, and they can be passed on at no charge. SLPs should be aware of sources of public domain software. One source is the *Software Shopper* (48). This catalog lists and reviews public domain software available for educational usage. The *Software Shopper* was originally developed by

Gallaudet University to assist teachers in Gallaudet's Pre-College programs. Later, it was determined that this information was of universal use in the education of deaf children. There is an abundant amount of software available in this catalog that can be used by the SLP in dealing with children and adults with normal hearing. This catalog contains listings by category, and programs may be used for articulation or other speech disorders. Public domain software, because of the limited cost, should always be an option for the school SLP. The quality of these programs may vary, however.

Shareware Software

This is a new method of marketing directly to users (46). Shareware may be examined without a fee, but the user is expected to pay a fee if the software is used. This fee for usage is usually far less than the cost of commercial software. Shareware users are often entitled to special updates, support, and access to future software. The cost of shareware is often as inexpensive as $5.00. The real advantage with this software is in the fact that the user is allowed a trial period to determine the worth of a specific program.

In order to obtain the best programs, it is necessary to evaluate them or find a source for reviews. A notebook might assist in the review of software. Each SLP could devise one specific to his or her needs. A form such as the one illustrated in Figure 8-1 might be appropriate. It was devised so that the majority of the evaluation would require only single words or a checkmark. These reviews can either be filed in a notebook or kept on a data disk by targeted usage. For example, these disks could be numbered and filed under language, articulation, specific concept, or any method deemed desirable. This type of system would allow for easy access to specific need.

As noted at the outset computer hardware and software may be very expensive; therefore, the school SLP must be cautious in selecting software. Next consideration is given to the application of computer technology in assessment, intervention, and reporting in the school setting.

Assessment

Computers have been employed successfully in the identification of children with communicative disorders. Fritch et al. reported on utilization of computer-assisted strategies in the screening of Head Start children in Alabama (49). The *Preschool Speech and Language Screening Test* was administered to fifty children between the ages of 3 and 6 under two conditions: (1) that trained graduate students in speech-language pathology administer the test in the conventional manner and (2) that Head Start personnel employ a computer-assisted version of the test. On the three language subtests, agreement levels of 88 percent, 88 percent, and 90 percent under the two conditions were achieved. Less consensus was seen in the articulation subtest, where only 56 percent agreement was reached; Head Start personnel failed more students than did the graduate SLPs. In terms of time effectiveness, the computer-managed test reports were printed in five minutes or less. "One person remarked that doing

FIGURE 8-1   Software Assessment

Disk File #_____   Target Usage: _____

                                    Cost: _____

                                                        Commercial – Public Domain

Name of Software: _____

Publisher: _____

Address: _____

Age Range: _____   Time Factors: _____

# of Users: _____

Usage

Diagnostic: _____   Therapeutic: _____

Enjoyment: _____   Administration: _____

Augmentative: _____   Other: _____

Description

Pictures: _____   Color: _____   Directions: _____

Ease of Use: _____   Other: _____

Scope/Handicap: _____

Rating

Useful: _____   Not Useful: _____

Possibly Useful: _____

Purchase: Yes – No

just one aspect of the report by hand – that of calculating chronological age – could take hours" (49).

The Fritch et al. study demonstrates the two types of software utilized in assessment: the administration software and programs that analyze results (50). A perusal of commercial catalogs suggests that software to complete the latter function is more readily available.

Intervention
Although the marketplace is becoming flooded with programs designed to assist clients with all types of communicative disorders, the school SLP must

consider the needs of the individual, the student's IEP goals and objectives, and his or her learning styles. Further, the specific service delivery model must be taken into account. Finally, the child's experience with computers and attitude toward computer use should be considered.

Schetz and Sheese suggest that the school SLP must also determine whether the intended use of the computer program is to instruct, supplement, or enrich (44). With regard to the purpose of intervention, does the SLP "want to provide computer-managed drill and practice, computer-managed tutorials, computer-managed instruction, computer-managed stimulation, or computer-managed problem-solving?" (44). Finally, it must be determined who will be involved: the SLP with the child, the child alone, or the child with another student. Only after considering the intent and purpose of using the software and deciding what approach will be appropriate can informed decisions be made.

Little doubt exists that computer-assisted intervention may be effective with some clients. Programs may provide motivation and stimulation, as well as visual and auditory feedback. Some software also allows students to work independently or semi-independently. SLPs are cautioned, however, to select and utilize intervention software with care, remembering that the communicative needs of the child, not the ease of implementation, are paramount.

Report Writing

Perhaps the most common use of the computer by today's SLP is in preparation of IEPs, record keeping, report writing, and word processing. Systems have been designed that are capable of generating due process materials and copies of IEPs, as well as storing data for research and administrative purposes (51). Reportedly, such systems have been time and cost efficient. Along with computer-assisted augmentative communication systems, the utilization of the computer for report writing may be most frequent.

In summary, computers have the capabilities to assist SLPs in most aspects of their professional endeavors. They will not transform a mediocre SLP into a competent professional but can be an asset to an already proficient individual delivering quality services. Despite the reluctance of some SLPs to become involved in the computer revolution in the 1980s, it is predicted that SLPs in the 1990s will be "looking for better things not just more things" (52). Technology will change at a rapid rate, and SLPs must take advantage of these advancements. "In a sense, our major challenge will be to take an activist posture to develop effective applications and integrate them into clinical practice" (52).

Summary

In this chapter, a number of contemporary issues has been considered. Included were innovative reimbursement strategies and ways in which the SLP can market speech-language services in the school setting. Increasing utilization of augmentative communication systems is apparent in the field, and that topic was considered next. Contemporary SLPs must be aware of the cultural and communicative differences presented by a growing number of groups, including Asian and Hispanic children. Some speech-language and pragmatic characteristics of these students were discussed. SLPs must be familiar with the speech and language disorders presented by individuals of a variety of ages, including little ones and not-so-little ones. In addition, the school professional must be prepared to work with students who have been abused or neglected, head-injured, or who are emotionally or behaviorally disturbed. Finally, SLPs in the school setting are making increasing use of technology; computer-assisted strategies in assessment, intervention, and reporting were discussed.

Endnotes

1. Individuals with Disabilities Education Act, *Education for the Handicapped Law Report,* (Horsham, PA: LRP Publication, 1990).

2. S. Dublinske, "Third Party Reimbursement for Speech-Language Pathology Provided in the Schools: The History" (Prepared for the ASHA Committee on Governmental Affairs, July, 1990).

3. *Education for the Handicapped Law Report,* supplement 222, SA-185-86 (Horsham, PA: LRP Publications, 1988).

4. Committee on Governmental Affairs, "Identification and Definition of Issues Regarding Third (sic) Billing and Procedural Guidelines" (1990).

5. N. P. Huffman, "Use of Third Party Funds to Pay for Speech-Language-Hearing Services Identified on a Student's IEP" (1990).

6. B. Hunt, Unpublished survey of teacher attitudes toward SLPs (1990).

7. J. Johns, "Marketing in the Schools: A Class Act," *Asha* 32(1990): pp. 40–41.

8. J. Viggiano, "Consumers Speak out on the Life of the Nonspeaker," *Asha* 23(1981): pp. 550–552.

9. "Position Statement on Nonspeech Communication," *Asha* 23(1981): pp. 577–581.

10. F. Carlson, *Alternate Methods of Communication,* National Student Speech Language Hearing Association (1981).

11. "Special Issue on Nonvocal Communication," *Language, Speech, and Hearing Services in Schools,* 12(1981).

12. C. R. Musselwhite and K. W. St. Louis, *Communication Programming for the Severely Handicapped* (Houston: College-Hill Press, 1982).

13. F. H. Silverman, *Communication for the Speechless,* 2nd ed. (Englewood Cliffs, NJ: Prentice Hall, 1989).

14. "A Decision-Making Strategy for Severely Handicapped Students" in *Program Suggestions for Speech and Language Services,* Michigan Department of Education (1982).

15. S. W. Blackstone, "Augmentative Communication Services in the Schools," *Asha* 31(1989): pp. 61–64.

16. L. Cole, "E Pluribus Pluribus: Multicultural Imperatives for the 1990s," *Asha* 31(1989): pp. 65–70.

17. L. L. Cheng, "Cross-Cultural and Linguistic Considerations in Working with Asian Populations," *Asha* 29(1987): pp. 33–37.

18. N. G. Bountress, "The Ann Arbor Decision in Retrospect," *Asha* 29(1987): pp. 55–57.

19. "Social Dialects Position Paper" (Reprinted from *Asha,* 1983), *Asha* 29(1987): p. 45.

20. O. L. Taylor in L. Cole and V. R. Deal, *Communication Disorders in Multicultural Populations* (Rockville: American Speech-Language-Hearing Association, undated).

21. *North Carolina Public School Guidelines for Speech-Language Programs,* (North Carolina Department of Public Instruction, 1985).

22. R. R. Ruiz, *Counseling the Culturally Different,* D. W. Sue (ed.) (New York: John Wiley & Sons, 1981).

23. D. L. Calvert, *Descriptive Phonetics* (New York: Thieme, Inc., 1986).

24. C. M. Wise, *Applied Phonetics* (Englewood Cliffs, NJ: Prentice-Hall, 1957).

25. C. Berg and H. R. Cox, "Austin Independent School District Bilingual Speech-Language Pathology Services," *TEJAS* 16(Spring/Summer 1990): p. 29.

26. B. Clark, "A Team Approach to the Speech-Language Evaluation of Bilingual Children," *TEJAS* 16(Spring/Summer 1990): pp. 29–30.

27. V. McAdams, H. Orr, and D. Price, "Description of Bilingual Services in the Fort Worth Independent School District," *TEJAS* 16(Spring/Summer 1990): pp. 30–31.

28. L. Cole, "ASHA Commitment to Cultural Diversity," *TEJAS* 16(Spring/Summer 1990): pp. 22–23.

29. N. I. Mickelson and C. G. Galloway, "Cumulative Language Deficit Among Indian Children," *Exceptional Children* 36(1969): pp. 187–190.

30. S. S. Berman, "Speech and Language Services on an Indian Reservation," *Language, Speech, and Hearing Services in Schools* 7(1976): pp. 56–60.

31. "Infants and Toddlers: Communication Assessment and Intervention," ASHA (Minneapolis, 1988).

32. L. M. Rossetti, *High-Risk Infants: Identification, Assessment, and Intervention* (Boston: Little, Brown, 1986).

33. N. L. McKinley and V. L. Larson, "Neglected Language-Disordered Adolescents: A Delivery Model," *Language, Speech, and Hearing Services in Schools* 16(1985): pp. 2–15.

34. V. L. Larson and N. L. McKinley, *Communication Assessment and Intervention Strategies for Adolescents* (Eau Claire, WI: Thinking Publications, 1987).

35. L. Fox, S. H. Long, and A. Langlois, "Patterns of Language Comprehension Deficit in Abused and Neglected Children," *Journal of Speech and Hearing Disorders* 53(1988): pp. 239–244.

36. S. N. Sparks, "Letter to the Editor: Speech and Language in Maltreated Children: Response to McCauley and Swisher (1987)," *Journal of Speech and Hearing Disorders* 54(1989): pp. 124–125.

37. R. DePompei and J. Blosser, "Strategies for Helping Head-Injured Children Successfully Return to School," *Speech, Language, and Hearing Services in Schools* 18(1987): pp. 292–300.

38. J. S. Taylor, *The Communicative Abilities of Juvenile Delinquents: A Descriptive Study,* doctoral dissertation (University of Missouri-Columbia, 1969).

39. B. M. Prizant, L. R. Audet, G. M. Burke, L. J. Hummel, S. Maher, and G. Theadore, "Communication Disorders and Emotional/Behavioral Disorders in Children and Adolescents," *Journal of Speech and Hearing Disorders* 55(1990): pp. 179–192.

40. Education Turnkey Systems, *Microcomputer Use in Special Education,* unpublished report (Fall Church, VA, 1986).

41. C. S. Hyman, "The 1986–1987 Omnibus Survey: Current Information for Sound Planning," *Asha* 29(1987): pp. 29–33.

42. G. R. Houle, "Computer Usage by Speech-Language Pathologists in Public Schools," *Language, Speech, and Hearing Services in Schools* 19(1988): pp. 423–427.

43. M. W. Palin and C. G. Cohen, "Technology in the Schools," *Asha* 28(1986): p. 35.

44. K. F. Shetz and R. J. Sheese, "Software That Works in the School Setting," *Asha* 31(1989): pp. 65–68.

45. *Apple II GS Owner's Reference* (Apple Computer, Inc., 1989).

46. *Apple Computer Resources in Special Education and Rehabilitation* (DLM Teaching Resources, undated).

47. *The Best of Apple Public Domain Software,* edition II (The Public Domain Exchange, 1987).

48. *Software Shopper* (Washington, DC: Gallaudet College).

49. J. L. Fitch, L. A. Davis, W. B. Evans, and D. E. Sellers, "Computer-Managed Screening for Communication Disorders," *Language, Speech, and Hearing Services in Schools* 15(1984): pp. 66–69.

50. J. Sanders, *Microcomputer Applications for Speech-Language Services in the Schools* (San Diego: College-Hill Press, 1986).

51. B. Krueger, "Computerized Reporting in a Public School Program," *Language, Speech, and Hearing Services in Schools* 16(1985): 135–139.

52. A. H. Schwartz, "A Look at the Needs for the Application of Microcomputers in the 1990s," *Journal for Computer Users in Speech and Hearing* 5(1989): pp. 114–124.

9

Epilogue

"Men have forgotten this truth," said the fox, "but you must not forget it. You become responsible, forever, for what you have tamed."*

Throughout this text I have tried to avoid expressing personal opinions and biases, and I hope my effort has been successful. This book is not intended to be a "how-to" manual, but a "what's possible" text. It is difficult, however, to discuss the subject of public school speech-language pathology services without creating some reactions. Those of you reading this text should have positive feelings about a career in public schools. There was a time when working in such an environment was somewhat tedious; physical needs were not always met, equipment was inadequate, and materials were in short supply. Moreover, the children seen by the SLP either presented "garden variety" articulatory defects or exhibited problems (specifically in the area of language) that the professional was unprepared to handle. Today, some of these same problems may exist, but contemporary SLPs are better equipped, have more sensitive testing tools and materials, and have training and experience that have prepared them to work effectively with children and adolescents presenting a variety of problems. With the advent of state and federal legislation that requires that all handicapped children must have access to a free, appropriate education in the least restrictive environment, there is little doubt that the public school setting presents a tremendous challenge to SLPs. In this final chapter, as a means of summarizing the text, I will permit myself the luxury of offering some personal observations about public school speech-language services.

In the Foreword, Dana LeTempt Jerome, a graduate with a variety of school experiences, discusses the field from a student's perspective. I think that her comments are rather typical, particularly as she recalls how overwhelmed she felt as she began her student teaching experience. Certainly, the require-

*From *The Little Prince* by Antoine De Saint-Exupery. New York: Harcourt, Brace and Company, 1943, p. 71. Reprinted by permission of Harcourt Brace Jovanovich, Inc.

ments of the EHA/IDEA have contributed to this sense of being inundated by regulations and paperwork; however, students prior to federal legislation also experienced insecurities as they student-taught. Mrs. Jerome was quite candid in her exposition and offered some very useful suggestions to those students preparing to embark on a school career.

The first chapter of the book dealt with historical aspects of the profession, qualifications of public school personnel, and professional titles. Little comment is needed on the origins of the profession, but the last two topics should be thought provoking. A question still to be answered is whether the preparation of school personnel should differ from the preservice preparation of students who plan to work in other settings. As of this date, the American Speech-Language-Hearing Association (ASHA) has not generated a certificate for public school personnel although other areas of specific certification are under consideration. States are in some disagreement about requirements for certification; perhaps SLPs in the Midwest require more education courses to function effectively in the schools than their counterparts in the South. Uniformity in certification requirements throughout the states would certainly facilitate the mobility of school SLPs and decrease the problem of preservice academic advisement. On the other hand, states, by virtue of their diverse populations, have varying needs. For example, Texas SLPs may need a knowledge of Hispanic languages and cultures, a need not felt by Maine SLPs. North Dakota personnel may require some background in native American customs and communication patterns. There is, therefore, some logic in the diversity of requirements for state certification. Licensure has been adopted by some states although school-based SLPs are exempted by the majority; this exemption has the potential of creating two classes of SLPs. One group includes health care professionals, with school personnel comprising the second. A solution, not without inherent problems, is universal exemption-free licensure. In sum, academic and clinical requirements for school-based SLPs are diverse and are likely to remain that way.

Regardless of whether certification or licensure ever become uniform, other qualifications of SLP candidates should be evaluated. Effective SLPs, in addition to meeting specific academic and clinical requirements, should relate well with clients, their families, and colleagues. They must be empathetic, patient, nonjudgmental, and sensitive; it is also essential that SLPs be active listeners. Without these and other personal characteristics discussed in Chapter 1, the SLP may be technically sound but ineffective.

Once these specialists have been appropriately educated and found to possess positive interpersonal skills, what should their professional title be? ASHA has recommended that "speech-language pathologist" be the designated title, and this has been employed throughout this text. However, if one consults the professional titles used in various states, it becomes apparent that SLP is not used with any degree of consistency. For example, California guidelines refer to language, speech, and hearing specialists, and North Carolina employs speech-language specialists; Indiana and Missouri, on the other hand, use SLP in their guidelines. Although I have conformed with the ASHA-designated title, this does not imply approval of its use in the school setting. Not only is it cumbersome, it is also somewhat difficult to include a - (dash) in oral conversation. Thus, speech-language pathologist becomes "speech (pause) language pathologist" or "speechlanguagepathologist." It is interesting that a profession that deals with oral communication has a title that is not easily communicated orally. If given a choice of titles, it would seem that "speech and language clinician" might be preferable to "speech-language pathologist." All areas of disorders would be included, and less imposing terminology would be employed. Unfortunately, what professionals choose to call themselves is sometimes irrelevant in the school setting; SLPs may still be "speech teachers" or, when spoken by children with articulatory disorders, " peech teacher."

Throughout this text, numerous references to ASHA were made. Even though individual states establish guidelines, regulations, and requirements for their school personnel, there is little doubt that ASHA has been influential in assisting the states through model certification requirements and a variety of position papers. For these reasons, it seemed appropriate to present the evolution of the association as seen through the eyes of Van Riper. Chapter 1 closed with that history.

Chapter 2 considered state and federal legislation involving the education of children with disabilities. There is little doubt that such legislation has contributed to public awareness of the problems of the disabled and has improved the quality and quantity of services provided to them. The landmark case of *PARC* v. *the Commonwealth of Pennsylvania* of 1971 was critical in establishing a need for reform of the education of handicapped children. Although other public laws were enacted prior to Public Law 94-142, it was the Education of the Handicapped Act (EHA/IDEA) that influenced the education of children with disabilities to the greatest extent. Amendments to the law have clarified, strengthened, and broadened its impact. A natural outcome of the EHA/IDEA has been the occurrence of violations of the regulations. Such violations have included infractions in the type, amount, and frequency of services, as well as the place of service delivery.

School-based SLPs, along with other educators, had some reservations when the EHA/IDEA and related legislation were enacted. Questions concerning parental involvement, IEPs, informed consent, and the availability of records arose. Additional concerns resulted when due process hearings occurred. It is understandable that SLPs are somewhat anxious; the laws are complex and continue to evolve. However, the conscientious SLP who remains abreast of state and federal legislation and who seeks to provide appropriate services to each communicatively disordered individual should view the EHA and related regulations as a challenge rather than a threat.

Chapter 3, by virtue of the contents, is likely to be controversial. By law, SLPs are required to identify and evaluate students who may be communicatively disordered; this has been a function of SLPs for years. The controversy arises over how to identify such individuals and which tools and procedures are most appropriate. My experience with case finding included both screening and teacher referral techniques. We routinely screened at a specified grade level while encouraging teachers to refer children with suspected communicative disorders. Undoubtedly some students were missed during screenings, but it is more probable that we overidentified potential candidates. By the same token — perhaps because we did not provide adequate information to teachers — teachers frequently made inappropriate referrals. Children who repeated "I" once were referred as stutterers; the child who could not pronounce "spaghetti" had a lisp. The SLP, in these situations, had the option of informing the teacher that her or his observations were incorrect (thus discouraging future referrals) or of working with the child and performing a miracle cure. Contemporary requirements demand more formal management of referrals; however, the potential problem remains the same. Nevertheless, SLPs must determine which methods of case identification should be employed.

Once students with suspected problems have been identified, the next challenge is to determine how these individuals should be evaluated. In Chapter 3, a variety of assessment tools and procedures for infants, toddlers, children, and adolescents was presented. Since this is not a book on assessment, no attempt was made to include all available instruments. Therefore, the student reader may find familiar tools excluded; the utilization of specific tests and procedures may depend upon instructor preference, institution preference, or even state preference. The availability of a tool within a school system is also a factor. Finally, there are those who feel that most instruments assess splinter skills or are culturally biased or do not evaluate what they purpose to assess; these persons may find few of the available tools to be appropriate.

As SLPs increase their involvement in the educational process, they must also increase their understanding of tools employed by other professionals. Some of these tests were identified in Chapter 3. Just as it is important to recognize that individual SLPs favor certain tools and procedures, it is equally important to realize that individual districts, special educators, and regular educators have similar preferences. Therefore, students and SLPs must familiarize themselves with tools employed within the school district.

One final word of caution seems necessary before leaving the topics of identification and assessment. SLPs, when meeting a person for the first time, tend to listen to how the speaker is speaking rather than to what the speaker is actually saying; it is an occupational hazard. As a result, we may be more critical than necessary. For this reason, it is important that the SLP be realistic in identifying children with communicative disorders. Some students with minor problems may not be disabled in the layperson's judgment; they are disabled only in the eyes (or ears) of the SLP. Many famous individuals (including politicians and newscasters) have been successful in spite of nonstandard communicative styles. Once children have been carefully identified as having suspected communicative disorders, evaluative procedures must be chosen sensibly. Numerous tools are available for the formal testing of such children, but the wise SLP will make extensive use of clinical judgment. Observation of the child and analysis of language and speech samples must comprise the better portion of the diagnostic. As many of you know, not all individuals respond well to formal testing, and it is the application of communicative abilities in real-life situations that should be considered.

Chapter 4 is concerned with case selection and service delivery options. Initially, the SLP must be aware if state or district caseload regulations exist; let's hope that none will be found since caseload size should be dependent on a number of variables that are difficult to factor into a formula. A draft of Illinois guidelines that identifies service delivery units based on the severity of the clients' communicative disorders offers some hope for equitable caseload decisions.

Once the SLP knows the guidelines for caseload determination, the next step is to determine if eligibility criteria exist. Some states, such as California, have specific guidelines, and both Illinois and Indiana have proposed similar criteria. Regardless of whether guidelines exist, SLPs must employ clinical judgment in determining which students require and will benefit from intervention. For example, I once saw a third-grade female beg to be seen for intervention because she was convinced (or had been convinced) that her /s/ was deviant. Given the range of acceptability of /s/ production, this student was well within normal limits. Nevertheless, she thought that she had a problem. Strict case selection criteria would have excluded her from intervention, but clinical judgment would suggest that intervention would be desirable. Eligibility according to the EHA/IDEA might be problematic, however. Sound clinical judgment must augment established criteria.

The plight of our third grader may have been altered by having today's variety of service delivery options available to her. Instead of determining whether students require direct intervention or none at all, contemporary SLPs have a continuum of models from which to choose. Granted, many SLPs, including the author, experimented with such options as consultation and collaboration for years; however, legitimacy and structure have now been given to numerous delivery models.

In Chapter 4, the continuum of service options available in California was highlighted, and model programs in other parts of the country were presented. It is difficult to know how frequently opportunities for diverse service delivery are available or how widespread their utilization is. For example, one SLP reported that her building principal was quite willing for her to become involved in collaboration as long as she continued to service her regular caseload of eighty. If this is the rule rather than the exception, it may be some time before the full range of options can be employed by school personnel. For that reason, it was necessary to review scheduling models associated with traditional pull-out intervention. Included was a hypothetical model that incorporated several service delivery options.

Change and innovation should be viewed by SLPs in a positive manner, and it is apparent that both are occurring in the public school setting. In addition, more structure in terms of guidelines is available. Students should remain aware, however, that not all change is appropriate, nor is structure intended to supplant clinical judgment.

The decision to discuss IEPs after assessment and service delivery options was an arbitrary one; it might just as easily have been Chapter 3 as Chapter 5. However, it seems that in the real world, it is important to know the types of problems that you are dealing with (assessment) and the options available to you prior to devising an IEP, hence, the placement of IEPs in Chapter 5.

As the reader is well aware by this time, the EHA/IDEA mandates IEPs, and some states have expanded upon the minimum requirements of that document. Nothing required in IEPs should be considered excessive since they include basic information necessary for adequate intervention. Forms included in the Appendix constitute examples of IEPs although some districts use computer-generated IEPs, and I have seen some that resemble "Peel and Put" materials.

IEPs are legally prepared in a meeting whose attendees include the SLP, the child's parents and teacher, a representative of the public agency, and when appropriate, the child. I have some reservations about the value of these meetings. It has been demonstrated that parents are somewhat reticent in IEP meetings; this is quite understandable especially when the professional participants employ highly technical language. On the other hand, parents know their children best and should be encouraged to share relevant information with the group. In the same vein, it has been found that teachers sometimes hesitate to contribute when the building principal conducted the meetings. Nevertheless, there is little doubt that IEP meetings are intended to serve an important purpose; at this point, skill in achieving the goal continues to evolve.

Chapter 6 explored the competencies of SLPs and their responsibilities as counselors and supervisors. In the past, we were somewhat haphazard in describing the expectations of school-based SLPs; as a result, we were similarly haphazard in assessing how closely they met these expectations. Currently, states are devising specific performance expectations guidelines; these criteria should continue to improve the accountability of school personnel.

Another issue addressed in Chapter 6 was the status of school-based SLPs. I must admit that, as an undergraduate, I had the dreaded white-coat syndrome; my ambition was to work in a hospital setting and perform miracles with stroke victims. Fortunately for me and my potential clients, hospital opportunities did not present themselves, and I ended up in the school setting. (I later learned that I did not tolerate hospital or nursing home settings well; I would have been quite ineffective.) I was quite content in the schools and functioned much better with potential and real delinquents than I would have with CVA patients. Like many others, I understand the challenges of the public schools and am pleased to have had the experience. Also, like many others, I believe that school-based SLPs are "a class act."

A great deal of attention was afforded the counseling function of the SLP. Anticipating some reader's lack of background in this area, I attempted to reiterate key concepts; hence, the reader may have noted some redundancies.

My experiences and the reports of practicing SLPs suggest that much intervention incorporates counseling; for example, up to 75 percent of the work done with adolescents involves counseling. As was obvious throughout this book, I believe that an effective SLP must be a good listener. This skill is particularly critical in counseling. There are those who play down this responsibility and some who question if we should be involved. My only question for these individuals is how can we or why should we avoid it?

SLPs as supervisors was also considered in Chapter 6. At this point in your preparation, supervision of others must seem a long way down the road. Nevertheless, it may be a role for which you should be prepared, particularly with regard to the supervision of paraprofessionals. For this reason, a great deal of emphasis was placed on the utilization of paraprofessionals and, by inference, your supervision of supportive personnel. Finally, student perception of their supervisors was presented; I suspect that more than one supervisory face reddened during this concluding discussion.

Chapter 7 dealt with familiar, yet evolving, roles of the school-based SLP: consultation and collaboration. One of the major problems in discussing these functions is that of terminology. Do SLPs consult, collaborate, engage in collaborative consultation, or a little of each or none of the above? The probable answer is that we do a little of each. We serve as consultants when we advise a teacher on methods of managing a dysfluent child in the classroom. Collaboration occurs when the SLP and classroom teacher compare observations of the child and devise strategies to be implemented by both professionals; the dysfluent child also might be included in the collaborative effort. The term *collaborative consultation* might be employed to describe either or both of the interactions presented above.

As one looks at the literature, it would appear that consultation and collaboration are being employed with increasing frequency. Whether that observation is accurate remains to be seen. Historically, these forms of intervention have been used by SLPs for years. What seems to differentiate contemporary consultation/collaboration from that employed in the past is structure. Formerly, SLPs met with teachers on an informal and usually erratic basis to discuss problems displayed by the latter's students and to determine what could be done in the classroom to ameliorate these problems. Today, structure has been superimposed. In addition, the various educational reforms have encouraged SLPs to look beyond what was happening to the child in the speech room and to provide intervention that meshed with classroom work and interactions. All these innovations in the consultative/collaborative efforts are viewed as positive.

What must be avoided by SLPs as they become involved in consultation and collaboration is overuse and misuse of these service delivery options. It is easy to become excited about a concept and attempt to employ it without proper preparation and analysis. Not all administrators or teachers will accept the consultation/collaboration model even after you have done your best to sell the concept through appropriate documentation and inservicing. In addition, this model is not suitable for all students, nor should it be employed as a means of providing services to large numbers of students due to excessive caseload size. Like all other delivery models, consultation and collaboration should be employed as an appropriate option, not one of convenience or necessity.

Finally, Chapter 8 attempted to cover relevant issues that seemed to have no other logical place in the book but that warranted attention. I am particularly indebted to ASHA president-elect Ann Carey who provided hot-off-the-press information regarding third-party payments; it was most convenient to have an inside source whose university office is adjacent. As was stated in the chapter, these sources of funding have been available for some time but are just recently being considered viable reimbursement channels. At this point in time, it may be safest to acknowledge that the nuances of third-party payment continue to be identified and that SLPs must remain abreast of developments in this area.

Marketing of speech-language services in the schools was the second topic considered. Although the concept of marketing seems foreign to some professionals, it is an endeavor in which SLPs have engaged throughout the years. With a knowledge of marketing strategies, the SLP can be even more effective in promoting speech-language services, the profession, and speech-language professionals in the school setting.

Augmentative communication is not new to the field, but its level of sophistication and expanded application is somewhat new. Early SLPs were admonished that nonspeech communication was a last resort for those individuals who were deaf; little consideration was given to the facilitating possibilities of augmentative systems. Today, such systems are being employed not only with the deaf but also with developmentally delayed persons and those who exhibit autistic tendencies. Moreover, elaborate gestural, gestural-assisted, and neuro-assisted systems have been devised to meet the communication needs of the speechless. This is an exciting extension of the field, one that has finally worked itself into the school setting. Students and professionals alike are obligated to familiarize themselves with augmentative possibilities if they are to service all of their clients adequately.

Many students are exposed rather early in their lives to class and cultural differences; others do not experience these differences until later. I fell into this latter category and was, therefore, quite unprepared to adapt to the class and cultural characteristics of the students with whom I worked as a student teacher. My cooperating teacher was itinerant and serviced a lower socioeconomic school in the mornings and went to a middle-class school in the afternoons. Although I observed her working successfully with both groups of students, I had problems when I assumed responsibility for the children. Board activities, which were quite popular at the time, were very successful with the middle-class children; students in the other school were quite baffled by them. These students had little concept of turn taking, and considerable therapy time was consumed by explanation of the purpose and rules of the activity. Needless to say, I quickly changed my approach with these children.

In today's society, it is somewhat difficult to remain as naive as I was as a student teacher. Many children have culturally rich neighborhood and school experiences. For those SLPs without the benefit of multiclass and multicultural exposure, it is important to understand that differences exist and to be open to these differences. In Chapter 8, some characteristics of Asian, black, Hispanic, and Indian students were presented; many of these characteristics are significant in the therapeutic setting. This area of multicultural and class differences is important to SLPs since they evaluate a variety of children and provide intervention. The discussion in Chapter 8 should be considered merely as an introduction to multicultural issues.

Until recently, SLPs viewed infants and toddlers as sweet young things to hold, love, feed, and diaper. Today, we must accept the fact that some members of this population require our early intervention, and we must view them as potential clients. Much of the service delivery to these infants and toddlers will be transdisciplinary, and the targeted population will be parents and caregivers. This area of study for SLPs is in its infancy (pun intended), and we will I am sure become more adept as additional literature becomes available.

Adolescents comprise a population that has been neglected by SLPs, partially because we thought that early intervention resolved initial communicative disorders and partially because we were unprepared to identify these disorders. As a profession, we have become aware that some problems do not surface until adolescence; at the same time, we have learned more about adolescent development and methods of assessing the adequacy of this development. Let's hope that intervention strategies for these clients will continue to be devised.

A population that should not exist, but does, includes children who have been abused and neglected. Many of these students will display communicative disorders and will find themselves in the SLP's caseload. As indicated in Chapter 8, SLPs and other school personnel are mandated reporters and are obligated to contact the proper authorities when signs of abuse or neglect are apparent. Early research suggests that neglected children are more depressed in linguistic competence than children who have been abused. It is critical to our understanding of these students that SLPs collect and share information about the communication characteristics of this population.

Head-injured students are also finding their ways back into the school setting and into the SLP's caseload. It is conceivable that some of these students were abused, or their injuries may be the result of accidents. This population is unique because these are formerly "normal" students who were functional in the school setting. Now, they are returning to the same situation in an impaired state. As with infants, toddlers, and multiply handicapped students, head-injured children and adolescents require a transdisciplinary approach, and SLPs must prepare themselves to function intelligently on such teams.

I have always had a particular affinity for juvenile delinquents and an interest in their communicative disorders. Of similar interest have been students who are classified as behaviorally disordered. Not all SLPs share my enthusiasm for this group of students who have the potential to be verbally and physically abusive. However, they are as needing and deserving of the SLP's intervention as the well-behaved five-year-old with an articulatory disorder.

It is with some fear that I embarked upon the next topic—the utilization of computers. My primary experience with computers was with a Macintosh; Macwrite, Macpaint, and I had a wonderful relationship until Mac died. I was self-taught and did not really understand how computers worked, only that they did—most of the time. Paula Baima, one of our graduate students, came to my rescue, however, and I am grateful to her for the computer information she supplied for Chapter 8. Little doubt exists that computers should play significant roles in the functioning of SLPs. Caution must be exercised, however, lest programs dictate your approach or remove the client–SLP interaction that is so critical to successful intervention.

In the Foreword, Dana Jerome spoke of the differences between intervention in the university and public school settings. She stated that this text should help students make a smooth transition from the artificial to the real world. It is my hope that she was correct.

Appendix
Resource Materials
and Forms*

*Reprinted, by permission, from *Program Guidelines for Language, Speech, and Hearing Specialists Providing Designated Instruction and Services*, copyright 1989, California Department of Education, P.O. Box 271, Sacramento, CA 95802-0271

General Classroom Modifications

In the appropriate box give the date when classroom modifications were made to accommodate students with speech, language, or hearing difficulties.

Date

Date	
	1. Provide a home-school checklist.
	2. Provide peer partners or a "buddy" system.
	3. Provide preferential seating.
	4. Provide cross-age tutoring.
	5. Increase routine and predictability.
	6. Move about room to maintain attention.
	7. Touch students occasionally to reward or orient.
	8. Use visual aids and examples liberally.
	9. Provide parent/teacher conferences.
	10. Consult with fellow teachers.
	11. Use easier material or shorter assignments than those usually given.
	12. Provide classroom contracts.
	13. Begin the day by reviewing the schedule and expectations.
	14. Study check sheets.
	15. Decrease change.
	16. Create a quiet study area.
	17. Provide breaks during the instructional day.
	18. Provide period-by-period reinforcement.
	19. Change teacher or grade.
	20. Modify the schedule or shorten the school day.
	21. Increase student participation in commitment and decision making.
	22. Obtain adult tutor volunteers.

Speech and Language Modifications for the Regular Education Program
---

In the appropriate box give the date when the activities listed below were completed.

Date   **Articulation**

1. Provide sound discrimination activities.

2. Provide sound awareness activities.

3. Develop a sound book.

4. Identify a target sound of the week.

Language: Listening

1. Keep directions simple; use short sentences.

2. Provide visual cues and examples.

3. Ask students to repeat or paraphrase directions to determine whether they have been received.

4. Supervise initial work on a new activity.

5. Demonstrate directions.

6. Shorten amount of verbalization.

7. Gain the student's attention and limit other movement when directions are being given.

8. Give directions at the student's eye level.

9. Check for understanding before proceeding.

10. Encourage questions.

11. Speak directly, loudly, and clearly.

12. Use a written checklist or sequence.

13. Color code the routine and sequence.

Language: Vocabulary Concepts

1. Teach vocabulary words in context.

2. Encourage use of dictionary.

3. Teach categorization or classification activities.

Fluency

Date

	1. Discourage interruptions when the student blocks on a word.
	2. Do not fill in words; wait patiently showing interest.
	3. Minimize competition.
	4. Remove time pressures in speaking.
	5. Avoid calling on students alphabetically or according to seating arrangements.
	6. Gain the student's attention.
	7. Observe the degree of fluency in speaking situations and encourage participation in fluent situations.
	8. Do not ask the student to stop and start over; accept whatever quality of language is expressed.
	9. Allow considerable flexibility in mode of responding (taped book reports, reports from seats, and so forth).
	10. Model acceptance for individual differences; for example, strengths and weaknesses.
	11. Talk and act calmly.
	12. Communicate positive regard for the content of the communication and accept any quality.
	13. Facilitate nonverbal activities in which the student can succeed.
	14. Call on students randomly.

Voice*

	1. Seek medical interventions as appropriate by consulting with the school nurse regarding possible medical concerns (injuries, allergies, or hearing loss).
	2. Monitor and note different situations for excessive yelling, screaming, shouting, or other verbal abuse; then reduce instances of abuse.
	3. Observe voice in various situations; too loud or soft, tense, strained, and so forth. Develop lists and charts of situations and review with the LSH specialist.
	4. Consult with the parents; are they concerned? Is the problem continual or seasonal?
	5. Observe for unnatural use of voice; e.g., imitates cars, squealing, and so forth. Discuss this behavior with the student. Monitor and reward reductions in vocal abuse.
	6. Check whether the student participates in any activities requiring excessive vocal use (e.g., choir or cheerleading). Discontinue such activities as appropriate.

---

*The points listed above are suggestions rather than modifications. The intended emphasis is on observation and data collection.

Structured Interview
(Sample Questions and Tasks)

1. Identifying information/declarative sentences
    a. What is your name?
    b. What are your brother's and sister's names?
    c. What do you watch on television?
    d. Can you tell me about it?

2. Imitation skills
    a. Repeat digits.
    b. Repeat sentences.

3. Sequencing skills
    a. Tell the days of the week, months in the year, seasons, and holidays.

4. Classification (production/processing)
    a. Name in ten seconds as many animals (or fruits) as you can.
    b. Identify which of three to four items go together and describe why.

5. Question format
    a. Can understand *wh* questions.
    b. Can use *wh* questions.

6. Directionality/laterality
    a. Tell how to get to your house.
    b. Show right and left.

7. Temporality (past and future tense verbs)
    a. Tell me what you did yesterday.
    b. Tell me what you will do tomorrow.
    c. Tell me what your mother will do tomorrow.

8. Expression
    a. Can understand whether a phrase is incorrect.
    b. Can use sentences of six to seven words.
    c. Can speak with native sound system under control.

9. Understands humor/inferences/absurdities
    a. Can tell jokes.
    b. Can understand peer-level jokes.
    c. Can explain absurdities.

10. Prepositions
    a. Can understand basic prepositions: *in, on, under,* and *behind.*
    b. Can use prepositions appropriately: *in, on, under,* and *behind.*

11. Adjectives
    a. Can understand some colors, shapes, and textures.
    b. Can use colors, shapes, sizes, and so forth to describe items.

Suggested Language Sample Collection Techniques*

Elicited/Imitation	Elicited	Storytelling	Spontaneous
Carrow Elicited Language Inventory	*Multilevel Informal Language Inventory*	Responding to story sequence cards	Responding to open-ended questions
Northwestern Syntax Screening Test	*Structured Photographic Expressive Language Test*	Responding to pictures in storybooks	Describing familiar items
Clinical Evaluation of Language Functions (CELF) Diagnostic Battery: Model sentences	*Fullerton Language Test for Adolescents (FLTA), Experimental Edition:* Morphology competency	Responding to pictures depicting typical scenes	Relating how to perform familiar activities
Test of Language Development (TOLD): Sentence imitation		Story reformulation	*Detroit Tests of Learning Aptitude (DTLA):* Verbal absurdities
Oral Language Sentence Imitation Screening Test		*Detroit Tests of Learning Aptitude (DTLA):* Story construction	*Detroit Tests of Learning Aptitude (DTLA):* Social adjustment

*This list of techniques is not inclusive. Other techniques may be used.

Eligibility Criteria for Speech and Language Disorders

California Code of Regulations, Title 5, Education, Section 3030 (c):

(c) A pupil has a language or speech disorder as defined in Section 56333 of the *Education Code,* and it is determined that the pupil's disorder meets one or more of the following criteria:

(1) Articulation Disorder

(A) The pupil displays reduced intelligibility or an inability to use the speech mechanism which significantly interferes with communication and attracts adverse attention. Significant interference in communication occurs when the pupil's production of single or multiple speech sounds on a developmental scale of articulation competency is below that expected for his or her chronological age or developmental level, and which adversely affects educational performance.

(B) A pupil does not meet the criteria for an articulation disorder if the sole assessed disability is an abnormal swallowing pattern.

(2) Abnormal Voice. A pupil has an abnormal voice which is characterized by persistent, defective voice quality, pitch, or loudness.

(3) Fluency Disorders. A pupil has a fluency disorder when the flow of verbal expression, including rate and rhythm, adversely affects communication between the pupil and listener.

(4) Language Disorder. The pupil has an expressive or receptive language disorder when he or she meets one of the following criteria:

(A) The pupil scores at least 1.5 standard deviations below the mean, or below the seventh percentile, for his or her chronological age or developmental level on two or more standardized tests in one or more of the following areas of language development: morphology, syntax, semantics, or pragmatics. When standardized tests are considered to be invalid for the specific pupil, the expected language performance level shall be determined by alternative means as specified in the assessment plan, or

(B) The pupil scores at least 1.5 standard deviations below the mean or the score is below the seventh percentile for his or her chronological age or developmental level on one or more standardized tests in one of the areas listed in subsection (A) and displays inappropriate or inadequate usage of expressive or receptive language as measured by a representative spontaneous or elicited language sample of a minimum of 50 utterances. The language sample must be recorded or transcribed and analyzed, and the results included in the assessment report. If the pupil is unable to produce this sample, the language, speech, and hearing specialist shall document why a 50-utterance sample was not obtainable and the contexts in which attempts were made to elicit the sample. When standardized tests are considered to be invalid for the specific pupil, the expected language performance level shall be determined by alternative means as specified in the assessment plan.

Eligibility Criteria for Individuals with Exceptional Needs, Aged Birth to Four Years Nine Months

California Code of Regulations, Title 5, Education, Section 3031(a) and (b):

(a) A child, age birth to four years nine months shall qualify as an individual with exceptional needs pursuant to *Education Code* Section 56026 (c)(1)(2) if the individualized education program (IEP) team determines that the child meets the following criteria:

(1) Is identified as an individual with exceptional needs pursuant to Section 3030, and
(2) Is identified as requiring intensive special education and services by meeting one of the following:

(A) The child is functioning at or below 50 percent of his or her chronological age level in any one of the following skill areas:

1. Gross or fine motor development;
2. Receptive or expressive language development;
3. Social or emotional development;
4. Cognitive development; and
5. Visual development.

(B) The child is functioning between 51 percent and 75 percent of his or her chronological age level in any two of the skill areas identified in Section 3031(2)(A).

(C) The child has a disabling medical condition or congenital syndrome which the individualized education program team determines has a high predictability of requiring intensive special education and services.

(b) Programs for individuals with exceptional needs younger than three years of age are permissive in accordance with Section 56001(c) of the *Education Code* except for those programs mandated pursuant to Section 56425 of the *Education Code.*

Infant and Preschool Developmental Age Equivalents

Chronological Age	Developmental Age with 50 Percent Delay	Developmental Age with 25 Percent Delay
0 years 6 months	0 years 3.00 months	0 years 4.50 months
0 years 7 months	0 years 3.50 months	0 years 5.25 months
0 years 8 months	0 years 4.00 months	0 years 6.00 months
0 years 9 months	0 years 4.50 months	0 years 6.75 months
0 years 10 months	0 years 5.00 months	0 years 7.50 months
0 years 11 months	0 years 5.50 months	0 years 8.25 months
1 year 0 months	0 years 6.00 months	0 years 9.00 months
1 year 1 month	0 years 6.50 months	0 years 9.75 months
1 year 2 months	0 years 7.00 months	0 years 10.50 months
1 year 3 months	0 years 7.50 months	0 years 11.25 months
1 year 4 months	0 years 8.00 months	1 year 0 months
1 year 5 months	0 years 8.50 months	1 year .75 months
1 year 6 months	0 years 9.00 months	1 year 1.50 months
1 year 7 months	0 years 9.50 months	1 year 2.25 months
1 year 8 months	0 years 10.00 months	1 year 3.00 months
1 year 9 months	0 years 10.50 months	1 year 3.75 months
1 year 10 months	0 years 11.00 months	1 year 4.50 months
1 year 11 months	0 years 11.50 months	1 year 5.25 months
2 years 0 months	1 year .00 months	1 year 6.00 months
2 years 1 month	1 year .50 months	1 year 6.75 months
2 years 2 months	1 year 1.00 month	1 year 7.50 months
2 years 3 months	1 year 1.50 months	1 year 8.25 months
2 years 4 months	1 year 2.00 months	1 year 9.00 months
2 years 5 months	1 year 2.50 months	1 year 9.75 months
2 years 6 months	1 year 3.00 months	1 year 10.50 months
2 years 7 months	1 year 3.50 months	1 year 11.25 months
2 years 8 months	1 year 4.00 months	2 years 0 months
2 years 9 months	1 year 4.50 months	2 years .75 months
2 years 10 months	1 year 5.00 months	2 years 1.50 months
2 years 11 months	1 year 5.50 months	2 years 2.25 months
3 years 0 months	1 year 6.00 months	2 years 3.00 months
3 years 1 month	1 year 6.50 months	2 years 3.75 months
3 years 2 months	1 year 7.00 months	2 years 4.50 months
3 years 3 months	1 year 7.50 months	2 years 5.25 months
3 years 4 months	1 year 8.00 months	2 years 6.00 months
3 years 5 months	1 year 8.50 months	2 years 6.75 months

Checklist of Eligibility Guidelines for
Non-English Background Students

Student's name: _____ Date: _____

Place a checkmark in the appropriate box.

Indicators

Agree	Disagree	N/A	
☐	☐	☐	1. A language disorder exists in the student's native language (corroborated by a combination of specialist's assessment, interpreter or translator, and parent).
☐	☐	☐	2. The student is slow to acquire English despite ESL and school interventions (verified by ESL personnel, regular classroom teacher, and so forth).
☐	☐	☐	3. Cultural or experiential differences and economic disadvantages are not the primary cause of the student's learning problems (verified by interview).
☐	☐	☐	4. The student is noticeably slower than siblings are in rate of learning at home (verified by interview).
☐	☐	☐	5. Poor academic progress was noted in the student's native country (if applicable, verified by interview).
☐	☐	☐	6. The student's academic achievement is significantly below his or her English language proficiency (certified by ESL and special education alternative assessment).

Conclusions (Based on the Above Indicators)

Agree	Disagree	N/A	
☐	☐	☐	1. Other school resources have been used and found insufficient to meet the student's needs (e.g., Chapter 1, Bilingual/ESL class, tutoring, and so forth).
☐	☐	☐	2. Limited-English-language acquisition is not the primary cause of a child's learning problems.
☐	☐	☐	3. After the above information has been considered, the student appears to meet the special education eligibility criteria of California Code of Regulations, Title 5, Education, Section 3030 (c).

Form 1
Speech and Language Assessment, Secondary Level

Identify:
Name: _____
Address: _____
    Number   Street
    City   State   ZIP code
Telephone: ( )

Birth date: _____
Parent's name: _____
Chronological age: _____
Grade: _____
Examination date: _____

Current program: _____
School: _____
Examiner: _____

Name of test or subtest	Raw Score		Assessment Results				
			Severe	Moderate	Mild	Average	Strength
		Percentile	2	7	16	50	84
		Standard deviation	-2	-1.5	-1	0	+1
		Age					
		Grade					
Oral Language Skills							
Morphology (use of prefixes and suffixes):							
FLTA (morphology competency)*							
Informal language sample							
Story reformulation							
Syntax							
FLTA (grammatic competency)							
CELF (formulated sentences)†							
Informal language sample							
Semantics (use, comprehension, and manipulation using vocabulary)							
DTLA (story construction)‡							
DTLA (verbal absurdities)							
FLTA (convergent production)							
FLTA (divergent production)							
Story reformulation							
Pragmatics (conversational skills):							
Informal observation checklist							
"Let's Talk" Inventory for Adolescents							

*FLTA represents Fullerton Language Test for Adolescents, Experimental Edition.
†CELF represents Clinical Evaluation of Language Functions—Diagnostic Battery.
‡DTLA represents Detroit Tests of Learning Aptitude.

Observed Behavior

- ☐ Has limited attention or focus
- ☐ Responds impulsively
- ☐ Delays responses
- ☐ Seeks clarification often
- ☐ Reauditorizes
- ☐ Needs repetition
- ☐ Fails to ask for clarification
- ☐ Has difficulty finding words
- ☐ Restarts
- ☐ Perseverates
- ☐ Uses stereotypic language patterns
- ☐ Uses tangential language
- ☐ Uses circumlocution
- ☐ Is verbose
- ☐ Is unable to switch tasks
- ☐ Has limited eye contact
- ☐ Uses interjections
- ☐ Initiates conversation freely
- ☐ Is cooperative
- ☐ Is attentive
- ☐ Asks for clarification

Developing a Severity Rating Scale and Minimum Contact Schedule

The following guidelines may be used to develop a severity rating scale for speech and language. However, such scales should be tailored to the student's individual needs.

1. Develop the severity levels for the rating scale.

   a. Mild, moderate, severe
   b. Normal, minimal, mild, moderate, severe, profound
   c. Mild, mild-moderate, moderate, moderate-severe, severe
   d. Priority: 1 (prevents), 2 (limits), 3 (interferes)
   e. Mild, moderate, severe, profound, multiple
   f. Numerical scale (one to ten)

2. Determine behavioral characteristics or assessment scores that are appropriate cutoffs for each level of the severity scale.

   a. Age-level norms
   b. Standard deviation
   c. Number of errors
   d. Rate
   e. Scaled score composite

3. Develop cutoff scores by severity level for articulation, language, voice, and fluency. Determining cutoff scores for each level of severity can be done by using suggested criteria, if any, included with standardized assessments or by analyzing records of communicatively handicapped children previously enrolled and dismissed. Once proposed cutoff scores are developed, they can be ratified by staff and then become the standard for professional practice.

4. Review a sample of records from communicatively handicapped children who have been dismissed and determine the severity rating. Using the accepted cutoff scores for each severity level, determine the severity for each student. Obtain 25 to 50 records for each severity level. Categorize the records by severity level and by communicative disorder, including articulation, language, voice, and fluency. Make sure you have records for each disorder.

5. Review the categorized student records and obtain the following data:

   a. Average number of hours of direct instruction provided from enrollment to dismissal. Direct instructional time is computed on an individual rather than on a group basis; e.g., if a child were enrolled in a group of three students for 30 minutes per session, the direct instructional time would be ten minutes (30 divided by three equals ten).
   b. Average total hours of service received (This amount includes total session time for individual and group service from enrollment to dismissal.)
   c. Average number of sessions from enrollment to dismissal
   d. Average number of school days from enrollment to dismissal
   e. Average number of hours of direct instruction and average number of sessions for each change in severity; e.g., from profound to severe, severe to moderate, and so forth

Example

Severity	Profound	Severe	Moderate	Mild	Normal
Hours to reduce to normal	100	70	40	10	0
Average number of sessions	300	210	120	30	0

Form 2
Language, Speech, and Hearing
Referral, Assessment Plan, and Notice of Meeting

Student Information

Student's name: _____
                            Last   First   Middle

Birth date: _____ Chronological age: _____ M: ☐ F: ☐

Name of parent: _____ Phone: ( ) _____ ( ) _____
                            Last   First   Home   Work

Address: _____
                     Street   City   State   ZIP code

Primary language: Student's: _____ Home: _____ Language proficiency status: _____

Referral

Person referring: _____ Referral date: _____
                            Name   Position

Reason for referral: _____
_____

Prior interventions and/or modifications of the regular education program (Include SST actions or screening data.)
_____
_____

Assessment Plan

The proposed assessment is to help us learn more about the educational needs of your child. Assessments will be conducted by qualified staff. No decision on program placement will be made without your written consent.

☐ Language/speech communication development: Assessment in this area measures the student's ability to understand, relate to, and use language, speech, and nonoral communication clearly and appropriately. Tests may include, but are not limited to: observation; *Illinois Test of Psycholinguistic Abilities; Peabody Picture Vocabulary Test (Revised);* language sample; *Clinical Evaluation of Language Function, Elementary and Advanced Screening;* and *Assessment of Phonological Processes (Revised).*

☐ Alternative assessment: (Use of criterion-referenced tests, behavioral observations, and so forth)

☐ Recent assessments/independent assessments (descriptions): _____
_____

Your written consent is required before assessment can begin.

☐ I hereby give my consent for the assessment listed above.

☐ I have received a copy of my rights.

Parent's signature: _____ Date: _____

Notice of Meeting

A meeting will be held after the assessment has been completed to discuss the results and review your child's possible need for special education services. An administrator or designee and the language-speech specialist will attend.

Date: _____ Time: _____ Location: _____

☐ I will attend the meeting as scheduled.

☐ Please reschedule the meeting: Date: _____ Time: _____ Location: _____

☐ I will not attend, but I agree to the meeting's being held in my absence. Send a copy of the IEP to me for my review, approval, and signature.

Parent's signature: _____ Date: _____

Form 3
Language, Speech, and Hearing
Assessment Report and Individualized Education Program

Student's
name: _____
              Last   First   Middle

Birth date: _____ Chronological age: _____ M: ☐   F: ☐

Assessment report (Include required components.)

Signature: _____ Date: _____
    Language, speech, and hearing specialist

IEP   ☐ Initial IEP ☐ Annual review ☐ DIS speech-language services

Date: _____ Date of initiation: _____ Date of annual review: _____

                   Duration: _____ Frequency: _____

Present level of performance: _____
_____

Annual Goals	Short-term Objectives	Review of Objectives
1.		Date: _____ Achieved ☐ Revised ☐
2.		Date: _____ Achieved ☐ Revised ☐
3.		Date: _____ Achieved ☐ Revised ☐

Signatures
Parent or guardian: _____ Date: _____

Language, speech,
and hearing specialist: _____ Date: _____

Administrator or designee: _____ Date: _____

☐ I agree.   ☐ I do not agree with the individualized education program (IEP).

☐ I agree to part of the IEP.

Parent/guardian/surrogate: _____

Form 4
Student's Referral Form

Student's name: Last	First	Birth date:	Chronological age:

School:	Grade:	Teacher/Counselor:	Sex:

Name of parent or guardian:	Phone number: ( )

Address: Number Street	City	State	ZIP code

Language spoken at home: ☐ English   ☐ Spanish   ☐ Both   ☐ Other: _____

Referred by (name):	Date:

Position:	Phone number: ( )

1. Specify reason for referral:

2. Describe any attempted interventions (educational, psychological, medical, and so forth):

3. Describe any known significant health problems:

4. Provide current test information (screening, other):

5. List other agencies involved with the student and the name of the person to contact:

   a. _____   _____
            Agency   Person to Contact

   b. _____   _____
            Agency   Person to Contact

Form 5
Assessment Plan

☐ Original referral
☐ Three-year reassessment

To parent of : _____   Date: _____

School: _____   Grade: _____   Birth date: _____

Primary language: _____   Language proficiency status: _____

To meet your child's individual education needs, the following assessment may be required. Assessment will be conducted by qualified staff and, when appropriate, suitable interpreters. You will be asked to participate in a meeting of the individualized education program (IEP) team following completion of the assessment. You may receive a copy of the assessment findings, on request, prior to the IEP team meeting. The result of completing these assessments may be a recommendation for special education placement or services. No placement in special education will be made without your written permission. All information and assessment results will be kept confidential.

☐ **Academic Achievement**
Purpose: These tests measure current reading, spelling, arithmetic, and/or oral and written language skills. Tests may include, but are not limited to: *Wide Range Achievement Test, Peabody Individual Achievement Test*, and *Woodcock-Johnson Psycho-Educational Battery, Part 1*.

☐ **Social/Adaptive Behavior**
Purpose: These tests will indicate how your child copes and how he or she gets along with other people. Scales may include, but are not limited to: an interview, *Adaptive Behavior Scale for Infants and Early Childhood, Vineland Social Maturity Scale*, and Alpern-Boll-Shearer *Developmental Profile II*.

☐ **Psychomotor Development**
Purpose: Instruments in this area measure how well your child coordinates body movements in small-muscle and large-muscle activities. Visual and perceptual skills may also be measured. Tests may include, but are not limited to: *Frostig Developmental Test of Visual Perception*, Beery-Buktenica *Developmental Test of Visual-Motor Integration*, and *Bruininks-Oseretsky Test of Motor Proficiency*.

☐ **Language-Speech Communication Development**
Purpose: These tests measure your child's ability to understand, relate to, and use language and speech clearly and appropriately. Tests may include, but are not limited to: observation; *Illinois Test of Psycholinguistic Abilities (Revised Edition); Peabody Picture Vocabulary Test (Revised)*; language sample; and *Clinical Evaluation of Language Functions, Elementary and Advanced Screening Tests*. This assessment will be conducted by an LSH specialist.

☐ **Intellectual Development**
Purpose: These tests measure how well your child remembers what he or she has seen and heard and how well he or she will perform in school. Verbal and performance instruments are used also, when appropriate. Tests may include, but are not limited to: *Wechsler Intelligence Scale for Children (Revised); Stanford-Binet Intelligence Scale; Leiter International Performance Scale*; and *Kaufman Assessment Battery for Children*. Tests yielding IQ scores cannot be administered to black students.

☐ **Other Tests**
Examples of other tests are hearing, vision, vocational, orientation, projection, observation, or interview.
Proposed methods: _____

☐ **Alternative Means of Assessment**
Proposed methods: _____

In the preceding boxes at the left, place the number for the professional who made the assessment. For example, if an LSH specialist made the assessment for "Academic Achievement," place a *4* in that box.

1. Audiologist	3. Nurse	5. Special education teacher	6. Adapted physical education specialist
2. Psychologist	4. Language, speech, and hearing (LSH) specialist	7. Other: _____ (Specify)	

I will submit a written report(s) from: _____
(Name and title of person or agency that has assessed my son/daughter)

If you have any questions about the above assessment plan, please call:

Name and position: _____   Phone number: _____

This form must be signed before assessment can begin. Please read the statement of parents' rights on the back of this form before signing.

Please check one of the following and sign:

☐ I have read and understand the assessment plan outlined above.
☐ I consent to having the assessment indicated above made. I understand that the results will be kept confidential and that I will be invited to attend the individualized education program team meeting to discuss the results. I also understand that no special educational placement or service will result from this assessment without my written permission.
☐ I do not consent to the assessment described above.

_____   _____
(Signature of Parent/Guardian/Surrogate)   (Date)

Form 6
LSH Specialist's Assessment Report

☐ Initial assessment
☐ Three-year reassessment

Name of student: _____ School: _____

Date(s) tested: _____ Birth date: _____ Age: _____ Grade: _____ Sex: _____

1. Tests administered, scores, and language sample:

2. Interpretation of assessment, including relevant behavior noted during observation:

3. Relevant environmental, cultural, health, medical, attendance, or economic factors, as appropriate:

4. Conclusions and recommendations (including the need for specialized services, materials, and equipment for pupils with low-incidence disabilities, if appropriate):

_____   _____
Signature   Title of specialist   Date report completed

Form 7
Notice of Meeting

☐ Initial review   ☐ Annual review   ☐ Three-year review   ☐ Other: _____

Dear _____

A meeting of the individualized education program team is planned concerning your child:

_____ .
                First name   Last name

The purposes of this meeting are to discuss and review your child's assessments, to recommend appropriate educational services if special education is necessary, and to develop an individualized education program.

You are requested to participate in this meeting. The meeting is scheduled for:

Date: _____ Time: _____ Place: _____

We anticipate that the following people will attend:

☐ Special education administrator or designee   ☐ Speech and language specialist

☐ Regular classroom teacher   ☐ Psychologist

☐ Student   ☐ Other: _____

You may bring someone with you, or you may designate another person to be your representative if you are unable to attend. Please review the attached copy of your rights and procedural safeguards. If you would like further information about your rights or the purposes of this meeting, please contact:

_____

                                 Sincerely,

                                _____

                                School or district: _____

                                Phone: _____ Date: _____

Please detach and return the bottom portion as soon as possible:

☐ I plan to attend the meeting.   ☐ I do not plan to attend the meeting.

☐ I request the following time and date: _____

☐ Please contact me. Phone: _____

☐ I will be accompanied by: _____

                                 _____
                                        Parent's signature

Form 8

Individualized Education Program Language, Speech, and Hearing (DIS)

Nonintensive ☐   Intensive ☐☐   Voice ☐   Articulation ☐   Birth to three years ☐☐
Review ☐   Terminate ☐☐☐   Three to five years ☐☐
(IEP) New ☐   Language ☐   Stuttering ☐   Assessment date: _____

Name: _____ Last _____ First _____   Sex: ____   Birth date/ID number: _____

Chronological age: _____ Grade: _____ School: _____

Parents: _____   Residence / Attendance _____
Phone number: (___) _____

Address: _____   Ethnic code* ☐☐

Primary language: _____ Home _____   LEP ☐☐
Interpreter required: _____ / Pupil _____   FEP ☐☐

Records filed (location): _____ Foster home: _____
_____ Licensed home: _____

Statement for eligibility/termination: _____

Areas of Need in Communication Development
(Present levels of functioning)

	Receptive	Expressive
Language:		
Syntax:		
Semantics:		
Morphology:		
Pragmatics:		
Specific auditory processing deficit:		
Fluency:		
Voice:		
Oral motor:		
Articulation:		
Hearing loss:		
Areas of need:		

Other related information regarding student's present levels of performance: _____

DIS Service	Original date of initiation	Expected duration	Session/week	Minutes/week
Language, Speech, and Hearing				

Extended school year Yes ☐ No ☐   Consultative: _____

I have received my rights at the time of referral, assessment, and placement. I agree to the individualized program for my child and give permission for my child's placement.

Members:
Parent(s): _____   Date: _____
_____   Date: _____
Administrator: _____ Date: _____
LSH Specialist: _____ Date: _____
Other (position): _____

Goals	Objectives: Specify time, observable behavior, evaluation conditions, and criteria.	Monitoring of Goals and Objectives
1.	1. Initiation date: _____	Date: _____ Reviewed: _____ Achieved: _____ Revision Recommended: _____
2.	2. Initiation date: _____	Date: _____ Reviewed: _____ Achieved: _____ Revision Recommended: _____
3.	3. Initiation date: _____	Date: _____ Reviewed: _____ Achieved: _____ Revision Recommended: _____

*Ethnic code: 1 = Native American, 2 = Asian, 3 = Pacific Islander, 4 = Filipino, 5 = Hispanic, 6 = Black, and 7 = White.

INDEX